ON THE TRAIL OF THE
GREAT WAR
BIRMINGHAM: 1914-1918

ON THE TRAIL OF THE
GREAT WAR
BIRMINGHAM: 1914-1918

Alan Tucker B.Ed M.A.

BREWIN BOOKS

BREWIN BOOKS
56 Alcester Road,
Studley,
Warwickshire,
B80 7LG
www.brewinbooks.com

Published by Brewin Books 2014

ISBN: 978-1-85858-527-7

Printed and bound in Great Britain
by MWL Print Group.

Contents

Foreword

THIS BOOK is the result of many years study and research by its author, Alan Tucker. Alan was passionately interested in the history of the Great War, being a local historian, a battlefield guide mainly working with school parties and a member of, and for the last six-or-so years, secretary of the Birmingham Branch of the Western Front Association.

In that role, Alan consistently produced a monthly lecture list notable for the quality of the invited speakers and the diversity of subjects covered. Alan had a deep personal interest in the Warwickshire Regiment, particularly its Birmingham battalions, knowledge of which flows through this book.

The branch was deeply saddened to learn of Alan's untimely passing at the age of 64, in September 2013. With the encouragement of his brother, Michael, and of Jonathan Dale, Birmingham Branch chairman, it was decided to seek to ensure publication of the book by then in its final draft. It was a privilege to be asked to read through the final proofs.

This book is a revelation of Birmingham's involvement in that terrible conflict of the Great War. As such it is a book, not just of local history interest, but of national importance. It reveals, section by section, Birmingham to have been one of the major powerhouses of the British war effort, without which the ultimate outcome may have been very different indeed. Not only was it a major recruiting centre with many battalions of the Warwicks raised and trained from here, but the harnessing of Birmingham industry was of vital importance. From the mighty Kynochs shell and ammunition factory to the small workshops we see making engine dynamos for vehicles and radiators for aircraft, and any one of a thousand other components, to tank and aircraft production including the largest aeroplanes of the war, the huge twin-engined Handley-Page 0/400 bomber, all of which were a vital component in ensuring ultimate victory.

Other unexpected aspects are the city's role as a major medical centre for ill and wounded servicemen. Also Alan does not ignore those who exhibited bravery of another kind, those who opposed the war and those whose conscience would not let them serve, many of whom experienced persecution, imprisonment, and even threat of death as a result.

I am sure it will stand in future years as the major reference book for those seeking knowledge of the city's role in the Great War. It stands as a fitting tribute to its author and I know Alan would feel justly proud at its production in print.

Christopher John,
Vice-Chairman, Birmingham Branch,
Western Front Association,
March 2014

Preface

WE DO not know when the last 'Brummie' survivor of the trenches of the First World War passed away or even the last one to serve on the home front but plenty of evidence survives from that period to tell the stories of Birmingham men and women caught up in the first major conflict of the 20th Century. That evidence lies buried in contemporary books, newspapers, magazines, maps, photographs, directories and medal index rolls as well as the database of the Commonwealth War Graves Commission and the census returns of 1901 and 1911. There is also the physical evidence on the ground in the city centre and the city's suburbs. There are many impressive memorials in the city to men and some women who were killed or who just served. As well as obvious church memorials there are those dedicated to units like the Pals and the Territorials or to occupations like the tram workers, brewery workers or employees of Cadburys. Buildings, grand and lowly, also survive from that period whether of the 'great and good' of the city elite in Edgbaston or the humble two up two down of a VC winner just off the Soho Road in Handsworth. Some are still of great importance in the modern city such as the Hall of Memory. It is also a story of the fate of buildings relevant to the war that have disappeared as Birmingham constantly re-invents itself and of the institutions of the wartime city; Corporation, hospitals, schools, churches etc.

This could have been a standard history of the city at war from 1914-1918 but Reginald Brazier and Ernest Sandford were there first with their very informative 'Birmingham and the Great War 1914-1919' published by Cornish Brothers in 1921. Instead this study is driven by place and is therefore divided by areas of the city so that modern 'Brummies' can easily locate what is or was near them.

The range of experience reflected here is a reflection of life on the home front in any typical British city during the period of the war. Men who served or died in all three services feature strongly and examples are drawn from memorials of those who saw combat at sea, in the air or on the Western Front and other theatres of war. Inevitably the army dominates. Some men were officers but many more just followed orders. Often overlooked are the 1447 men and women commemorated by the CWGC in the five major municipal cemeteries. A few were the bravest of the brave and were awarded the Victoria Cross. Others held positions of responsibility in recruitment, the administration of war, hospitals and politics. The city elite is recorded in families like the Chamberlains and Martineaus but there are also those from the court dwellings of the working class. The role of women is emphasised by their work in the city's great munitions factories. Some women stand out for other reasons such as Matron Katy Beaufoy and Lady Mayoress Bowater. Apart from the sacrifice of too many of its manhood the city's major contribution to the national war effort was as a huge manufacturing base of the weapons of war. Metal-bashing was adapted to produce tanks, aircraft, machine guns, rifles and the Mills Bomb was invented and then made by William Mills, the adopted 'Brummie' from Wearside. The overall munitions production statistics are too monumental to really grasp. Here are the great names of the time such as Kynoch, Austin and Wolseley. Sir John French had referred to the war as 'a struggle between Krupps and Birmingham'. Significant trade unionists of the time are not neglected, particularly concerning the intense debates over conscription.

There were other sides to the war on display. A large number of Belgian refugees were welcomed into the city and the 'Brummie Germans' were, largely, not treated as badly as in many other cities and some professed their adopted patriotism as strongly as any 'native'. In a city where the Quaker influence was far greater than its small numbers warranted there were strong opponents of the war such as Joseph Southall, Alfred Barrett Brown and Beatrice Cadbury. The anti-war movement quite rightly features here as without them the overall picture of the city at war would be incomplete.

Here too we can find the stories of 'Brummies' that were on the Lusitania, the fate of one of the greatest child actors of the day, cricketers and footballers and an Olympic gymnast. Also the officer who was on the ship which rescued the survivors of the Russian royal family and a man who drove Lawrence of Arabia around the desert. The first and last 'Brummies' to be killed in the conflict are identified. The airman who shot down the last Zeppelin to attack Britain and the three City councillors who did not return are noted along with those killed on the first day of the Somme or in the Blyth beach drownings. Birmingham's technical and scientific contribution to the war is exemplified by those who worked at the Stratford experimental station in London. Overall over 470 men and women are detailed which can stand for them all. Some participants have left their own testimony in letters and diaries and the memories of Hilda Moss about her wartime childhood are particularly valuable. A final thanks to all those authors who had helped with their histories of the city or of any of its suburbs. There are too many to mention.

It is appropriate to end with the words of Birmingham's Lord Mayor at the end of the war cited in Brazier and Sandford.

> "Those who peruse the following pages cannot fail to be impressed with the whole-hearted desire of the citizens of Birmingham to help their country to the utmost of their capacity. During that eventful time Birmingham lived up to its highest traditions. The sacrifices of those days should be an incentive to a corresponding effort on the part of present and future citizens to secure the fruits of victory and to work together for the well-being of the community. Thus Birmingham should maintain and strengthen its position as one of the leading cities of the Empire. Success in war must be followed by success in peace: otherwise our soldiers have fought and suffered in vain."

Readers should note that some of the buildings which have been identified are private homes and the privacy of those living there should be respected.

A final word of definition. The city is defined as the modern boundaries which includes Sutton Coldfield which was, of course, not the case in 1914. Further contact with information can be made via the Birmingham Branch; Western Front Association.

Alan Tucker
January 2013

"They nobly responded to the Call of Duty and died that Britain might honour her pledged word to protect the weak and defenceless against aggression and that good faith, truth and justice should prevail among the Nations"

Stechford War Memorial

1.

City Centre

Birmingham Town Hall. The building acted as a recruiting station at the outbreak of war. In her wartime diary entry for August 17 1914 Cordelia Leigh of Stoneleigh Abbey wrote….

> "Went to Birmingham for the afternoon to a Diocesan Meeting. The streets were crowded near the Town Hall where recruiting seemed to be going on and a military band was playing loudly. The Bishop's Meeting was held at the Queen's College near the Town Hall and the noise in the street was so loud that we had to move from the large hall into a small room on the quieter side. Though the Meeting was entirely on Diocesan affairs the Bishop of Worcester opened it with a prayer for victory and final peace."

In January 1919 a farewell gathering took place for Flemings and Walloons, who had been Belgian refugees in the city, with about 3000 people present. In 1919 the Corporation received from Belgium a marble tablet which is now in the Council House foyer and was dedicated to the 'Belgian exiles' who recognised 'the generous spirit of amity' with which they were received. On the afternoon and evening of April 22 1915 a 'Serbian Relief' was held. The organisers, the Women's Volunteer Reserve, wanted gifts of necessities, defined as medical supplies and clothing, which would be forwarded to Prince and Princess Alexis Karageorgeovitch. There was an entrance fee, sideshows and entertainments.

'Edgbastonia' April 1915. Library of Birmingham.

'The Diary and Scrapbooks of Cordelia Leigh 1914-1919. A Strange Time'. Edited by Sheila Woolf and Chris Holland. Warwickshire Great War Publications. 2012.

Victoria Square. Local battalions such as the Birmingham Pals and Territorials regularly paraded there. The Italian colony celebrated Italy's entry into the war on June 2 1915; there were at least 600 Italians living in Birmingham at that time. Several fund raising events for war bonds were held including Tank Bank Week, December 31 1917–January 5 1918 during which Lord Mayor Brooks presented an address to Sergeant A.J Knight V.C. Birmingham competed with Liverpool and Manchester with regard to the amount raised and beat them with a total of £6.5 million. Dreadnought Week took place between March 4-9 1918 (when a captured German reconnaissance plane was exhibited), and 'Big Guns Week', October 21-26 1918, when a number of artillery pieces were exhibited. Win the War Day was held on September 21 1918. During Win the War Week RAF aircraft dropped leaflets over Birmingham which acknowledged the city's contribution to the equipping of the air force. They were entitled 'First Message from Mars'.

The square was the focus for Armistice Day celebrations on Monday November 11 1918. The official news reached Birmingham at 10.36 a.m. The news spread with 'lightning rapidity'. A loud exploding maroon helped spread the message as train whistles and factory sirens joined in. Behind the dominant feeling of 'wild and unrestrained joy' there was a note of sadness for the bereaved and anyone in uniform were the 'heroes of the hour'. Union Jacks and the flags of Allies appeared over public buildings. With Victoria Square crowded the Lord Mayor appeared on the bandstand. His words included…"We have won the cause for which we have struggled for the last four years. I am sure the news will be received in a spirit of deep thankfulness that the sacrifice of further lives has been avoided. You will naturally rejoice that the war is over. Show your joy in an orderly and becoming manner. Do not forget in this supreme hour the men who have died and suffered for their country that you and I might live in safety and the world be free." An 'intense silence' followed and then the National Anthem.

National and patriotic airs were played from the bandstand for the rest of the day. Almost everyone wore a rosette or carried a flag and processions of lorries started to come into the square filled with British, Colonial and American soldiers. The 'exuberant joy' continued until evening. Near dusk the square was lighted and the crowds spilled into nearby streets. There may have been 100000 people in the neighbourhood of the Council House. There were more speeches and at the end there were cheers for the King, the City Battalions, the Warwickshire Regiment and the Lord Mayor. Celebrations continued on the following day with crowds pouring in from the suburbs.

Tank Bank Week in Victoria Square, December 31 1917- January 5 1918

The Belgian colony marched along New Street and Corporation Street. About 150 'Old Contemptibles' also paraded the streets.

Birmingham Weekly Post November 16 1918.

Council House. There are plaques to men killed in the City Council Departments – Board of Guardians, Public Works, Electricity Supply, City Treasurer, Veterinary Department as well as a plaque commemorating Belgian refugees. Three city councillors were killed – Norman Chamberlain, Thomas Silver and Henry Lynn Shaw. The Council House was the HQ of the Citizens' Committee which aimed to alleviate war distress. During the war it spent over £170000. 6034 Council employees joined the Forces. 11.5% were killed. 1792 Tramways men served and 1239 from Gas – the highest totals. Twelve women are listed on the Board of Guardians memorial in the foyer as having seen some war service.

Sister Rose Kendall is described elsewhere. The majority were members of the Territorial Force Nursing Service. One of these was Adelaide Bottrill who lived in as a nurse at the Birmingham Workhouse Infirmary in 1901 and 1911. This was adjacent to the main workhouse at Dudley Road and, according to its plan had nine wards. She was born in Australia in 1862. Her sister lived at Woodville, South Australia. She stayed on as a Sister when the building became part of the 1st/2nd Southern General Hospital also called the 'Dudley section'. The annual reports compiled by the matron on Sister Bottrill were very complimentary. She continued her military nursing until August 1919 when age meant retirement. Her matron wrote letters to ensure that she was invested with the Royal Red Cross Medal (2nd class) for war service at Buckingham Palace on November 6 1919 before returning to Australia. At one point during the war she had lived at 'The Retreat', Royal Road, Sutton Coldfield, the home of Mrs Buckler.

Sister Rose Leary also continued from the same Infirmary into its military role in the same nursing service on May 3 1915 . She had been born into a family of seven children at Salford in 1887 where her father was a greengrocer. Matron's reports were more critical. In July 1916 she was allowed to resign giving her reasons as "she cannot stand the unavoidable spells of inactivity and that she feels it is very wrong to be taking pay and be doing as little work as she is at present." Ironically this was just before Somme casualties started to arrive. Winifred Slatford was also a member of the Territorial Force Nursing Service. She was born in London in 1878. On the 1901 census she was a visitor at an Atkinson Home which was a refuge for children at Broughton, Lancashire. By 1911 she was a charge nurse at the Kings Norton Union infirmary at Selly Oak which was built in 1897 to accommodate 250 patients. Before being mobilised at the 'Dudley Road' section on May 3 1915 as a charge sister she was the second assistant matron at the Dudley Road infirmary. She served throughout the war and earned praise in her confidential annual reports from the matron although she was also believed to be 'dictatorial'. It appears that she remained as a Territorial nurse until 1933.

Two other women named on the Guardians memorial were also working at Selly Oak in 1911 as probationer nurses. Clara Latham, aged 28, was born at Barrow in Furness. Ten years before she had been a millinery assistant there. Isabel Morrish, then aged 22, was Welsh born. Sister Lucy Bentley of the Dudley Section from May 1915 was also named on the Guardians memorial. She was born c1867. Her brother, William, was named as nearest relative. He lived at two different Edgbaston addresses and at Bennetts Hill during the war. She remained a Territorial nurse until 1924 when she resigned and gave up active duty in July 1919. At that time she gave her address as Canonbury, London. In October 1917 she began to suffer from periostitis in the left radius and had to undergo treatment in the General Hospital. After recovery and light duty she returned to the Dudley section.

At the start of the war Agnes Patterson was a sister at the Dudley Road infirmary and became a war nurse at the same time as the infirmary became a war hospital. In December 1916 she was transferred to the Monyhull section after three months absence due to appendicitis which included an operation for removal. While convalescent she went to live with her sister in Liverpool where her mother was old, an invalid and had fallen downstairs and also where her sister was semi-invalid with a husband at the front. She had already had requests to transfer to a Liverpool hospital turned down but her wish was granted in April 1917 and she joined the 1st Western General Hospital in April 1917. She was still in the city in January 1919 and in charge of an Auxiliary Hospital when she was discharged to become a matron in infant welfare. She had been born in Forfar in 1878 and in 1891 was a weaver in a factory. In 1911 she was a nurse at the Liverpool Stanley Hospital.

Although it is not totally clear the Birmingham Local Tribunals under the Derby Scheme at the end of 1915 and the first Military Service Act of February 1916 probably met in the Council House. Appeal courts against a Tribunal decision were definitely held in the Council Chamber from March 1916. Ordinary tribunals were initially held in the morning and afternoon and then, as the volume of appeals increased, were held simultaneously. During the first year 745 courts were held and 47538 applications were registered. Many applicants were able to show good grounds for remaining in civil occupations. As the demand for manpower increased the conditions of exemption became more severe until questions of personal hardships received secondary consideration. Trade advisory committees were formed to help decide who were essential men. In most cases where the conscript was fit for military service the call up was only postponed. In October 1916 the tribunals were expanded to a total of thirty members. The courts remained busy until the end of the war. 38% of men making an appeal were made available for the army and 8.5% received temporary or conditional exemption certificates. Amongst the latter were 82 conditional conscientious objectors and only 9 absolute 'conchies'. The appeal tribunal faced a difficult task as its members had to decide disputed points arising out of six Acts of Parliament, eight sets of regulations, several lists of certified occupations, numerous instructions from the Local Government Board and 103 decisions of the Central Tribunal. Appeals came from those seeking exemption as well as the Military or National Service representative.

The examples which follow are from cases reported in the Birmingham Daily Post in March 1916. The names of appellants were never given.

An assistant librarian who was unwilling to fight but was willing to do work of national importance in agriculture which was allowed.

A time expired Territorial who had joined at 16 before the war was against the 'slaughter of human life' and was refused exemption.

A reporter on a Birmingham newspaper applied for absolute exemption as a Quaker. He had already served in the Friends Ambulance Unit in France but had returned ill. He was willing to work for the War Victims Relief Committee or in agriculture. He was given a 14 day exemption to consider the kind of work of national importance.

An engineer appealed and contended that a conscientious objector was a marked man and had to suffer more through public opinion being against him than the soldier in the trenches. He was made exempt anyway because of his occupation.

A tinsmith declared that he was a socialist and was asked what he was prepared to do to help the nation. "I am not a member of the nation, I am only a slave… hundreds of people were in agony before the war as a result of capitalism. As long as you have capitalism you will have war". He was refused.

A tailor's machinist who was born of unnaturalised Russian Poles in England was refused exemption.

'Birmingham and the Great War 1914-1919'. R.H Brazier and E. Sanford. Cornish Brothers. 1921

Nurse service records – National Archives

Three memorials are located just inside the building in the foyer of the entrance to the Council House located nearer to the Town Hall than the main entrance – Belgian refugees, Board of Guardians and Veterinary Department.

Birmingham Central Library/Library of Birmingham.

Six Library staff were killed in the war and are commemorated by a plaque. Four served in the 1st Birmingham Pals – Percy Garner, Thomas Riley, Henry Checketts (also on the Carrs Lane Church memorial) and Frank Izard. The first three named died on the Somme in 1916. The Library archives hold a photograph album dedicated to those killed and thirty other staff from Branch Libraries and the Central Library. The Central Library also holds the very important War Poetry Collection which was originally presented by William Cross of Rubery in memory of Private John Billington of the London Regiment. The latter was killed in Palestine in March 1918 and had lived at 11, Robert Road, Handsworth.

Art Gallery and Museum. The Art Gallery Extension was opened as a special recruiting office of the City Battalions on September 7 1914. From January 1917 the Feeney Art Gallery became the central centre for the Lady Mayoress Depot which provided comforts and clothing for serving Birmingham men. It also provided parcels for POWs.

Hall of Memory. The foundation stone was laid on June 12 1923 by the Prince of Wales. It was opened on July 4 1925 by Prince Arthur of Connaught. The former was the son of King George V and said at the time that it would "symbolise to generations to come all that Birmingham stood for during a period of great national crisis – work of every kind unflinchingly given, compassion to the sick and wounded, courage and resource in adversity and, above all, self-sacrifice in the face of death". He used a special silver trowel with a carved ivory handle designed in the city. The latter was a grandson of Queen Victoria; his father was Arthur, Duke of Connaught, her third son. His mother was Princess Louise of Prussia. One of the bas reliefs in the building notes 150000 Brummies 'answered the call' and 12320 fell and 35000 came home disabled.

There had been a considerable debate of how the city should commemorate its war dead with views ranging from an artistic monument to a major hospital extension. The final solution was a hall of memory in the city centre but post-war depression put a ceiling on cost. About £100000 was spent in the acquisition of a site between Easy Row and Broad Street. The work to demolish the old buildings of the Easy Hill Estate was begun in July 1922. £35000 was allocated to the cost of the building. In 1921 an architectural competition was held with a prize of £500 judged by Sir Reginald Blomfield. This was won by Messrs Cooke and Twist of Queen's College for an octagonal design in the Doric style using Cornish granite and Portland stone.

The Roll of Honour of the fallen housed in the Hall of Memory began under Lord Mayor William Bowater in 1914. Names were recorded in the Lord Mayor's Parlour. The idea developed that there should be a more permanent memorial. In October 1917 a War Memorial Museum was suggested but little happened and in 1919 such a building was proposed for Cannon Hill Park. The actual building work was carried out by the firm of John Barnsley and Sons. Four bronze statues, the work of Albert Toft, are placed on granite pedestals at the four corners of the main building – they symbolise the work of the Navy, Army, Air Force and Women during the war. Inside there are also bas-reliefs showing three aspects of the war – men leaving home to join up, a party of men in the firing line and maimed and wounded returning to their homes. Inside is a shrine which supports a bronze casket and within it lies a superbly inscribed and illuminated Roll of Honour designed by Sidney Metyard of the Birmingham Central School of Art.

There are also two stone laurel wreaths which commemorate Birmingham's role as 'godmother' of Albert on the Somme in the 1920s. One dated from 1926 and the other from 1933. The latter reads "To the children of Birmingham who fell in the cause of right and liberty from the people of Albert in gratitude". Carl Chinn in his first 'Brum and Brummies' describes how Suzanne Scott still had her late mother's programme for the opening. It was treasured because her mother lost her eldest brother, Private G.W Carter, on June 7 1917 in the 8th London Regiment, the Post Office Rifles. He was aged 21 and his parents, William and Rose, lived at 20, St Paul's Avenue, St Paul's Road, Balsall Heath. For many years Suzanne's mother visited the Hall of Memory and she had also gone there to look at her uncle's name. She had also visited his grave at the Voormezeele Enclosure, Belgium, on four occasions.

'The Hall of Memory'. H.J Manzoni. Public Works Committee, 1937. Held in the Library of Birmingham.

'Birmingham: Godmother of Albert in Picardy'. Alan Tucker. Stand To No 82. Western Front Association.

Curzon Hall. Built in 1864 this building was known for holding the city's first cinema shows and was still showing films in 1914 when it opened on October 26 1914 as a recruiting centre and remained the most important one for the rest of the war. It originally stood on the corner of Holliday Street

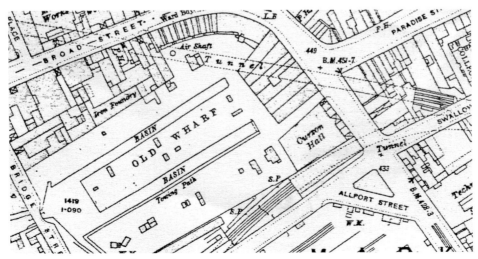

Location of Curzon Hall in 1918

and what is now Suffolk Queensway and was close to the Old Wharf canal basins.

St Martin's Church. There is an impressive memorial to the fallen comrades of the three city-raised battalions of the Birmingham Pals. Old Contemptibles plaque. There is also a plaque "in memory of General French's Contemptible Little Army" dedicated by the Birmingham Branch of the Old Contemptibles Association and the men who fought at Mons, the Marne, the Aisne and at Ypres in 1914.

St Philip's Cathedral. There is a memorial to the 1/5th and 1/6th Territorial battalions Royal Warwicks who were based at the Thorp Street drill hall. There is also the ensign flown by HMS Birmingham during the war and which was presented to the City on Nelson Day 1921 with the help of the Birmingham Branch of the Navy League. The ship, a light cruiser, was the first to sink a German submarine on August 9 1914 when its first shot hit the periscope forcing the submarine to surface when a second shot hit the conning tower. The submarine sank. Three successive services held on November 12 1918 to celebrate the end of the war with large numbers in the churchyard who could not fit into the main building.

Moor Street Station. In the autumn of 1914 Battle of Mons wounded arrived here before being taken to the 'University' hospital. In the modern booking office hall there is a memorial to railway workers who were killed.

Snow Hill Station. The local Territorial Battalions arrived here on recall from summer camp in North Wales at the outbreak of war. It soon became an important rest centre for ambulance trains passing through the city, one of the biggest in the country. It began operation on September 7 1914 and was staffed by the Voluntary Aid Detachment. In her diary entry dated August 12 1914 Cordelia Leigh of Stoneleigh Abbey, Warwickshire, detailed how Miss Murray, the Ashow schoolmistress, had returned with difficulty from her holidays in Birmingham and reported on women crying at Coventry Station as their menfolk departed. In Birmingham they were not allowed on the platform. The entry may have referred to New Street Station. She also described the station in a diary entry on March 21 1916 when in Birmingham for a meeting – "saw a long ambulance train which was built for the French Government at Swindon and was being shown at a shilling a head. I think the showman said it was about 960 feet long and could take 750 patients.

There were berths over each other in some compartments and seats for less badly wounded men in others – no cushions were allowed. There was a small operating compartment. Also a dispensary, storeroom and kitchen".

'The Diary and Scrapbooks of Cordelia Leigh 1914-1919. A Strange Time'. Edited by Sheila Woolf and Chris Holland. Warwickshire Great War Publications. 2012.

New Street Station. The King arrived here for his two day tour of Birmingham on July 22 1915. He was greeted by the Lord Mayor, William Bowater.

Old Contemptibles Pub. This building is situated in Livery Street opposite Snow Hill Station. The pub sign is a Mons Star, the medal given to those who had seen active service in 1914. In March 1977 the Birmingham branch of the Old Contemptibles Association still had 23 members, seven of whom were housebound. They used to meet on the last Wednesday of the month in the Old Contemptibles in Livery Street. It was originally named the Albion but was renamed in 1953 as the Old Contemptibles used to meet there for much of its 49 year history. In 1965 they still had 200 members. Bruce Bairnsfather, the famous wartime cartoonist, who had served in the 1st Warwicks until the Second Battle of Ypres, took an interest in the Old Contemptibles Association and, in the early 1950s, painted a magnificent pub sign in oils for the meeting place of the Birmingham branch then called The Albion. It showed a Tommy warming himself by a coal brazier.

Tom Morgan remembers helping to organise a Christmas dinner for about 300 veterans from the Midlands at the Longbridge branch of the Royal British Legion. Fred Page of the Birmingham Old Contemptibles was given the job of making a speech of welcome. He talked about comradeship, remembering the cold and the wet, the misery of feeling in your pocket and finding only one 'fag' left and breaking it in two and giving half to the man next to you. There was thunderous applause and beer glasses were banged on tables. Fred had served in the Artillery, won the Military Medal and had been an army boxing champion. He joined under-age and was nicknamed 'Lucky Page' due to the number of horses that were killed under him. He remained in the army after the war and left as an RSM. At his funeral his coffin was draped in the Union Jack and the Last Post was played.

The Bairnsfather sign is not the current one which shows a Mons Star.

Sunday Mercury March 20th 1977.

Tom Morgan and Joanna Layton, Great War Forum.

Municipal Technical School Suffolk Street. Trained munition workers in tool-setting, gauge-making and the manufacture of tools. It opened originally in 1895 and in 1897 was renamed as Matthew Boulton Technical College.

It was demolished in the late 1950s to make way for the Inner Ring Road.

Thorp Street. In 1914 there was the Drill Hall of 1/5th and 1/6th Royal Warwicks, both Territorial battalions. It was too small for both when they mobilised in 1914 so the 1/5th moved to the Midland Railway sheds in Suffolk Street. The Drill Hall was originally built in 1881 for the 1st Volunteer Battalion of the Warwicks and extended in 1893. Its large hall could hold 2000 men mustering at the same time and there were also administrative offices, mess rooms and an armoury.

It is now a car park having lost its roof.

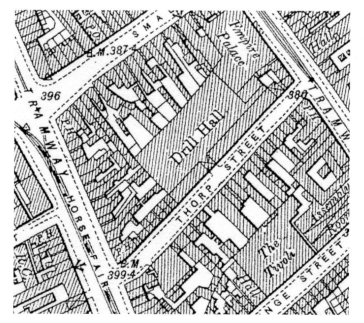

Thorp Street Drill Hall area in 1905

Carrs Lane United Reformed Church. There is a wooden memorial board with thirty-seven names. Second Lieutenant William Wheeler died on the Somme on July 2 1916 whilst serving in the 1/6th Warwicks. He was aged twenty and lived at Wylde Green. His father, Edward, was the agent to Sir Arthur Steel Maitland, the Conservative M.P. for Birmingham East. He is also commemorated on the Thiepval Memorial. Private Clifford Buckley, aged 21, was killed three weeks later on the same battlefield whilst serving in the 1st Birmingham Pals. His home was at The Dispensary in Monument Road, Ladywood. His parents made an appeal for news of his fate in the 'Missing Soldiers Bureau' column of the Birmingham Weekly Post but would have been relieved that his body was recovered and he now lies buried in Caterpillar Valley Cemetery, Longueval. Corporal Harold Wall was killed in the 10th Worcesters , aged 19, on July 22 1916, also on the Somme, and he is also commemorated on the Thiepval Memorial. He had lived with his parents in Dartmouth Street. Second Lieutenant Wilfred Cooksey was serving with a Special Company (B) of the Royal Engineers when he was killed, aged 27. His father had been a mining engineer of 'West Bromwich and Handsworth'. Corporal Henry Checketts is also listed on the Central Library memorial as he had worked in the Central Library as a senior assistant. He lived in Oldfield Road, Balsall Heath, and was killed when the 1st Birmingham Pals attacked Falfemont Farm on the Somme on September 3 1916 aged 30. He had attended King Edward's, Camp Hill, and Birmingham University.

Theatre Royal, New Street, just below Ethel Street. During the war this theatre, the fourth on the site and opened in 1904, was managed by Philip Rodway who lived at 62, Princess Road, Edgbaston. As his biographers noted – "Could footlights continue to shine in England while Verey lights were flickering over No Man's Land? Could Life go on with Death all-powerful?". The answer was a resounding yes as the first phase of the war was often called 'Business as Usual'. "Every man in the trench or the gunpit was dependent for his efficiency on the many men and women and factories, workshops, hospitals, camps, laboratories, offices, farms and bakeries of England. The home army needed services to keep it vigorous and cheerful. It needed amenities, relaxations, distractions which would refresh it mentally and physically, renew its determination, strengthen its courage". "The cry was soon – let us get away from this horror for a few hours; let us forget". The plays of the war years cheered and heartened and men returned to the front singing 'If you were the only girl in the world'.

In September 1914 Lewis Waller appeared at the Theatre Royal and added to the play being performed an impassioned rendering of Henry V's speech to the troops before Harfleur. In August 1916 a novel matinee was held there when a full house of 2200 convalescent servicemen were entertained by fellow soldiers and airmen. The money raised from the restricted number of paying customers in the dress circle enabled the purchase of a motor coach to carry wounded men to places of amusement.

The programme included several chorus songs for audience participation. Solo items were given by Sapper Gerrard (RE), Air mechanics Butt, Bone and Milburn (RFC), Sergeant Major Barlow (Royal Warwicks) and Piper Daniel Laidlaw VC (Kings Own Scottish Borderers) – 'the piper of Loos'. Philip Rodway helped to organise weekly garden parties for war charities in the Botanical Gardens. A military band played, there were teas and organised games and competitions. In either 1915 or 1916 Neville Chamberlain as Lord Mayor mentioned in a speech that over 30000 wounded men had already been guests at the Royal. In 1917 Rodway was publicly presented by Bishop Wakefield with an album containing the signatures of grateful men. The first signature was W. Powell, 2/Worcesters, who had been wounded in the 1st Battle of Ypres on November 1 1914. The names reflected innumerable units in the navy, the army, the 'colonial contingents' and the flying corps.

The 1917 programme included George Robey in 'The Bing Boys are Here', one of the hits of the war, and in April a special Lady Mayoress' matinee (Mrs Brooks) to raise money for the Lena Ashwell fund for concerts at the front. In January 1918 Philip Rodway made one of the speeches in support of Tank Bank Week from the tank in Victoria Square. The theatres publicised the campaign and sent artists to entertain the waiting crowds. One of these was Billy Merson, the comedian. On October 28 1918 a Mary Anderson charity matinee raised a staggering £6200 for the Lady Mayoress' Prisoners of War fund for men from the Royal Warwicks. Mary Anderson was the star attraction with the balcony scene from Romeo and Juliet and four extracts from Macbeth. An autographed letter from the Prime Minister was auctioned. Similar letters from Field Marshal Haig, General Pershing and President Wilson raised £25, £30 and £85 respectively. An autographed photograph of Marshal Foch raised £60. In 1911 Philip Rodway was living at 62, Princess Road, Edgbaston with his wife, Ethel, and daughters Phyllis and Lois. He was born at Aston Hall in 1877 as one of twelve children and where his father was a Park Superintendent. The family lived in the South Wing.

'Philip Rodway and a tale of two theatres'. Phyllis Philip Rodway and Lois Rodway Slingsby. Cornish Brothers. 1934. Library of Birmingham.

Both theatres have long since gone.

Queen's College, Paradise Street. The Birmingham Trades Council met here for most of the war until February 1918 when they moved to Bristol Street Schools. In 1911 their secretary, Joseph Kesterton was living at 48, Merrivale Road, Smethwick. He was a machine minder. During the war the

Trades Council became divided over its attitude to the conflict, particularly conscription of manpower, whilst at same time acting as a social shield for working class Brummies as their rents rose and food became expensive. In the early patriotic tide the Council agreed to work for the 'triumph of Empire'. For a group led by Eldred Hallas, the founder of the Municipal Employees Union, everything should be subjected to the primary task of defeating Germany. For others the extension of state activity was welcome. The doubters were divided between those who would assist voluntary military recruitment and would reluctantly accept conscription if voluntaryism failed and those against compulsion at all costs. On August 6 1914 a deputation met the Lord Mayor to discuss the economic dislocation of the war.

The Trades Council also called for government control of the food supply. The demand was renewed in June 1916 as food prices rose and profiteering and hoarding increased. In 1917 the 'submarine menace' placed further pressure on supplies. A Town Hall protest meeting had taken place at the end of 1916. After being ignored a protest resolution in December 1917 which remarked on the 'scarcity and unequal distribution of food in Birmingham' carried a threat of strike action on the issue. There were serious shortages of margarine, butter, tea and bacon and queues outside grocers' shops had become common. Within a week the Birmingham Food Control Committee was given permission to introduce a scheme of rationing in the city which began operation on January 1 1918. It became the model of a national scheme which began in July 1918 for sugar, butter, margarine, meat, lard, tea and jam. 870885 ration books were issued in Birmingham to individuals including children.

Joseph Kesterton, Secretary of the Birmingham Trades Council from 1913 to 1918

By 1916 demand had forced up rents and insecurity of tenure was common. The Trades Council carried on a public agitation for rent control and helped to set up tenants' associations. A 1915 Rent Act lacked teeth but another in 1917 was the result of the Trades Council winning a legal case in 'Sharpe Bros and Knight v Chant'. The Council also campaigned on old age pensions and secondary education for all in the post-war world. The Trades Council also played a part in helping Belgian refugees in the city. Their efforts were praised in November 1914 when Emile Vandervelde, the Belgian socialist leader, visited.

As conscription grew nearer a Labour Recruiting Committee was set up in 1915 to save the voluntary principle. A campaign was launched in the Town Hall and around a further 30000 men came forward to enlist. This did not prevent the Military Service Acts of 1916. In March and July 1915 there had been the Treasury Agreements and the first Munitions Act whereby those in war industries gave up the right to strike and agreed to the introduction of 'diluted' labour including the employment of women. Workers were forbidden to change jobs without a 'leaving certificate' from the employers.

Such agreements put workshop practice and working men at the mercy of their employers. A factory floor 'troublemaker' could be sacked and was then liable to military service. The withdrawal of protection cards, whereby a skilled munitions worker was given a trade card by his union which gave exemption from military service, made all workers liable to conscription. Into the vacuum came the Shop Stewards Movement eventually based in 45 of the biggest factories. In the engineering industry a central co-ordinating committee was formed with Percival Bower as its secretary. The Ministry of Munitions issued an order that every factory should have a licence to employ skilled men and placed an embargo upon employing skilled men without such licence. Skilled men therefore could not leave and had to accept whatever their employers demanded because they could not leave. On July 25 1918 150000 men downed tools demanding the withdrawal of the 'embargo'. Two days later there was a threat to withdraw protection cards from the strikers and after two more days there was a return to work. By the end of 1916 the Trades Council represented nearly 100000 workers in 182 branches of 79 affiliated unions.

The political divisions between the anti-conscriptionists and those in favour of any step which would assist the war effort led to a split in 1918. Tensions had been growing for some time when F.W Rudland was elected President as a supporter of the former position and Joseph Kesterton, the secretary, on the other side of the argument. The 'antis' took the view that conscription meant 'obedience to orders which any fool, brute or bully might give if dressed in an officer's uniform'. It was 'Prussian' and an attack on liberty. In July 1918 a breakaway group formed the Trade Union Industrial Trades Council. W.J Davis of the Brassworkers had stated that "the money contributed by the trade unions in the Birmingham district for organisational purposes was utilised to put pacifists in every possible position". Those who remained with the Trades Council were seen as 'politicians first and trade unionists a long way second'.

'The Birmingham Trades Council 1866-1966'. John Corbett. Lawrence and Wishart. 1966.

The building was later demolished but its 1904 listed façade was incorporated into an office and residential block called 'Queen's Chambers' opposite the Town Hall entrance.

In Newton Street. The City Council lent premises for the Birmingham Soldiers' and Sailors' Club modelled on the Union Jack Club in London. It aimed to provide men with lodging and refreshment at reasonable prices in congenial surroundings so that they avoided public and lodging houses. It was opened on August 4 1915 by the Earl of Neath. It became particularly popular with Colonial troops. The committee which planned the initiative was chaired by Godfrey Nettlefold and included Colonel Hart, Major Hall-Edwards, Professor Gilbert Barling and seven others. An appeal was made for money to equip and furnish the premises which would include several bedrooms.

St Basil's, Heath Mill Lane, Deritend. The wooden memorial plaque in the chapel lists the names of 112 men. One was Private T.W Attenborrow who was killed four days before the Armistice in the 48th Divisional Mechanical Transport in Italy. Private Robert Drennon, aged 26, was killed in Belgium just two weeks after landing at Zeebrugge with the 2nd Warwicks, a Regular Army battalion. Rifleman George Gandy was killed on the first day of the Battle of Loos on September 25 1915 whilst serving in the 2/Kings Royal Rifle Corps. Another man listed was Serjeant Edwin Jeynes, aged 28, who was killed at the Battle of 2nd Ypres on April 25 1915 whilst serving in the 1/Warwicks. His parents lived close to the church at 13 Court, 6 House, Heath Mill Lane. He was a regular soldier who was on the North West Frontier in 1908.

The Church is no longer consecrated but is a church social centre.

St Thomas, Bath Row. This bomb damaged church from December 1940 is now the site of the original colonnade of the Hall of Memory as part of the Peace Garden. On the walls are memorial plaques from later conflicts.

Steelhouse Lane Police Station. In June 26 1915 over 50 unnaturalised Germans of military age were held there before leaving under escort for New Street Station and a 'concentration camp' in Cheshire. Some of their English born wives looked on and there were no hostile demonstrations.

Digbeth Institute. Opened in 1917 and did similar work to the Birmingham Soldiers' and Sailors' Club in Newton Street. Now a nightclub.

Cheapside, Digbeth. Thomson-Bennett Ltd had a small factory there at the start of the war. They were making 25 magnetos a week at this Arden Works. Being aware that 98% of magnetos used in Britain for aero and motor engines came from Bosch of Germany Harry Lucas bought the firm and ran it as a separate company. In the second half of 1915 the Admiralty gave war orders for motor cycles, the six cylinder tank engine and four cylinder engines for transport vehicles as well as aero engines. Production moved to Lucas at Great King Street in 1916.

St Gabriel's, Barn Street, Deritend. On Saturday October 7 1916 the Bishop of Birmingham blessed the street shrine to the fallen on the wall of the church which included the names of two clergymen and two nurses. He was assisted by other clergy including the Reverend Canon Adderley, the vicar of the parish. After the ceremony those attending blessed eight other shrines in the parish. These were at Pickford Street, Fazeley Street, Floodgate Street, Milk Street, Oxford Street, Meriden Street, Bordesley Street, Little Ann Street, Coventry Street and Digbeth.
Birmingham Weekly Post October 14 1916.

St Gabriel's no longer exists as a result of damage in the Second World War.

Rea Street, Deritend. The Albion Works of Fisher and Ludlow Limited, tinmen's furniture manufacturers, was here in 1913. In simple terms they were metal bashers. During the Boer War they had helped to supply the army with camp kettles, brass buttons and mess tins. During the First World War the Albion Works and a new premises nearby moved into war work. A wide range of munitions were produced – Stokes mortar bombs, Lewis Gun parts, field kitchens, exhaust manifolds for aircraft, brass shell cases, ammunition cases, camp kettles and mess tins. Women workers were involved in turning, soldering, japanning, packing and operating power presses. Later in the century the company became well known for producing car bodies at Castle Bromwich.

'Brum and Brummies Volume 3'. Carl Chinn. Brewin. 2002.

Police Station residence, Moseley Street which ran parallel to Cheapside. During the war it was the home of Superintendent Daniel Long of 'E' Division of Birmingham Police. His son Second Lieutenant Bernard Long was killed near Zonnebeke on August 16 1917 serving in the 2/West Yorkshire Regiment. During the war Bernard regularly wrote home to his father, his mother, Mary, and his sisters Ethel and Hilda. Many of the letters survive and were published by his niece in 1995. Born on May 10 1896 the young Bernard had won a scholarship from Loxton Street Council School to Waverley Road Secondary School in 1907 at the age of 11. He then won a scholarship to Birmingham University in 1912 and achieved a BSc. He had joined the OTC there and obtained a commission in the West Yorkshire Regiment in January 1916. His officer training was at Keble College, Oxford and at Brocton Camp, Cannock Chase.

On July 13 1916 he left for France and served as an intelligence officer (he called it a 'snip of a job') until wounded at Givenchy on September 20 the same year. His unit was also known as the 1st Bradford Pals. In a letter dated July 30 he asked Ethel for "some stuff to get rid of lice" and "a small metal flask to hold brandy in as it is jolly necessary to burn horrible smells and tastes out of your mouth". In a letter to his father dated August 29 he wrote that "I see that many of the fellows who left Brocton on the day I did have now passed away. Of course they went down to the Somme – unlucky beggars". Around this time he had a 'near squeak' with a shell. He promised Ethel some souvenirs in a letter dated September 1. He had forgotten that he now had his own horse. At this time he received a parcel of food, toffee and mittens from home. On September 20 he was wounded in the right arm by a sniper while inspecting a crater. He was sent to a small hospital near Cambridge. He told his mother that "I've got a very cushy sort of wound just above the elbow, went clean through and it doesn't hurt a bit".

By February 1917 he was convalescent at the Royal Hotel at 'dreary' Whitley Bay, near Newcastle. He was still there on March 22 but within a month was at No 1 Officers Company, Command Depot, North Camp, Ripon. The base was to get men fit to return. He heard the Dean of Ripon, Mansfield Owen, preach at the Cathedral; he had been vicar of Edgbaston. Bernard also visited Harrogate and Fountains Abbey and went for walks on the moors. Still there on May 10 his parents had sent him a ring and his sisters a pipe for his 21st birthday. In May he spent £100 on 130 War Savings Certificates. By mid-June he was back at the Royal Hotel, Whitley Bay. He returned to the front in July 1917 but was now sent to the 2/West Yorks. He thought it was 'swanky' battalion with strict discipline and dress. As a new officer he spent a month at a Corps Reinforcement Camp and was not sent into the trenches. Bernard's final letter as to his mother on August 11th five days before his death. In it he wrote "I shall be thinking of you when I'm up there and I know you won't forget me. We're fighting hard now and it's a serious game. We're all ready to lay down everything if need be, and if God wills I'm ready. So goodbye and wish me luck". He is buried in Buttes New British Cemetery, Polygon Wood, near Zonnebeke, Belgium. In 1901 Daniel had been living with his family at 40, Miller Street, Clifton Grove, Aston. His father was then a police sergeant. Ten years later his father was now a police inspector in charge of the Bloomsbury Street Police Station where he lived and which housed twenty-two constables. In 1913 Daniel Long was a Chief Inspector at Kings Heath.

'First World War Letters of 2nd Lt Bernard Wilfrid Long 1896-1917'. Valerie A. Hawgood (ed). 1995

Broad Street Chambers. The showroom and basement were given by the Old Wharf Properties Co Ltd as the main centre of the Lady Mayoress Depot which supplied comforts and clothing for serving Birmingham men. It is also provided parcels for POWs. It operated until January 1917. The Depot was established as a result of a public meeting at the Council House on August 18 1914 under the aegis of Mrs Ernest Martineau, then Lady Mayoress. Amongst those attending were women from needlework guilds and sewing parties. Eventually over 200 centres affiliated to the central body with thousands of volunteers. The Broad Street premises were partially opened on August 31 1914. In its first four months 40146 articles were despatched to the Forces. By the end of the war the Depot had handled 273553 garments.

On September 8 Mrs Bowater became the driving force as the new Lady Mayoress of the central body which could co-ordinate the work of other organisations. On October 26 1914 a separate depot was opened at 6, Great Charles Street, for the collection and distribution of garments to meet civilian distress in the city. In June 1917 its work was taken over by the Citizens' Committee. The three local county regiments were beneficiaries before conscription and second-hand clothing was sent to Belgians, Serbians and the French. An RAMC Lieutenant at No 9 Stationary Hospital wrote that "some of the poor fellows' clothes are in an awful mess. Can we have fifty shirts, some socks and Woodbine cigarettes". Considerable help in terms of medical supplies was also given to local hospitals and from early 1916 other hospitals in Britain, particularly for 'our Allies'. The latter work was conducted at Clyro House, 176, Broad Street which was lent by Mr John Nettlefold and then at the Assembly Rooms, Francis Road, Edgbaston. Two base hospitals in France also received help.

On May 14 1915 a Prisoners of War Sub-Committee was formed and each POW was sent a fortnightly parcel at an average cost of four shillings. The parcels included items such as bread, cake, biscuits, dried fruits, tea, sugar, beef, fish paste, cigarettes, jam, tobacco and milk. The bread was sent from Denmark and Switzerland. Newspaper appeals enabled the Depot to collect details of POWs. By mid-June 1915 632 names had been submitted. They were adopted by their relatives and friends or by other subscribers. Mrs Neville Chamberlain organised a series of concerts in the suburbs to collect money for this cause; just over £1000 was raised. By May 1916 there were 850 men on the list of whom 542 had been adopted. On October 14 1916 a flag day to defray cost raised £2574. From late 1916 the Depot worked under the guidelines of the Central Prisoners of War Committee. A citizens' meeting was held on September 20 1917 with escaped POWs present to relate their experiences. Further flag days were held a week later and on May 4 1918.

School children in city schools were also active in raising money. For all its activities the Depot raised £111754, a modern value of nearly £5 million. Despatch of items were halted as Germany's allies succumbed in 1918; five Warwickshire men were affected when Turkey was defeated and 41 Royal Warwicks when Austria-Hungary left the war. Parcels to Germany were ended on Armistice Day for 1485 men. Throughout the war the Depot had sent 130162 parcels. The returning prisoners were invited to five special entertainments in the Town Hall between December 1918 and February 1919. In early 1916 the organisation received a windfall of nearly £4000, the surplus from the City Battalions' Equipment Committee. Some of this money provided the Birmingham units with indoor and outdoor games equipment and musical instruments. Sixty-seven gramophones were supplied; some provided by employees of various firms and Corporation departments for particular battalions closely associated with them.

In November 1915 Mrs Chamberlain took over the responsibility as the new Lady Mayoress. In July 1916 she broadened the responsibilities when a new sub-committee was set up to support convalescent soldiers in war hospitals with amusements and simple occupations. In February 1917 a further sub-committee was formed, chaired by Charles Hyde, to oversee the graves of Colonial and other soldiers dying in local hospitals. A special plot was set aside in Lodge Hill Cemetery. In January 1917 it was the turn of Lady Brooks who served for the rest of the war. She organised a Gift Day on December 5 1917 which was an appeal to Birmingham women to provide at least one article each for the Front. 3426 gifts were given including socks, scarves, mittens and shirts.

'Edgbastonia'. November 1915. Library of Birmingham.

'Birmingham and the Great War 1914-1919'. R.H Brazier and E.Sanford. Cornish Brothers. 1921.

Municipal Bank, Broad Street.
It was opened in November 1933 by the Duke of Kent but the bank had been founded in 1916 to enhance war savings by wage-earners. In this way it raised money for loan to the Government war effort. The original proposal became law on August 23 1916 after ten months of negotiations. The first branch was in the basement of the Council Water Department in Edmund Street and opened on September 29 1916. The wooden counter and screen still existed there in 2001. Before it opened circulars were sent to 2350 employers who would assist saving via a coupon scheme when wages were paid. A pioneer of its kind in the country in its first twenty months 30000 depositors opened accounts.

Its driving force was the Lord Mayor, Neville Chamberlain. In October 1916 he made twelve factory speeches in twelve days including BSA, Cadburys and Kynochs. BSA produced over 1000 depositors in the first month with an average weekly save of five shillings. Also of crucial importance was Labour Councillor Eldred Hallas who also campaigned and secured trade union support. He told one meeting at the BSA that "we do not want you to be only one week removed from the workhouse when this business is through......When the war is over and our men come home with nothing in their pockets and no job for them to do, can you allow them to enter your houses to a bare cupboard and an empty larder". Alderman W.E Lovsey was also an active campaigner. In total over a thousand meetings were held. Factory branches were soon established in workplaces including BSA, Austin, GKN, Dunlop, Wolseley and all City Council Departments. The wartime Bank officially closed on November 17 1919 with over 24000 accounts and £600000 in deposits. It quickly re-opened on a new basis with a head office and 17 branches. In July 1925 a new head office in Edmund

Street was opened and known as 'Swissles' as the building had formerly been the premises of the Nestle Swiss Chocolate Company. In 1919 there were 280000 accounts. In 1966 the Municipal Bank had 68 branches. The bank became the TSB in 1976 and the 1933 building is now owned by the City Council.

'Aspects of Birmingham'. Edited by Brian Hall. 2001. Chapter 7 by C.J Brockie.

'Britain's First Municipal Savings Bank. The Romance of a Great Achievement. J.P.Hilton. 1927. Library of Birmingham.

School of Art. Situated at the corner of Edmund Street and Margaret Street opened in 1895. During the First World War it became the headquarters of the local Food Control Committee. Birmingham piloted rationing in December 1917.

It has a similar use today and it is the Department of Fine Art for the Birmingham City University.

Blucher Street. Here is the historic home of the Birmingham Jewish community – the Singers Hill synagogue. The British Jewry Book of Honour lists 167 men who served in the Royal Warwicks in the First World War. Twenty-three were killed or died on active service. Some were honoured for their bravery. Major R.A Raphael gained the Military Cross; Lance Corporal H.Aaron, Corporal W.T Klein and Private L.Y Marks each won the Military Medal; Serjeant W.C Jacobs was awarded the DCM; and Private W.J.C Solomon gained the Meritorious Service Medal. Jacobs was in the 2nd Birmingham Pals and was awarded his medal for continually repairing broken telephone wires under intense artillery fire. Betty Browne gave information about her father, Harry Cohen, who later became a well-known tailor next to the Birmingham Hippodrome, served in the 1/6th Warwicks.

'Brum and Brummies Volume 3'. Carl Chinn. Brewin. 2002.

73, Bromsgrove Street. This was the family home of Sergeant Clarence Steane of the 1/5 Royal Warwicks who were based at the Thorp Street Barracks. He was living there in 1911 and the house is recorded as the parental home in CWGC records. His father Joseph was a stamper in 1911 and worked in metal. At Ovillers on the Somme on July 16 1916 he carried out a brave act in holding a barricade in a captured German trench despite repeated counter-attacks. He was wounded but also recommended for a Military Medal. On August 22 his parents received a telegram which said that their son was very ill and that they could visit him at No 18 General Hospital in France at Camiers near Etaples. Two days later he died of his wounds at the age of 22 and never knew that he was to be awarded the MM. He is buried in Etaples Military Cemetery. His father later received the medal on his behalf.

'Brum and Brummies Volume 4'. Carl Chinn. Brewin. 2005.

Newbury's Old Square. These were a notable firm of drapers, furnishers and furniture removers. They also had workrooms in Dale End, the furniture department was at 40, Bull Street and the 'removers' were at 67 and 68 Great Hampton Street. It was later the site for Lewis's store. On the 1911 census James Newman Townsend was named as a retired director of the drapery warehouse. He also comes to our attention for his exploits in the 1/8th Battalion of the Royal Warwickshire Regiment, particularly on the first day of the Somme. He had gone to France with the battalion in March 1915 as a major. On May 2 1915 Lieutenant Sherwood, Signals officer of the 1/7th Warwicks recorded a humorous incident…."Cpl and 4 men of 7th R.Warwicks told to arrest spies and snipers. Finally arrested a man with a shotgun dressed as a British major – identified as Major Townsend, 2 i/c of our 8th Bn!".

Charles Carrington, an officer of the 1/5th, though not an eye-witness to July 1 1916, later wrote about the 1/8 Second-in-Command, Major Townsend who was…..."a sporting type of the 8th, went over the top with a shot-gun – no bad weapon for trench fighting – and a terrier to flush the game. He survived and told me afterwards that he had two or three brace". Lieutenant Sherwood, who was now the Brigade signals officer, also remembered him on July 1… "he had a bag of cartridges, and no Sam Browne, respirator or anything…". Private Stanley saw him later that day… "my partner signaller and I had to get on top with a drum of telephone wire, each holding one end of a piece of wood which went through the drum. Jim Riddings was hit and went down with the drum of cable…Came across Major Townsend of our battalion lying wounded in a shell hole with another man…I asked if there was any message I could take back. He said yes, 'bombs needed urgently Quadrilateral'". This was a fortified German position near Serre.

Private Fred Lewis , Colonel Innes's runner, remembered that…"Major Townsend used to give me five francs for every shell nose-cap I got. The shell would explode but the nose-cap would fly off and bury itself. He wanted them for souvenirs. I even dug up a milestone for him. He had them all sent back to England for his shop in Corporation Street. The milestone had 'Foncque-villers' on it – and that place was flattened". Michael Renshaw in his book on Redan Ridge states the following about Townsend on July 1…."was Australian by birth but had settled in Birmingham, in business. He carried a Browning automatic into the battle with him, a bottle of whisky and a terrier dog. He lost direction but got into a German trench where he carried on the fight. He was wounded twice and returned to the British lines for more whisky. He was, however, bundled protesting into an ambulance".

Renshaw also states in the caption to a photograph of Townsend that he 'liked his drink and was liable to lead astray any junior officer who fell into his path and it was felt that he set a bad example. He was made salvage officer for the 48th Division'. In addition the 11th Brigade war diary 'narrative' of July 1 reported…."The 8th Royal Warwickshire Regiment advanced at 'zero' hour. The two left companies suffered heavily from machine gun fire from their left flank and apparently very few penetrated beyond the German front line trench. The right companies advanced with small casualties until approaching point 92 in which it is reported there were three machine guns. They pushed on beyond this trench. The Officer Commanding the leading right company states he believes he reached the trench 49-05. This trench was not nearly so much damaged by shell fire as the others he had passed over……A report timed 3.35 p.m. was received from Major Townsend, 8th Royal Warwickshire Regiment, that he still had some men in the third German trench i.e. near Point 92, but apparently shortly after this they were all back with the other units of the 11th and 10th Infantry Brigades in the German front line trench 22-56".

In early September Townsend rejoined the battalion as second-in-command; his wounds had not been dangerous. On January 1 1917 he was awarded the DSO presumably for his work on the Somme. On June 13 1917 a ceremony took place in the Birmingham Council Chamber to commemorate the "heroism and self-sacrifice of two officers of the Warwickshire Regiment and sorrow at the loss which has fallen to wife and mother as the toll of war". The Lord Mayor, A.D Brooks, presided and the opening remarks were by Major Townsend DSO, the second in command of the battalion. On behalf of his brother officers he asked the Lord Mayor to present to the wife of Lieutenant-Colonel Innes and the mother of Major Caddick a framed and illuminated address and an enlarged photograph. On his own award of the DSO a Birmingham newspaper stated that he was "fearless and brave…loved by rank and file – a typical example of a real English officer and gentleman".

In 1911 Townsend,aged 47, was living at 'Lisshicawn' in Birmingham Road, Solihull. Also living there was his wife, Nellie Gertrude, aged 40, who was the daughter of the head of the household, Ellen Newbury, a widow aged 60. They were married in the Birmingham area in 1893. There were also three servants and two nurses. Both Townsend and his mother-in-law were born at Bampton, Oxfordshire, five miles from Witney; for Townsend this contradicts Renshaw giving him an Australian birth although there is a later connection to the country. The house was originally owned by Charles Newbury, a pioneer of mail order shopping. He employed about 400 people and also established a sports club for his employees. He died in 1907. It was later demolished and became the site of Cedar Mansions, 617, Warwick Road, Solihull. Only two stone gate piers survive. Ellen Newbury died on January 5 1921, aged 70. James Townsend was living at Leam Grange, Warwick New Road, Milverton, near Leamington when he died on May 3 1925. His estate was worth just over £1100.

His early military experience was as a private with the 1st Battalion of the Berkshire Regiment in the Egyptian War of 1882. He was severely wounded in a reconnaissance in force. In 1885 he served in the campaign in the Eastern Sudan and then on the Upper Nile. A service record exists for a James Townsend which backs up the Birmingham newspaper report at the time of his DSO which details his earlier military career, also in the regiment named, and finally in terms of place of birth and approximate age. According to this evidence he enlisted in the Berkshire Regiment on July 23 1880 with an age of 18 at his last birthday and a former trade of baker. He was 5 feet 6½ inches in height. His service history lists the following places…

Reading November 23 1880
Parkhurst September 1 1881
Gibraltar September 30 1881
Malta July 12 1882
Egypt July 27 1882
Gibraltar May 20 1883
Egypt August 29 1884
Cyprus June 1 1886
Malta February 3 1888

A conduct sheet was signed by a Lieutenant in the 1st Royal Berkshires. He was discharged in 1892, a year in which he had two short spells in hospital with fever and bronchitis. He saw service in the Boer War and gained a commission; we cannot be totally sure of the regiment. He was mentioned in despatches for his efforts in the Western Transvaal. He then served with the New South Wales Imperial Bushmen in the Eastern Transvaal. This explains why he cannot be traced on the 1901 census. He is then mentioned in the London Gazette of November 6 1908 which noted that he was to be Captain in the newly formed 8th Battalion of the Royal Warwickshire Regiment. It also stated that he had been a Honorary Lieutenant in the 6th Imperial Bushmen of Australia. When the Territorial Force was formed in 1908 Captain Townsend offered his services to Colonel Ludlow who raised the 8th Battalion at Aston. Townsend raised the first company which at that time was entirely recruited from the drapery and textile trades. He was selected in 1911 to command the representative detachment of his battalion at the coronation of King George V. He was at camp at Rhyl when the war broke out and he set to work improving the discipline and efficiency of his 'A' company.

Lewis's later bought the neighbouring Newburys store.

95 and 96 Charlotte Street. On the south side at the 'Parade' end was the location of the Belgian Consulate in 1914. The consul was Adolph Myers who lived at 'The Oaks' in Richmond Hill Road. He was Birmingham born, as was his father, and he had attended King Edward's Grammar School and a school in Hanover. He then joined the pen factory in Charlotte Street which had been founded by his grandfather. He married Annette Nathan from London. His daughter was working at the Harborne Hall VAD Hospital in 1916 and his son, Lieutenant Ronald Myers, went to the continent as a despatch rider early in the war but by 1916 was an officer in the Intelligence Corps on account of his linguistic ability. Adolph became Belgian consul in 1903. For many years this was an 'almost nominal' role. This changed with the outbreak of war and Myers led the arduous work required. In 1916, for example, upwards of forty men a day visited the Consulate in order to obtain a provisional certificate of Belgian nationality. He worked on all the local com-mittees connected with Belgian relief. The early city response to help Belgian refugees had lessened by 1916 despite continued need. The Lord Mayor made a new appeal in the spring of 1916. Myers became the treasurer of the Birmingham branch of the National Committee of for Relief in Belgium.

'Edgbastonia', June 1916. Library of Birmingham.

155, Alcester Street. Runs from Highgate towards Digbeth. This was the family home in 1901 of the Barker family. Many Brummies had emigrated to other parts of the Empire before 1914 and two brothers, Jesse and James Barker, provide typical examples. They served in the Australian (ANZAC) forces in the First World War. In 1901 they were both Birmingham born young adults with five other siblings, the children of William Barker, a brass founder, and his wife Harriet. Jesse was a carpenter and at the age of 23 was already a widower, his wife and two sons having all died. He had served an apprenticeship with John Barnsley's building firm. James was a year younger and was a lamplighter. By 1911 Jesse had remarried and his second wife was Rebecca who was London born. He was then living at 8, Lilac Avenue, Runcorn Road, Balsall Heath. His occupation was now given as 'cabinet maker mantles'. James was still a single man and a lamplighter and was with his parents at 21, Hollier Street.

Jesse and Rebecca decided to emigrate to Australia. They left London on the 'Indrapura' on September 30 1912. James decided to join them later. James and Rebecca arrived in Melbourne via Cape Town just before Christmas 1912. In September 1913 they adopted a daughter, Roberta. On November 7 that year James left London. When he arrived he moved in with his brother and sister-in-law. James was the first to enlist which he did on October 1 1914 when he joined the 7th Australian Battalion. On his attestation papers he gave his religion as Wesleyan. On April 5 1915 he left Australia on the 'Cardiganshire' in an expedition of twelve ships bound for Gallipoli. They arrived at Imbros on April 24. James was injured two weeks after the landings at what became 'Anzac Cove'. He was sent on May 5 to the 3rd Field Ambulance and joined the Permanent Beach Party on July 8 where he remained until the evacuation at the end of the year. He now transferred to the 59th Battalion in Egypt in early 1916. On June 29 1916 he arrived at Marseilles and his unit was destined to join the newly formed 5th Australian Division. They took part in the fruitless attack on Fromelles on July 19 when James was killed. His body was never recovered and his name is therefore commemorated on one of the panels of the VC Corner Memorial there. His sister-in-law wrote to the authorities on September 16 1916 expressing anxiety and asking for any news.

Whilst James was in Egypt Jesse joined the Australian Imperial Force on February 21 1917, also into 7th Battalion. He was then living at Williams-town, Victoria. His attestation papers gave his height as only five feet two inches. He arrived at Etaples, France, on October 23 1916. He later saw action during the 3rd Battle of Ypres in 1917 where he was badly injured in hand to hand combat on September 20. He lay out in No Man's Land for two days before being rescued with arm, neck and severe leg injuries as well as deep shrapnel into his face. On September 26 he was admitted to the Queen

Alexandra Hospital at Cosham, Hampshire via Le Treport and Weymouth. On November 2 he was back at Weymouth in the 3rd Auxiliary Hospital. He recovered to a great extent and was able to visit his mother before leaving for Australia the hospital ship 'Llanstephen Castle' on February 15 1918. She was then either living at 139, Cattell Road, Small Heath or 20, Flora Road, Red Hill, Yardley. On May 21 Jesse was discharged as medically unfit. In June 1919 some possessions of Jesse were sent to his mother. They included a cash box, 13 coins, photos, letters, a purse, a key, a silver watch and chain and three sports medals. In 1920 the Barker family visited England and decided to stay. Jesse's health never really recovered from the effects of his wounds and he died in Birmingham General Hospital in 1954.

'Birmingham Anzacs', Valerie R.Kennedy. Birmingham Historian No 22, May 2002.
Service files of Jesse and James Barker – online at the Australian National Archives.

10, Easy Row. Here was the office of the Birmingham Women's Suffrage Society which was affiliated to the National Union of Women's Suffrage Societies. The organisation was the non-militant part of the women's struggle for the vote. Between at least 1909 and 1918 the local secretary was Florence Caroline Thorne Ring, better known as Carol. In 1911 she was living at 169, Bristol Road, Edgbaston as a 41 year old widow with her son Julius, aged 18, who was a laboratory assistant in the electrical engineering department of Birmingham University. She was Leeds born but her son had been born in New South Wales, Australia. Ten years earlier she was already a widow and was running a boarding house at 13, Francis Road, Edgbaston. There were five boarders and two servants and a daughter, Hyacinth, aged 7, also born in Australia.

Just before Christmas 1914 the Church League for Women's Suffrage, also part of the organisation, gave the NUWSS Workroom, then in operation in the city, an order for little frocks to be given as gifts to those young German children in Birmingham whose fathers had been interned. In 1915 the NUWSS became divided over its attitude to the war. Carol Ring as an organiser was part of the peace group as a Socialist. In May 1918 she chaired a George Lansbury meeting at the East Birmingham Labour Church. In 1918 she also became paid secretary of the Birmingham Women's Local Government Association. In the post-war election she supported Mrs Corbett Ashley for the Liberals in Ladywood against Neville Chamberlain and Councillor Kneeshaw. She lost her deposit. Her father had been a Liberal MP in 1906. In May 1920 Carol Ring went to Austria on behalf of the Lord Mayor's European Famine Fund and reported on the plight of the country.

Catherine Osler was another key member of the Birmingham Society and had also served on the national committee. Born in Somerset in 1854, a Unitarian, she was an active supporter of the cause of women's suffrage for nearly forty years. In 1873 she had married Alfred Osler, a wealthy glass manufacturer in the city. By 1901 she had become President of the Birmingham Society, a post she held until 1920. By 1911 she was a widow and living with one her daughters at 'Fallowfield', Norfolk Road, Edgbaston. During the war she was an executive member of the Citizens' Committee which acted as a control committee for distributing grants to alleviate distress caused by the war. In March 1917 she presided at a suffrage demonstration at the Midland Institute in favour of including women in the proposed Electoral Bill. In 1919 she was granted an honorary M.A by Birmingham University and in 1920 her portrait was presented to the Art Gallery and later moved to Highbury. When she died in 1924 her only bequest outside the family was to 'my friend Florence Carol Ring'.

'Socialism in Birmingham and the Black Country 1850-1939'. George Barnsby. Integrated Publishing. 1998.

30, Paradise Street. In 1918 this building became the local office of the Women's Party. Until November 1918 it was better known as the Women's Social and Political Union founded by Emmeline Pankhurst in 1903 and even better known as the suffragettes. After calling off its campaign for the vote when the war broke out it had become a 'jingoistic machine'. By January 1918 Miss Isabel Green of 91, Kingsbury Road, Erdington, had become the local organiser and that month Mrs Pankhurst spoke at the Temperance Hall. In February 1918 Isabel Green revived the idea of weekly open air meetings in the Bull Ring. She was very critical of "young fit men hiding in the factories and talking Pacifism. It was not British".

In June 1918 the Women's Party spoke out against a strike of engineers at a Birmingham factory where a man named Cogbill had been imprisoned for 'impeding the production of munitions'. They believed that the strike had been fomented by 'certain advanced and Socialistic members of the ASE'. That summer the Women's Party began to organise factory gate and canteen meetings including BSA, the National Shell Factory, Kynochs and Vickers. In the autumn of 1918 Green announced that the National Federation of Women Workers was an organisation led by pacifists and Bolsheviks. In October 1918 she spoke in Victoria Square during Big Gun Week. She was starting to say that there could be no peace until Germany capitulated.

In the December 1918 general election Christabel Pankhurst stood as a Women's Party candidate in the new constituency of Smethwick but was defeated by 775 votes. She was endorsed as a Coalition candidate by Lloyd George and Bonar Law having forced Major Samuel Thompson to withdraw. She faced a straight fight with John Davison, a union organiser for the ironfounders, who was the Labour candidate. The campaign was uneventful although she was rebuffed when claiming that she was being supported by all the discharged sailors and soldiers of Smethwick. Her platform was to secure a lasting peace based on obtaining material guarantees against future German aggression; to improve the social conditions of the working classes by a levelling up in society, by industrial salvation and wealth production; and to crusade against Bolshevism and 'shirkers'. She was also in favour of co-operative housekeeping and the provision in public houses of music and refreshment for women to enter.

2.

Edgbaston

Birmingham University. Became the 1st Southern General Hospital. There is a plaque dedicated to its use as a hospital above the entrance to the Great Hall. The agreement concerning wartime use dated from 1910 and there had been considerable planning in pre-war period. Detailed plans were drawn up for mobilisation as a Territorial hospital as the university was the only available building of suitable size. Within a week of the outbreak of war the university was ready, including putting in a large number of lavatories

The Great Hall of Birmingham University used as part of the 1st Southern General Hospital

and baths. The Principal Matron, Ellen Musson, then matron of the General Hospital, mobilised sisters and nurses, including the matron, Miss Kathleen Lloyd, who had been assistant Matron at the General Hospital. Miss Musson received the Royal Red Cross medal (1st class) in January 1916. The sisters moved into the Women's Hostel of the university. Twenty one medical officers were also mobilised.

The key administrator was Lieutenant Colonel Frank Marsh of the RAMC. He had previously served as a surgeon in the Turkish Army in their war against Russia in 1877-8. He came to Birmingham from his native Stafford in 1886 and served as a surgeon for fifteen years at the Queen's Hospital. He was an ear, nose and throat specialist and lectured at Queen's College until 1909 when he concentrated on his private practice. In 1913 he took over the command of all the Birmingham units of the RAMC. The first convoy of 120 sick and wounded were received at the new hospital on September 1 1914 from Moor Street Station but patients were soon brought in from Selly Oak goods station as it was more convenient. Two of the early convoys were Belgian soldiers. In November 1914 Mr E.M Tailby designed an ambulance trailer for two lying down cases and raised a large fleet of cars and ambulances. By the end of 1914 3892 patients had been dealt with and there were now 800 beds. There were also over 1000 beds in auxiliary hospitals controlled from Bournbrook. By April 1915 there were 1040 beds in the main hospital as a result of taking over the Chemistry block. A month later the Poor Law Infirmary at Dudley Road was taken over. In January 1916 an in-house journal was started, 'The Southern Cross', and ran to 32 issues. There are also three marble tablets to graduates who fell in the Great War in the main entrance to the Aston Webb building. Their details are on the University of Birmingham Virtual War Memorial.

The son of Sir Oliver Lodge (1851-1940), the 'Vice-Chancellor' and notable physicist, Second Lieutenant Raymond Lodge, was killed on September 14 1915, aged 26. Sir Oliver also served on the Admiralty Board

Matron Kathleen Lloyd of the 1st Southern General Hospital

of Invention and Research and assisted the development of sound ranging for artillery. The OTC at the University was the only officer training facility in the city. From a total membership of 504 commissions were obtained by 308. The King visited the Hospital on July 22 1915 and toured the wards and when he reached the Great Hall a patient played 'God Save the King' on the organ. On August 4 1915 about 1500 people attended a Church Parade taken by the Bishop of Birmingham on the anniversary of the start of the war. On June 13 1916 there was a well-attended memorial service to Lord Kitchener conducted by the Bishop of Birmingham. On May 19 1917 Princess Louise visited the hospital.

At the end of 1915 sections were opened at Stirchley and Kings Heath, both in converted elementary schools. In May 1917 the Dudley Road 'section' became independent. On the eve of this change the 1st Southern General had expanded to 8827 beds in five sections (5064), civil hospital beds (701) and auxiliary hospitals (3062). 77520 patients had passed through by that date. Towards the end of the war about 15 American medical officers joined the staff and over 300 American sick and wounded men eventually passed through. By the end of the war the hospitals had treated 130569 patients with 71% from the Western Front. Gallipoli, Palestine, Salonika and Mesopotamia were well represented.

In addition fifty seven German prisoners of war were treated. On November 13 1918 a thanksgiving ceremony was held in the Quadrangle for the signing of the Armistice with over 1000 present. British and Empire troops gave a gift of thanks to Matron Lloyd by means of a beautifully handmade white quilt which had regimental symbols stitched into it – Worcs, Warwicks, North Staffs, MGC, RFC, Tank Corps, Australian, New Zealander and Canadian. It is now in the University of Birmingham Department of Research and Cultural Collections.

Professor Henri Chatelain of the French Department had left for the French army to serve as a private in his native area; he died in a Paris hospital as a result of service at the front on 19 August 1915. He had joined the University in 1908. A Professor of German opted for naturalisation while his second assistant, Dr O. Intze, was on holiday in Heidelberg, Germany when the war broke out and was called up into the German Army. He ended the war as a captain on the Russian front suffering from shell shock. In 1915 an American journalist visited a Landwehr battalion in Poland and asked a spectacled sergeant what he did before the war. He replied that he was an Assistant Professor at the University of Birmingham and taught German literature. The story appeared in the New York Times.

Cordelia Leigh of Stoneleigh Abbey visited the hospital on January 29 1917 when she was in Birmingham for a meeting. She recorded in her diary "I took a tram to go and see Ernest Walford, formerly a Stoneleigh boy, wounded and now at the 1st Southern General Hospital, Edgbaston. It took about twenty minutes from New Street Station to the nearest point to the Hospital. I then had about five minutes walk to the entrance guarded by sentries who, however, let me pass through without comment and, after crossing a large courtyard, I found myself in the great hall of the huge building where I talked to a friendly hall porter. Walford's 'B Ward' was on the ground floor facing me and the porter went to enquire if I could see him but, rather unfortunately, he was out for a walk and I had not time to wait for his return so had to content myself with leaving a note and a box of sweets".

There were two notable patients during the war. Major Frank Buckley was an important figure in the 17/Middlesex, the Footballers' Battalion. Born near Manchester he had attended St Francis Xavier College for Boys in Liverpool. He had bought himself out of the army in 1903 for £18 after serving in Ireland in the 2/Kings Liverpool Regiment and after a Villa scout had seen him playing in an army match. He was an uncompromising centre half. However, his Villa career did not take off and he left for Brighton in 1905. After other clubs, including 55 games for Birmingham City, he was playing for Bradford City in 1914. The latter club had signed him from Derby County for £1000. As a junior officer in the Footballers' Battalion, which he had joined from its birth, his platoon was made up entirely of professional players. On July 28 1916 he was badly wounded at Delville Wood by shrapnel in his shoulder and lung. Some men thought he would not live even if he reached a Casualty Clearing Station. However, he was sent back to 'Blighty' and became a patient at the 1st Southern General. His wife, Madge, had always been very active in sending food parcels to men in the trenches. She followed him to Birmingham and was involved in entertaining wounded soldiers from local hospitals at Birmingham City home games. On September 16 1916, for example, she attended the home match against Sheffield Wednesday. He healed well but some shrapnel remained in his lung and he was advised to 'go slow' for a few years.

However, in January 1917 he returned to his old battalion in France to find that his lungs could not cope and he was sent home. Major General Tim Harington, Plumer's Chief of Staff, had been Buckley's company commander in South Africa. He had once written to the young Buckley praising his prowess on the football field. After the war Frank Buckley became a well known football manager for several clubs including Wolves (1927-44) and

Leeds United (1948-1953). In football circles he was known as 'The Major'. At Wolves he signed Stan Cullis and Billy Wright and at Leeds John Charles. Buckley died at home in Mellish Road, Walsall in 1964 aged 82. His funeral took place at Wolverhampton and his ashes were scattered on the Malvern Hills.

The second well known patient was J.R.R. Tolkien. On November 8 1916 he left France for Southampton after contracting trench fever whilst serving as an officer in the Lancashire Fusiliers. He was sent to the 'University Hospital' and arrived the following day where there was a reunion with his wife after five months. A medical board on December found him pale and weak with aches and pains in the legs although his temperature had returned to normal. He was unfit for service and was allowed to join his wife, Edith, at Great Haywood. On January 23 1917 he faced a second board at the hospital but recurrent fever attacks resulted in his being sent to Lichfield Military Hospital and then a convalescent home for officers at Harrogate. His fighting war was over.

Another notable patient was Private Robert Cruickshank VC who appeared in a photograph in the Southern Cross magazine in 1918, sitting in a wheelchair next to the standing figure of Private Sheridan DCM MM of the 11th Hussars. Although born in Canada in 1888 Cruickshank moved to England at the age of three. He lived in London and Essex and worked as a travelling salesman. After transferring from the RFC he was wounded on the Somme and in early 1917 joined the 2/London Scottish in Salonika and then Egypt. The VC action took place east of the Jordan River in Palestine on May 1 1918 when he volunteered to take a message to company headquarters from his platoon which was in the bottom of a wadi with most men and the officer as casualties. In trying to carry out his task he was wounded during each of three attempts. When examined he had sustained eight wounds. He was evacuated to England to recover. He received the VC at Buckingham Palace on October 24 1918. After the war he worked for Lever Brothers for thirty-four years and was active in the British Legion. In later life he lived near Leicester where he died on August 30 1961.

When the war broke out 32 year old Richard Archibald Jones was the Principal of Birmingham University Training College for Men and also the commanding officer of the University Officer Training Corps. He was also a member of Birmingham Education Committee. He had left King's College, Cambridge, in 1904 and became a lecturer at University College, Exeter and then Master of Method at the College, Sunderland. When war broke out he soon joined the 2nd 'Birmingham Pals' as a captain. He went to the front with the battalion and was a major and second in command when killed near Arras on May 21 1916. He had had a premonition that he would not return from France. He left a widow, Alice, and three young children. A press report after his death referred to "a career brilliant alike in its professional and military reaches".

Times obituary of Frank Buckley – December 24 1964.

University of Birmingham Virtual War Memorial.

Birmingham Weekly Post June 3 1916.

68, Hagley Road. This was the family home in 1911 of the Saundby family. Robert, the head of the household, was a consulting physician to the General Hospital in Steelhouse Lane and the Birmingham and Midland Eye Hospital in Church Street. In 1913 he was one of two Professors of Medicine at Birmingham University with a practice at 140B, Great Charles Street, very close to that of John Hall-Edwards. Both his Birmingham born sons were pupils at King Edward's. Magnus, born in 1896 whose first name was Robert, attended the school from 1910-14. His younger son William, born in 1898, was a boarder at the Woodbourne prep school at 63, Wheeley's Road, Edgbaston, at the time of the census but went on to King Edward's from 1912-15. Both sons saw active service in the First World War. Robert left school and joined the Traffic Department of the London and North Western Railway. He probably joined the 1/5 Royal Warwicks in June 1914 as a private and was commissioned into either the 1/5 or 1/6 as a second lieutenant in June 1915.

He saw front line service until transfer to the Royal Flying Corps in January 1916. On June 17 1916 he joined 24 Squadron as a flying officer. This unit was Britain's first single-seater fighter squadron and was commanded by the tactically aggressive Major Lanoe Hawker. They were active over the Somme battlefield. Robert Saundby's first success was on July 31 1916 when he drove down a Fokker Eindekker out of control and was slightly wounded himself. On November 23 1916 he took off from Bertangles as part of a flight of DH2s which included Major Hawker. Three planes spotted two German aircraft over Achiet. One was hit in the engine and glided out of the fight under Saundby's covering fire. Hawker was shot down and killed by the faster Albatross DII of Manfred von Richthofen. In January 1917 Lieutenant Saundby transferred to 41 Squadron and shared a victory over an Albatross. In April 1917 he transferred to home defence in Britain as a Flight Commander, including Orford Ness Armament Experimental Station. Whilst there he was flying one of three aircraft which intercepted a Zeppelin L48 which crashed near Theberton, Suffolk. Captain Saundby's DH2 fired two and half drums of his Lewis guns into the rear section. As a result he was awarded the MC.

Before the end of the war he served at No 11 Training Squadron at Scampton, near Lincoln. He remained in the new RAF after the war and rose to the rank of Air Marshal in the Second World War. In 1943 he became Deputy Air Officer Commanding in Bomber Command under Arthur Harris who had been his co-pilot in Iraq in the early 1920s. He retired in March 1946 and died at Burghclere, Hampshire, on September 25 1971. William, the younger brother, attended King Edward's from 1912-15 and then went to Sandhurst. He was gazetted as a subaltern into the Yorkshire Regiment but soon became attached to the RFC and joined 29th Squadron. He was missing in action on November 17 1916 and is commemorated on the Arras Flying Services Memorial.

The house no longer exists and the plot, with No 66, is now the site of the Radclyffe House office development.

'Service Record of King Edward's School, Birmingham during the War 1914-1919'. Cornish Brothers. 1920.

64, Wheeley's Road, Edgbaston.
The home in 1913 of Barrow Cadbury, the eldest son of Richard Cadbury. He was a notable peace advocate before and during the war and made generous donations to peace organisations, many associated with the Quakers. He also supported Quaker relief bodies such as those for Enemy Aliens and War Victims. He also helped the Friends' Ambulance which his son, Paul, joined. He was particularly keen to bring leaders together across national barriers. In 1906 he helped to welcome a party of German mayors who visited England and at Bournville addressed them in German. In 1915 he was present at the first two London meetings of the World Alliance for the Promotion of International Friendship through the Churches. On July 30 1914 he left with his family for a holiday in Holland but had to hurry home as war grew nearer. He was also enthusiastic about using the adult school movement to bring people together. He had already founded an institute for the local adult schools in Moseley Road. In May 1914 he visited Germany with a party which he co-led with his German born Leicester friend, Frederick Merttens. They visited Hamburg and Berlin. Barrow and Geraldine, his wife, led a deputation to the Reichstag where they were received by the Secretary of State, Dr Delbruck. In 1915 Barrow Cadbury joined Edmund Wright Brooks, chairman of the War Victims Committee, on a visit to devastated areas of eastern France

around the Marne and places which the Germans had withdrawn from in 1914.

The house no longer exists and there is a block of flats, 'Edencroft', on the site. The house next door still remains.

'Barrow Cadbury. A memoir'. Percy W. Bartlett. 1960. Library of Birmingham

'Penryn', Somerset Road. Opened in August 1918 as an officers' hospital as an offshoot of the 1st Southern General Hospital. There were 40 beds. The house was owned by Edward Greey in 1913.

7, Yateley Road, Edgbaston. This was the last permanent address recorded in the pocket book of Captain Charles Edmund Carrington M.C. who had arrived in England from New Zealand in 1914 in order to study for a year as a seventeen year old so that he could try for a scholarship to Oxford University. His father, the Reverend Charles Walter Carrington, was at Christchurch, New Zealand. Charles junior had two uncles in England and stayed with both of them. One lived in a country vicarage at Fleet near Aldershot and the other, Philip Halliley Carter, lived in Yateley Road. He was at Fleet when the war broke out and made abortive attempts to enlist. He soon paid a visit to his relatives in Birmingham and "persuaded his parents by cabling round the world, to let me enlist and, pretending I was nineteen, put down my name at the Town Hall on 6th September." Back at Fleet the same he wrote to a friend about committing 'perjury' about his age. "Three days later, as one of a long queue, I was 'attested', medically examined, sworn in, handed the King's symbolical shilling, and was dismissed to await the calling up order". He was an early joiner in the 1st City Battalion with a service number of 247. His first involvement was a voluntary church parade in St Martins on October 4 1914. He then set off for billets in Sutton Coldfield and training in the Park.

Philip Carter was a chartered accountant born c1867 and was living at Yateley Road in 1911 with his wife, Alice, two children, and three servants. Philip also had an office at 33, Waterloo Street. Philip had a longstanding involvement in the 1st Volunteer Battalion, becoming a second lieutenant, in 1896, which became the 1/5th Territorials in 1908 when he became a captain. Charles Carrington's Midland connections began in 1897 when he was born in West Bromwich where his father was the Vicar of Christ Church from 1894 to 1902. Charles senior had been born in Bath in 1859 where his father had been proprietor and editor of the Bath Chronicle. In 1903 the Carrington family left for New Zealand where Charles senior became

Principal of the Upper Department of Christ's College at Christchurch. In 1910 he became a canon and in 1913 a dean. Charles junior was educated at Christ's College.

In February 1915 Charles was commissioned into the 9th York and Lancaster Regiment but was left behind when they went to France in August 1915 because of his age. He was very frustrated when he was sent to a reserve battalion on Cannock Chase for ten weeks. He looked for an alternative and Philip Carter came to his rescue. Philip had sailed for France with the 1/5th in March 1915 and was now a Major. He persuaded his Colonel to apply for Carrington who was then sent to a reserve Royal Warwicks battalion in Birmingham. On December 25 1915 he arrived in France to join the 1/5th in France and spent his embarkation leave at Fleet where he was joined by his three older brothers who had come to England. Two had served with the ANZACs at Gallipoli. He met his new unit in the trenches facing Gommecourt Wood on the Somme. There is an interesting footnote to Carrington's relatives and the 1/5th Battalion. His Uncle Philip's nephew, Edward P.Q. Carter was a captain in the same battalion and produced the disciplinary record of Private Charles Britton at his court martial for desertion in August 1917 after he had been sentenced to be shot at dawn; this took place on September 12.

Charles Carrington later became one of Britain's most significant writers about the war based on personal experience. In 1922 he published his 'The War Record of the 1/5th Battalion of the Royal Warwickshire Regiment' which appears to be heavily based on the war diary. In 1919-20 he had written 'A Subaltern's War' under the alias of Charles Edmonds which was not published until 1929. In 1965 he published a broader view of the war in 'Soldier from the Wars Returning'. They are all worth reading today because he felt strongly that his generation of young soldiers were being misunderstood and misrepresented. As Brian Bond, the historian, has commented – "They had not gone to war gaily in 1914 in the spirit of Rupert Brooke, only to lose their faith amid the horrors of the trenches and to return in a mood of anger and despair". He disliked the books of disenchantment which came out between the wars. War was also about shared experience and the special bonds of comradeship. He always maintained that Britain's cause had been just; that there was no alternative to sticking it out until victory was won; and that the nation had reason to be proud of the Army's achievement.

He won the Military Cross for his leadership of 'B' company in his battalion's attack towards Winchester Farm during Third Ypres in 1917 and was also promoted to captain. After the war he went to Christ Church,

Oxford and taught at Haileybury before joining Cambridge University Press in 1929. He saw active service in the Second World War and ended as a colonel. Between 1954 and 1962 he was Professor of Commonwealth Relations at Chatham House. He died in 1990 aged 91.

The house still exists today.

Bishops Croft, Somerset Road. This was the residence of the Right Reverend Henry Russell Wakefield, the Bishop of Birmingham. His detailed account of a fortnight in France was published by The Times on September 14 1915 under the headline 'A Bishop at the Front'. He went within 35 yards of the German trenches and bases well behind the lines. In several places he addressed troops, both wounded and fit, sometimes on parade. He paid tribute to the special qualities of the British soldier, particularly the latter's adaptability, calm and sense of humour which included the anglicising of French and Flemish words. An officer of the Artists' Rifles acted as his escort. He felt that there was mutual respect between men in the Allied armies which was a 'true entente'. A constant question from the men at the front was whether the home front would show as much 'keenness as the men at the fighting front'.

He described his visit to the trenches and passing ruined villages to get there. The importance of keeping his head down was stressed. He met two men digging and asked them what they doing – 'souveniring' came the reply. "Dotted all about the country are little cemeteries which tell of devotion unto death and which remind one of all the sorrow this war has caused". He did not name it but he visited Albert on the Somme and saw the famous statue of the Virgin and Child at the top of the basilica but now at right angles. Soldiers "have been able to see God through the cloud of smoke raised by shot and shell and the presence of the Divine has not been obscured by the horrors of war". Religion was a 'stay in the hour of conflict'. He also paid tribute to the work of army chaplains. On his travels he met L'Abbe Le Mire, the Mayor of Hazebrouck who was also a member of the French Chamber of Deputies, and the Archbishop of Rouen the grounds of whose residence were used by a British medical unit.

Times September 14 1915

The Bishop's residence moved to Old Church Road, Harborne, formerly Harborne House, in 1921 and at some point the old residence became Queen's College, now an ecumenical theological college. Bishop Gore had called the building 'the ugliest villa in Western Europe'.

Mariemont, Westbourne Road, Edgbaston. This was the home of Sir Oliver Lodge, Principal of Birmingham University and his son Raymond, who as a Second Lieutenant in the 2/South Lancs was killed on September 14 1915, aged 26. He is buried in Birr Cross Roads cemetery, near Ypres and close to where he was killed. He was born in Liverpool, where he was father was then Professor of Physics, on January 25 1889. He had five brothers and six sisters. He was educated at Bedales School and the University of Birmingham from 1906. He studied engineering although there is no record of his graduation. After two years practical training at the Wolseley Motor Works he joined Lodge Brothers, the family engineering company. He was at Mariemont when he volunteered in September 1914 without the knowledge of his parents who were in Australia at the time.

He was commissioned into the South Lancs and left for Flanders on March 17 1915 and the 2nd Battalion. He was able to spend six hours at home as he travelled to the south coast from Liverpool. He saw his mother for only one hour as she had to rush back from London. Forty-two of his letters home survive, mainly to his mother, and they are full of information about trench life. He saw service in the Ypres Salient, including at Hill 60, St Eloi and Hooge. He commanded No 11 platoon of 'C' company and later became machine gun officer after attending a course near St Omer at the end of June 1915. His letters were always positive. On May 12 he wrote that "Things are very quiet and I am enjoying myself very much. If it wasn't for the unpleasant sights one is liable to see, war would be a most interesting and pleasant affair". He received a periscope and sniperscopes from home in addition to foodstuffs which he shared with the Mess.

Shortly afterwards his battalion impressed their Brigadier General with their digging ability so became 'Pioneers'. He became aware that the Germans had started to use gas. He had a short leave at home in mid-July. In September he commanded 'C' company as his captain had injured himself. He ended his penultimate letter before going back into the line with 'Cheer-ho, lovely weather, great spirits'.

He died of wounds soon after being hit by shrapnel when his company were temporarily leaving the front line to facilitate an artillery bombardment; the front lines were close together. A fellow officer, Alan Ventris, was killed alongside him. Ventris was the

*Second Lieutenant
Raymond Lodge*

son of a Major-General and ironically had attended Adams' Grammar School, Newport, Shropshire as did Raymond's father. Private George Gray, Raymond's servant, was also killed at the same time. Raymond's obituary appeared in The Times. One of the letters to his family after his death came from Norman Stallard of Small Heath who had worked alongside him at Wolseley Motors and had taken on Raymond's dog, Larry, when he joined up. His letters from the trenches were published in 1916 in a book written by his father entitled 'Raymond or Life and Death: With Examples of the Evidence for Survival of Memory and Affection after Death'. The book gives a detailed account of the family's attempts to contact him through mediums in the period after his death. Sir Oliver was convinced that these attempts were successful. Interest in spiritualism had been boosted by the war. The book was very popular and gave comfort to many who had suffered bereavement. He kept a diary which was returned to the family with his kit. The edges were soaked and some of the leaves stuck together with his blood.

University of Birmingham Virtual War Memorial (Douglas Bridgwater).

'Raymond or Life and Death'. Sir Oliver Lodge. Methuen. 1916.

Mariemont no longer exists as it was demolished in the 1950s except for the two stone pillars which were at the entrance to the drive which are in Westbourne Crescent and have the name engraved at the top of each. The site is now occupied by 'Mariemont' hall of residence on one of the campuses of Birmingham City University.

A memorial tablet to Raymond Lodge can be found in St George's Church, Edgbaston.

349, Gillott Road.

349, Gillott Road. This was the home in 1911 of three sons of William and Mabel Lamb. Each made a contribution through their differing war service. William was a Scottish-born surgeon. The family had lived there since at least 1898. In 1891 they were living at Moira House, Front Street, Arnold, Nottinghamshire, now an outer suburb of Nottingham. All three sons had attended King Edward's School. The eldest, John Henry, had been there from 1898-1901. In 1911 he was 28 years old and, like his father, was a surgeon. He had been born in Lewisham, Kent. Frederick Briddon was 21 and a student of engineering which explains the nature of his later war service. He had attended King Edward's from 1901 to 1907. The youngest, aged 16 and still at school, was Francis William Mason. He was a pupil from 1906-13.

John joined the Royal Naval Volunteer Reserve early in the war and from September 1914 to August 1916 served on HMS Calgarian which was part of 9th Cruiser Squadron which was based mainly in North America and the West Indies. The ship was an armed merchant cruiser of 17500 tons which the Navy had commandeered early in the war. Probably in early 1916 the ship took part in a blockade of the River Tagus which led to the internment of thirty-six German and Austrian ships in Lisbon. From August 1916 to July 1918 John Lamb served on HMS Arrogant at Dover, an old cruiser used as a submarine depot. He finished the war on the monitor HMS Sir Thomas Picton in the Adriatic Sea. A monitor was a small warship with dispropor-tionately big guns. 'Picton's' 12 inch guns had previously been on a pre-Dreadnought battleship. Its role at that time was to give close support to troops ashore at Valona in modern Albania and Durazzo in modern Croatia. Operations were taking place against the Austro-Hungarian army. On February 2 1919 the 'Picton' arrived at Malta and within a month had ended its and John's war in England. He ended the war as a Surgeon Lieutenant.

Frederick Briddon Lamb was commissioned into the Army Service Corps in October 1914 having been a cadet. He seems to have gone to France without delay and until September 1915 was a member of the 6th Divisional Supply Column. By the latter date he had received two promotions and was a Captain. From September 1915 to December 1916 he was attached to two different siege batteries of the Royal Garrison Artillery; the 50th with six inch howitzers and the 65th with twelve inch howitzers. In December 1916 he transferred to the Heavy Section of the Machine Gun Corps, which became the Tank Corps in July 1917, and became Engineer Officer to the 'B', later 2rd Battalion. He would have been involved in the first major use of tanks at Cambrai in November 1917. In February 1918 he became an Acting Major at one of the five Advanced Workshops at Dainville, Arras. In June he joined the HQ of the Tank Corps and in August joined the Tank Inspectorate when attached to Mechanical Warfare Design Department. In 1919 he ended his war in the Tank Design and Experimental Department of the War Office. His post-war medal index card gives two addresses – Cornwall House, Stamford Street, London SE and 88, Hagley Road, Edgbaston.

Francis Lamb, the youngest brother, was 19 when the war began and was probably doing his medical training. He was a RAMC lieutenant when he went to France in April 1918 and was attached to the No 7 Stationary Hospital at Boulogne. He was later attached to 26 and 25 Field Ambulance near Amiens and was in charge of a dressing station at Boves in the same area and was then based at a Divisional Rest Station at Dravegny between the rivers Marne and Aisne. He then rejoined 26 Field Ambulance which was part of 8th Division. However, on May 27 1918 he was temporarily attached to the 25th F.A in the same division when it was overrun by the German attack on the opening day of the 3rd Battle of the Aisne, and everyone, including Francis, was taken prisoner. As a prisoner he spent three weeks at Tastatt, Baden and three months in an officers's camp at Stralsund, Pomerania, on the Baltic coast. Tastatt was very unpleasant. A Royal Berkshire officer later wrote that the prisoners were treated like dogs and there was a 'starvation diet'. In September 1918 he was sent via Berlin with a guard to a camp in Silesia near the Austrian border. Here he took charge of all British sick in the camp until repatriation in January 1919. As a captain he then worked at the 2/1 Southern General Hospital at Dudley Road and the 1st Birmingham War Hospital at Rubery.

The house still exists and is semi-detached in a street of houses of similar style.
'Service Record of King Edward's School, Birmingham during the War 1914-1919'.
Cornish Brothers. 1920.

125, Ladywood Road. This was the home of Maurice and Florence Pollack. Maurice was a famous child actor of Edwardian Britain whose father, Oscar, was a noted Birmingham music and language teacher and, above all, music critic and whose uncle, Maurice, was Liberal Mayor of Birmingham in 1887 and a major steel pen manufacturer. Oscar was music critic for the Birmingham Mail for twenty-seven years. The two brothers were immigrants from Germany. Maurice was killed in the Syrian campaign on September 28 1918 whilst serving as a trooper in the Dorsetshire Yeomanry. Before the war he had worked for the Gas Department at Saltley. A Council Gas Committee report on October 28 1918 noted...

> "Pte Maurice Pollack of the Saltley staff. 1st Dorset Yeomanry, attached to the Egyptian force, died on the 28th ult. from wounds received in action. He joined the Staff of the department in 1907 and enlisted on the 29th February 1916."

He was born on September 14 1885 as the youngest son of Oscar and Melanie Pollack. Oscar was a German Jew born in Upper Silesia and arrived in Britain to join his older brother, Maurice, in 1855. Melanie was Austrian born and a singer. In 1885 Oscar's family was living at 56, Duchess Road, Edgbaston. Oscar was naturalised in 1870. Maurice first appeared in a charity show when he was seven. From 1895 he appeared in Christmas pantomimes, fairy tales and entertainments organised by his mother, who called herself Madame Pollack, as part of her Juvenile Dramatic Company.

He often gave powerful performances as the 'leading lady' and also did impersonations of music hall stars of both sexes. He could dance, sing and mimic. His first newspaper review was in January 1895 when he was nine and played the heroine in 'Sleeping Beauty'. Reviewers described his performances as 'astonishing' and 'the sensation of the evening'. In March 1896 he performed at the Prince of Wales Theatre in the pantomime 'Little goody Two Shoes'. One reviewer declared that "a special feature was the appearance in the palace scene of little Master Maurice Pollack, who gave his delightful and graceful song and dance 'Marguerite' which quite aroused the enthusiasm of the house and which he had to repeat in loud response to overwhelming applause".

In January 1897 the first performance of 'The Star in the East' at the Edgbaston Assembly Rooms led the Daily Post to write that "The Princess is impersonated by Master Maurice Pollack, who makes a charming Eastern beauty. He dances and sings with grace and vivacity, acts with spirit and intelligence, and in all is consistently girlish". Many performances were for charitable causes such as hospitals. On December 17 1897 The Dart carried an advertisement for young Maurice as a "Female Impersonator, Speciality Artiste, Drawing-room Comedian and Dancer, (who) is prepared to accept engagements for At Homes, Christmas Parties, Variety Entertainments and Concerts. An entirely novel, artistic, highly amusing and refined Entertainment and quick-changing of magnificent Costumes". The culmination of his career as a child actor came in 1899 when he played Cedric in a production of Little Lord Fauntleroy. One performance was watched by the American authoress, Frances Hodgson Burnett. When the Boer War broke out he became a soldier in 'Tommy's Appeal'. By this stage he had probably been involved in nearly one hundred engagements as a child actor. For six years after 1900 he devoted himself to male parts such as David Garrick, caused by the breaking of his voice. In 1901 he left Five Ways Grammar School after four years and just before his sixteenth birthday.

He still made ventures into the theatre and married Florence Moles (1886-1963) in 1904. He was described as a 'commercial clerk' on the marriage certificate. A daughter, Clara, soon arrived. In his appearances he had often appeared as several characters. His final performance was at the Grand Theatre on May 5 1906 as Hamlet where his acting produced his most unfavourable review. By then he had married Florence Moles on September 17 1904. His address was given as 355 Monument Road, which was the Duke of Wellington public house, and he was a 'commercial clerk'. Florence had been a dancer so they probably met through the theatre.

In the war Maurice had originally joined the Bedfordshire Yeomanry. After transfer he may have joined the Dorsets in Egypt. They were part of 10th Cavalry Brigade who were concentrated north of Jaffa by September 1918. They crossed the River Jordan on September 26 heading for Deraa. On the following day they became the advanced guard and were fired upon by Turks when approaching the village of Er Remte. It is likely that Maurice was killed in a cavalry charge which captured the village on September 28. A day later a patrol met Colonel Lawrence at Deraa. Damascus fell two days later and the Turks sued for peace a month later. He is buried in Damascus British War Cemetery. He had two brothers who both survived the war – Martyn in the Royal Navy and Montague in the Artists' Rifles. He is commemorated on the Birmingham Roll although misspelt as 'Pollock'. His father died in 1927, still at the same address, and his mother in 1935. Florence died in 1963.

'The Life of Maurice Pollack 1885-1918. A Birmingham actor'. Peter Farrer. Karn Publications. 1998.

Both Ladywood Road and Duchess Road, Ladywood, have been redeveloped.

St Bartholomew, Edgbaston parish church. Eveline Fidgeon Shaw is named on its war memorial. She was the only member of the FANY (First Aid Nursing Yeomanry) to lose her life there. This was on August 24 1918. She is buried in Sezanne Communal Cemetery in France. She was working as an ambulance driver with the French Red Cross. She was awarded the Croix de Guerre by the French government. The citation stated that she was "a driver of devotion and courage beyond all praise. She exerted herself selflessly, completely disdaining danger and fatigue, whilst carrying out evacuations, often in difficult circumstances and under enemy air attacks. She died as a result of a contagious illness contracted in the course of duty". Eveline was born in 1881 and was yet to be named on the census of that year – she was 'baby Shaw'. The family then lived at 195, Stratford Road, Aston and her Birmingham born father, Walter, was described as a 'manufacturer and merchant employing 28 men and 4 boys'. The 1891 census confirms that this was related to tools.

Eveline was not at the new family home at Uplands, Greenhill Road, Moseley when the 1891 census was taken despite her young age. Instead she was a visitor in the home of Charles Ellis, a gun manufacturer, at Greenfield House, Broom Hill, Handsworth. She may have been a friend of one or more of the five young children in the household. In 1901 the family had a new address – 2542, Bristol Road, Edgbaston. She was now 20 but without an occupation. Her older sister, Winifred, was a teacher of music and her brother, Archibald, was a student. She was still without an occupation in 1911 when the family had moved to 26, Priory Road, Edgbaston, close to St Bartholomew's Church. This house was next door to a house built for John Thackeray Bunce by J.H Chamberlain in 1893; the former was editor of the Birmingham Post and a historian of the city.

King Edward's School. The Roll of Honour was published in 1920 after diligent work by Charles Heath. 1403 former pupils had served and 243 had been killed. 321 had been wounded and 34 had become prisoners of war. 356 honours were awarded, including 14 DSOs. The fact that former pupils were more likely to become officers is shown by the disparity between 97 Military Crosses compared with 8 Military Medals. J.R.R Tolkien, a pupil from 1903-11, survived as did Major Hans Boeddicker of the South Midland Field Ambulance who attended the school between 1890 and 1894. Lieutenant Colonel Retallack who commanded the 1/5th Warwicks was a pupil from 1892-7. Lieutenant R.Q Gilson, son of the headmaster, was killed by a shell burst on July 1 1916 in the 11/Suffolks. He was a gifted artist and friend of J.R.R Tolkien. He had studied at Trinity College, Cambridge. G.Bertels was a Belgian refugee who attended the school in 1915-1916. In August 1917 he joined the Belgian Army and in 1918 saw service at the front in the artillery.

Further examples of former pupils who served show the range of experience different from the standard infantry soldier. D.Adams had attended the school from 1901-3 and went to Armentieres France in February 1915 as a driver with a British Red Cross Motor Ambulance Unit. In 1916 he assisted the French at Verdun in the same capacity. In June 1917 he was commissioned into the Royal Flying Corps as a pilot and second lieutenant. In November 1917 he was with 82 Squadron in the Arras area. This squadron was involved in the army co-operation work of artillery spotting and photo reconnaissance. He was wounded on March 22 1918 whilst flying at 7000 feet in a fight with nine German planes. Two Busby brothers were killed in the war. Vernon, born in 1895, had attended the school from 1905-10 and had also joined the OTC. Before the war he was an expert motor cyclist who had appeared in two TT races.

He went to France in August 1914 as a dispatch rider with the Royal Engineers. He was wounded but by the end of the year he was commissioned into a Motor Cycle Signal unit of the RE, initially based at Aldershot and

Dunstable. From 1915 to December 1916 he was a RFC lieutenant in France. A leg injury kept him in an English hospital for several months. He later became a flight commander and was employed at the Air Ministry. He was on special flying work on June 9 1918 when he was killed in a flying accident at Hendon. He was buried at Lodge Hill Cemetery. His younger brother, Eric, born 1898, had attended the school from 1919-13. In 1916 he joined the Royal Naval Air Service and went to France in April 1917. He was killed in action on July 10 1917 in 4th Squadron at Pervyse while engaging four Albatross scouts. He had previously brought down one kite balloon, four enemy machines, had driven down two and helped to destroy another two. He is buried in Adinkerke Churchyard Extension, Belgium. Their parents had been living at 'Fairfield', 5, Serpentine Road, Selly Hill, from at least 1901. Their family were comfortably off with their father a builders merchant and the home having two servants in 1911.

E.P.O Haughton joined the RNAS soon after leaving school in 1917. He saw service in 1918 with 222 Squadron based on the island of Lesbos which raided Turkish targets. He was brought down over Constantinople in October 1918 and taken prisoner. G.H Yates was only at school from 1901-2. In November 1915 he joined the 26/Royal Fusiliers otherwise known as the Bankers' Battalion. In August 1916 he was on the Somme and became partly buried. Later he was wounded in Belgium. In August 1917 he was attached to the Army Pay Corps and became a corporal at Boulogne. In December 1918 he was a lieutenant under the Field Cashier at 4th Army HQ. However, he then became a victim of the influenza epidemic and died at the age of 33 in 14 General Hospital, Wimereux on February 15 1919 and was buried in Terlincthun British Cemetery. Hilary Tolkien was the older brother of J.R.R Tolkien. He attended the school from 1905-10. He joined the 3rd City Battalion at the beginning of the war and trained at Spring Hill College and served as either a bugler or drummer which also meant, when in action, being a stretcher bearer. He was wounded on April 11 1916 in the trenches around Roclincourt north of Arras.

See 17, Lyttleton Road, Edgbaston, for Harold Harrison; Sherbourne Road, Acocks Green for Eustace Hill; 31, Francis Road, Stechford for Arthur Langley; 'Corris', Maney Hill Road, Sutton Coldfield, for Thomas Salter Price; 68, Hagley Road for Robert and William Saundby; 347, Gillott Road, Edgbaston, for the three Lamb brothers; 2, Amesbury Road, Moseley for the Alabaster brothers.

'Service Record of King Edward's School, Birmingham during the War 1914-1919'.
Cornish Brothers. 1920.

Edgbaston Cricket Ground. Percy Jeeves was a player who served in the 15th Royal Warwicks and was killed on July 22 1916 on the Somme aged 28. He had been struck in the back by a piece of shrapnel in an attack on Wood Lane. His parents lived near Dewsbury in Yorkshire where he was born in 1888. His father was a railway porter. He came to Warwickshire to play in 1912; in the 1913 season he took 106 wickets with his quick bowling and scored 705 runs and in 1914 he took 85 wickets and scored 403 runs. In 1914 he also helped the Players to beat the Gentlemen. Hobbs and Woolley were in his side and Fry, Fender and Warner the opposition. Wisden said that England had lost a player of whom very high hopes were entertained. P.G Wodehouse used his name for his butler in his novels having seen him play against Gloucestershire at Cheltenham in 1913. The name 'Jeeves' first appeared in a Wodehouse short story in 1915. His name never appeared on the scorecard of an England cricket team but, instead, he is commemorated on the Thiepval Memorial.

On October 26 1917 the Birmingham Local Tribunal sat with Sir William Bowater presiding. The Warwickshire Club asked for absolute exemption for their groundsman, who was not named, aged 36, and had been passed for garrison duty abroad. He was needed to manage twelve acres at the ground which was needed for charity matches, munition workers' matches and sports. He was the only employee left out of seventeen; seven were in the army and six were in munition works. Bowater told the club's representative that "You cannot claim that this man's work is essential in the national interest". A compromise of munition work and part-time care of the ground was turned down.

In the autumn of 1918 the Birmingham Special Constables played two matches against Warwickshire Club and Ground to raise money for POWs. Sergeant Samuel Bates had been born at the Edgbaston ground in about 1890 when his father, Henry, was the groundsman. He attended Tindall Street School and later played occasionally for the county. He was killed in the same battalion as Jeeves as a result of shelling near Falfemont Farm, also on the Somme. His brother, Len, survived the war, also in a City Battalion, and played 440 games for Warwickshire, mostly post-war. Another brother, Private Harold Bates, born 1889, served in the 2/7th Warwicks and was killed on July 19 1916 in the attack at Fromelles. He had lived in Bedworth.

Eric Hastilow, born 1895, also served in a City Battalion and played two games for the county in 1919 followed by a long playing career for other county teams and Moseley. In the early 1950s he was chairman of the county club. Today the Eric Hastilow Trophy is awarded to the most promising player under the age of 16. Second Lieutenant Esmond Hallewell Rogers, born 1891 and son of a City Alderman and chairman of BSA, had played some Second XI cricket for the county. He was killed on July 3 1916 in the 10th Warwicks on the Somme.

Birmingham Daily Post October 27 1917.

81, Harborne Road. This was the home in 1913 of Colonel Charles Joseph Hart. In late 1915 he was appointed to command all troops within the City of Birmingham as Birmingham had been recognised as a garrison town. At the outbreak of war he had been appointed Recruiting Officer and began his tireless work at the Technical School. Between August 14 and September 19 over 8000 recruits were enlisted there. He was assisted by Major Smith and Major Hall-Edwards and other officers who all faced an organisational challenge. Curzon Hall was then taken over under the Defence of the Realm Act. In the first fourteen months of the war over 32000 men were medically examined and over 25000 accepted there. In the first two years 35000 men were enlisted and a further 40000 under the Derby scheme. In the autumn of 1914 Highland battalions visited the city and Curzon Hall was fitted up as a recreation club for soldiers and concerts were arranged by Edgbaston ladies. Such provision led to the establishment of the Sailors' and Soldiers' Club in Newton Street; Hart served on its committee. His other role was to inspect and report upon the various Volunteer Rifle Corps in the district, perhaps 4000 in number. These men guarded bridges, factories and public works. He was also a strong early supporter of conscription as he was aware, even when making allowances for munition workers, that large numbers of men had not come forward. In 1915 he became a strong advocate of employing women to do men's work and by October 1915 the tramways had already responded.

On October 2 1915 Hart organised a 6000 strong march past in front of the Lord Mayor and the Council House as part of a national recruiting initiative. He was also the Competent Military Authority for the sale and manufacture of arms and ammunition in the city. In 1918 he completed fifty years service with the 5th Warwicks, where he was now honorary colonel, and its Volunteer predecessor. In the same year he was acting as President of the Northern Area Quartering Committee of Southern Command at Birmingham. This involved the negotiation and acquisition of buildings required for military purposes; by 1918 there were 61.

Charles Hart had been born in 1851 at Wandsworth, Surrey. He attended Haileybury School and afterwards spent six months in Paris in order to learn the language followed by four years of architectural training. In 1879, whilst living there, he formed the Harborne Volunteer Fire Brigade. In 1886 he was one of the honorary secretaries for the British Association meeting in Birmingham. He also did important work for the Harborne and Edgbaston Institute and the Queen's Hospital. He was a prolific speaker, particularly on decorative ironwork. In March 1868 he had become a private in the 1st Warwickshire Rifle Volunteers. In 1870 he became a lieutenant and, five years later, a captain. By 1894 he was an Honorary Lieutenant Colonel. In 1901 he took over command of the 1st Volunteer Battalion of the Royal Warwickshire Regiment. At that time he had nearly 1600 men. He was an excellent shot and studied and wrote on army tactics and manoeuvres. One of his lectures in 1898 was entitled 'How the War Game is played'. He initiated Easter route marches to Ledbury. He also wrote a 'History of the First Volunteer Battalion the Royal Warwickshire Regiment'. He helped to mould the local Territorial force after 1908, particularly the review of over 4000 men in the city streets in April 1909 by Sir Ian Hamilton. In 1909, just before his retirement, he was honoured with the Companionship of the Bath for his military contribution. He now became Honorary Colonel of the 5th Battalion.

He was always part of the art metal firm of Messrs Hart, Peard and Co.Ltd of the Grosvenor Works, Grosvenor Street West. They produced artistic iron and brass work. With his interests in design he had strong links with the Municipal School of Art. The business had originally been based in London but followed Charles Hart senior to Birmingham in 1867 although they kept a London showroom. Amongst their work was a Hagley Road fountain, gates for Hampton Court Palace, brass memorial tablets for churches, church plate and ornaments. Other work could be found at the Bank of England Head Office, Manchester Town Hall and Chatsworth. Many major buildings in the city also featured their artistic work. The firm exhibited with others in Bingley Hall at the 1886 British Association meeting. At the end of his life the Colonel, still unmarried, was living at South Bank, Warwick New Road, Leamington Spa. He died in 1925. His recreations were listed in 'Who Was Who 1916-28' as archaeology, golf and Leamington Tennis Club.

The house still exists today and is used as a business premises. The house next door was the home of Austen Chamberlain.
'Edgbastonia'. April 1903 and October 1915. Library of Birmingham.

Hill Crest, Richmond Hill Road. The house was opened in November 1914 as a St John Ambulance Brigade hospital in the Birmingham district.

The first patients on November 18 were ten Belgians. Eventually 75 beds were provided. In January 1916 the hospital moved to Harborne Hall. Hill Crest later became a hostel for the training of disabled ex-servicemen. In 1911 the house was the home of Joseph Rowlands, a seventy year old solicitor who was also a widower. He lived there with his son, Osbald, 39, who was a tube manufacturer. There were also three servants. In 1904 the house was called Lightfoot Hall and was adjacent to Hill Farm.

The house still exists as 37, Richmond Hill Road but now named as 'Aldorham'. It is near the junction with Farquar Road but on the other side of the road.

Mayfield Auxiliary Hospital. Of the 1st Southern General in Harborne Road was given by Colonel Arthur Parkes in early 1918 to provide more accommodation for officers. It had 40 beds.

17, Lyttleton Road. This was the home in 1901 of twelve year old Harold Cecil Harrison. He was born on February 26 1889 at Alton, Warwickshire, but was still a pupil at King Edward's School, which he attended from 1899-1907. His father, Edward, was a bank secretary. In 1907 he was commissioned into the Royal Marines and in 1911 the census recorded him as a Lieutenant in the Royal Marine Artillery Barracks at Eastney, Portsmouth. In May 1914 he was the assistant adjutant. He had already built a reputation for himself as a rugby player and had played for England four times, once in 1909 and against Scotland, Ireland and France in 1914. He had also represented both the Navy and Army teams. He was a 'massive forward' which accounts for his nickname of 'Tiny'.

When war broke out the Royal Marine Artillery sent three brigades to South Africa to train local troops. Lieutenant Harrison arrived with the 3rd Brigade under Lieutenant Colonel Peacock. They were attached to the South African Heavy Artillery which was sent into German South-West Africa in 1914-15. Before the end of 1915 he held the rank of Temporary Major. After a reorganisation Harrison's unit was known as the 71 Transvaal Siege Battery and in August 1915 he took over command with the rank of Major. He was mentioned in despatches for distinguished service in the field in the campaign in German South West Africa. South African heavy artillery were then sent to the Western Front via Lydd in Kent arriving in Le Havre in April 1916. In England during the previous month he turned out for a South African Heavy Artillery team against a New Zealand Army team at Queens Club, London.

His unit was now 44th Brigade Royal Garrison Artillery firing 6 inch howitzers and were at Beaumont Hamel on the Somme on the first day of the battle. He was gazetted for a DSO on August 25 1916 as a result of his actions at Pozieres. The citation noted that "he carried out two dangerous reconnaissances far in front of our foremost line and brought back valuable reports. On both occasions he was under heavy shell and rifle fire. He had previously been observing from a tree when it was struck with a direct hit from an enemy gun". On July 29 1916 he was gassed and became unfit for active service. He subsequently became an instructor in gunnery at Lydd and Salisbury from June 1917 to July 1918 when he returned to the front with XI Corps Heavy Artillery as a Brigade Major and was wounded in October 1918.

In May 1919 he was back at Eastney Barracks. That was not the end of either his army or rugby career. From 1919 to 1921 he was adjutant of the Royal Military Academy and in 1924 he transferred to the East Yorkshire Regiment. By 1927 he was a Brevet Lieutenant Colonel. A year later he was with the 1st Battalion in Tientsin, China. He was an instructor at the Staff College, Quetta, India from 1930-1 and a year later at the Imperial Defence College. He then commanded the 1/Green Howards from 1932-5 and was GSO1 of British troops in India from 1935-7, including another spell in China, when he left to command 14th Infantry Brigade. In rugby he had refereed the France Scotland game in 1922 and the Army Challenge Cup in 1928. He died on March 26 1940 at Marylebone, London. Twelve days before his death he had given a lecture at the Tower of London on 'The German Army'.

This large detached house, built in the late 19th century, still exists.
'Service Record of King Edward's School, Birmingham during the War 1914-1919'. Cornish Brothers. 1920.

112, Gough Road. This was the home of Major John Francis Hall-Edwards RAMC. When the war broke out he became Principal Medical Officer of the medical examiners at the recruiting stations, a post he held for fourteen months. He also addressed hundreds of meetings, travelled the city in recruiting motor cars, organised charity performances in aid of the various war funds and helped to look after the interests and amusements of regiments visiting the city. He was described as doing the "work of twenty men ever since the beginning of the war"and worked closely with Colonel Hart. After 1916 he was appointed Senior Medical Officer at the Military Command Depot at Sutton Coldfield, where he remained for seventeen months before being appointed inspector of the X-ray department of Southern Command. After this he was in charge of the X-ray departments at the military hospitals at Hollymoor, Monyhull and Rubery. He had also been consulting radiographer at the 1st Southern General Hospital.

However, by profession he was a surgeon and radiographer of distinction not just at the General Hospital in Steelhouse Lane but nationally. He had a practice at 141, Great Charles Street in 1913 and earlier had been based in Newhall Street. He was very much a Birmingham man and became the fifth eldest son in succession to join the medical profession. He was born at Moseley on December 19 1858 where his father was Dr John Edwards, at one time of Ash Mount, Sparkbrook. He attended King Edward's School from 1871-5 and Queen's College and stayed at the latter as Assistant Demonstrator from 1880 to 1882. He then qualified as a doctor at Edinburgh University in 1885 and started to practise in Moseley. He could easily have been a photographer, lecturer or journalist as his medical work took him into all these fields as 'sidelines'. He gained medals and prizes at photographic exhibitions, wrote prolifically for local newspapers and technical or medical journals. He travelled the country giving lectures on his work.

Major John Francis Hall-Edwards

As early as December 1890 he was involved in medical photography when he took before and after treatment photographs of a patient suffering from lupus in Birmingham Skin Hospital. In 1893 he was President of the Midland Camera Club. His real focus, however, was radiography and X-rays. Inspired by Rontgen's discoveries in 1896 he saw the possibilities and began his own experiments. He produced the first radiograph taken outside of London. He now sold his practice in Moseley to become a specialist in the new field. On February 14 1896 he worked on the first operation which followed an X-ray when Mrs Berry of Birmingham ran a needle into her hand which disappeared under the flesh. It was located by a radiograph and extracted. In the same year he submitted X-ray photographs to the Royal Photographic Society exhibition, including one taken through the chest of a five year old child. In January 1897 he wrote that he had been experimenting daily for the previous eleven months.

For over twenty years he was senior surgeon-radiographer at the General Hospital. He also worked at five other local hospitals, advised on setting up X-ray departments at others and invented pieces of apparatus used in X-rays, particularly to safeguard operators. He offered his services to the War Office when the Boer War began following practical experiments made with Surgeon-Major Freer of the 1st Volunteer Royal Warwicks. In spite of their conservatism he went to South Africa in February 1900 attached to the Imperial Yeomanry Hospital formed by Princess Alexandra. He had been offered the post by Mr A.D Fripp who attended the Prince of Wales after he injured his knee and was a leading civilian member of the Imperial Yeomanry surgical staff. Hall-Edwards had already devised a 'portable Rontgen-ray apparatus' for use on the battlefield. He travelled 23000 miles during his fourteen months of war and saved many lives. He was awarded the Queen's medal with four clasps. On his return he presented a series of slides to the Royal Photographic Society Exhibition taken in the Yeomanry hospitals at Deelfontein and Pretoria. In 1906 he became President of the British Electro-Therapeutic Society, just one of many honours.

He was also something of a showman. There is a well known undated photograph which shows him demonstrating X-rays in front of a crowd on Hodge Hill Common. There was, however, to be a personal cost. By 1902 he was developing painful sores and warts on his hands and at the BMA at Oxford in 1904 he urged young workers to take every possible precaution before it became too late. The pain was "as if bones were being gnawed away by rats". By 1906 his left arm was useless and carried in a sling. X-ray dermatitis deprived the doctor of his left arm and most of the other hand before he perfected his experiments. In June 1908 shortly after his first operation, he was granted a pension of £120 per annum on the Civil List by King Edward VII who in a letter to Mrs Hall-Edwards stated that "his services had been extraordinarily self-sacrificing towards the advancement of science and the benefit of humanity".

In May 1916 John Hall-Edwards was presented to the King and Queen, with others, in the garden of Buckingham Palace when the royal couple inspected an 'X-ray Motor-car' which had been presented to the St John Ambulance by Sir John Holder. He was there as the 'X-ray specialist'. After the war he did work as an official of the Comrades of the Great War which became the British Legion. In December 1920 Hall-Edwards was elected as a Unionist Councillor for Rotton Park Ward in a by-election. He was a useful member of the Public Health, Museum and Art Gallery and Public Libraries Committees. In January 1922 he received the Carnegie Hero Trust medallion which carried an annuity of £100. On one side were the words 'He serves God best who most nobly serves humanity'. Towards the end of his life he took up painting. One of his pictures was a sketch of the battlefield cemeteries in Flanders with poppies blooming at the foot of the wooden crosses. In April 1926 he was elected a life member of the Council of the BMA in recognition of his services to medicine. He died at his Edgbaston home on August 15 of the same year after two years of mostly agonising pain. His funeral service was held at the Cathedral before cremation at Perry Barr. The chief mourner was his adopted daughter, Violet. Press reports of his death called him the 'X-ray Martyr'.

John Hall-Edwards is commemorated by a Civic Society blue plaque on the exterior of the Children's Hospital in Steelhouse Lane. His house in Gough Road still exists today.

'Edgbastonia'. April 1915. Library of Birmingham. Times obituary August 16 1926.

Birmingham Biography 1926-7. Newspaper cuttings after his death. Library of Birmingham.

14, Church Road. William Mills, inventor of the Mills bomb, lived here during and after the war. He was born in 1856 at Southwick, county Durham. David Mills, his father had risen in fortune from a 'ship's joiner' because the 1881 census described him as a 'retired ship owner'. William left school at fourteen and had gone on to a seven year apprenticeship with Messrs George Clark, marine engineers of Sunderland. In 1891 David and Sarah Mills were described as 'visitors' at the home of David's son-in-law, Friend Shield, a farmer near Durham, who had married William's sister. William was also there as a 'visitor' with an occupation described as 'engineer, manufacturer of boat gear and ship fittings'.

William's earlier career was summarised in one of his later obituaries…

> "After a private education in his native town he obtained a first class certificate as a marine engineer and went to sea. His varied experience included the arduous work of salvaging ships and the laying and repairing of submarine telegraph cables. Once he ran a blockade and witnessed in Peru and in Chile the spiking of the old-fashioned guns. His experience

at sea resulted in his designing and patenting the Mills Patent Instantaneous Engaging and Disengaging Boat Gear, which in 1891, in competition with 15 other gears, carried off the 'Fairplay' prize of 100 guineas, the one and only prize of the kind offered at the Royal Naval Exhibition." (Birmingham Mail January 8 1932)

The gearing was approved by the Board of Trade and it came into worldwide use on naval and merchant vessels. An article in 1919 states that the boat gear was a life saver. The Chief Officer of the SS Drumberlie of Liverpool praised it after lifeboats were released quickly after the ship hit rocks in a storm and sank in ten minutes.

After the success of the boat gear William Mills turned his attention to the use of aluminium for mechanical purposes and set up the country's first aluminium foundry. In 1897 he was living at 17, St George's Square, Bishopwearmouth but regularly moved house in the Sunderland area. The 1911 census shows that he was at Northwood with his family. In 1914 he is no longer listed as having a Sunderland residence and had already moved to the Birmingham area where he had a factory in Smethwick.

In Durham in November 1891 William had married Eliza H Gandy, the widow of John Robert Gandy of Warrington. She was the daughter of a Manchester cotton spinner. On the 1911 census William was described as a 'managing director'. In 1912 we can definitely locate William in the Birmingham area for the first time as Kelly's Directory of Warwickshire shows him at Danesbury in Alderbrook Road, Solihull. The same address is also given on an American patent application dated July 20 of that year. At some point William Mills turned his attention to the application of aluminium to golf clubs. One of his obituaries in 1932 noted that "every golfer has heard of the Mills putter". The website of the British Golf Museum at St Andrews states that he "produced a whole range of aluminium clubs based on the long nosed clubs, also patented dual faced clubs, which were quickly termed 'Duplex'". He also invented a telescopic aluminium stool.

When Britain went to war in 1914 the demands of static siege warfare in the trenches meant a fresh look at the 'grenade'. In early January 1915 William Mills arranged with Major Banks of the War Office to help evaluate a Belgian hand grenade, the Roland. On January 26 Mills attended a trial with Albert Dewandre, a Belgian engineer who was familiar with the Roland grenade. The Belgian armed and threw four Roland grenades which Mills had fabricated for the trial, which went badly. Major Denn, the evaluator, rejected the Roland as unsafe and unreliable. On the following day Mills discussed the rejection with Major Banks. Banks made some vague suggestions about improvements and Mills soon came to believe that an improved Roland would serve the needs of the BEF in France. By the beginning of February William Mills had used his inventive engineering skills to devise a new hand grenade based on the Roland. He was able to turn something impractical into a workable grenade. The new 'Mills bomb' was successfully tested at Shoeburyness on February 20 1915.

The Birmingham Mail reported in 1932…

> "Only those who remember the primitive bombs used in the early days of the war can understand the delight with which the Allied troops hailed the appearance of the Mills grenade. Previously our men in the front line had been driven to strange shifts to meet the bombing raids of the enemy. Empty jam tins, even, were brought into service and proved almost as dangerous and uncertain in the hands of their users as they were to the Germans. The new missile imbued the users with confidence and even a knowledge of superiority. It was pre-eminently safe and easy to handle."
> (Birmingham Mail January 8 1932)

The 'Mills bomb' as it became known was an essential ingredient in arming the British and Allied infantry for the siege warfare of the trenches. Mills bombs had a cast iron body filled with explosive. A tube which consisted of a detonator, fuse and percussion cap ran down the centre of the grenade. An external lever, attached to a spring, restrained the striker. A pin, in turn, held the external lever. The user held the grenade so as to depress the lever, withdrew the pin and threw the grenade. With no pressure on the lever the striker was activated and detonated the grenade after four seconds. The first Mills was the No.5 with 'pineapple segments which would assist fragmentation'. It was later adapted to also become a rifle grenade. The shape of the No.5 fitted neatly into the clenched fist. It also had the huge advantage of being able to be safely transported with the grenade separate from the time fuse which was armed when required by front line soldiers.

Although the Mills was the best of the wartime grenades it had numerous teething troubles. As late as mid-1916 there was still one accident for every 3000 grenades. Although William Mills can only be proved to live in the Birmingham area in 1912 the 1908 Birmingham telephone directory lists William Mills Ltd at the Atlas Aluminium Works in Grove Street on Smethwick 9. This was the first aluminium foundry in the country. A 1912 Birmingham directory describes the works as producing 'aluminium castings of every description for motor car manufacturers a speciality'. In 1917 this aluminium works produced castings of 'every description for motor cars, aeroplanes and general trades'. In 1919 he chaired the James Watt Memorial Trust on the centenary of the steam pioneer's death. He was involved with the Council of the Birmingham Chamber of Commerce and various industry bodies. The 1920 electoral roll lists William and Eliza Mills as living at 14, Church Road, Edgbaston next to the Deaf and Dumb Institution.

After William Mills had developed his grenade in early 1915 he opened a works to manufacture it in Bridge Street West in Birmingham which became known as Mills Munitions Limited. With other firms perhaps 75 million were produced during the war. His firm was given no preference over others and probably made nearly four million of the total. For his services to the war effort he was rewarded with a knighthood in June 1922 and received £27750 from the Royal Commission on Awards to Inventors. He failed in his expensive legal claim that he was not liable to pay income tax on that sum and often stated that he had lost money by the grenade. Just before his death he told an interviewer that he had lost £30000 on it.

He was a collector of pictures, china and antiques and a member of Moseley Golf Club. His wife Eliza died in May 1930 and William died at Edgefield, Broadoak Road, Weston-super-Mare, on January 7 1932 where he had gone for health reasons instead of his usual winter at his Riviera villa. He still owned the house in Edgbaston. A memorial service was held at Edgbaston Old Church in Birmingham where Canon Blofeld spoke of his 'inventive genius' and he was cremated. He was worth £37829 at his death which equated to about £1.26 million in 2005 values.

Oxford Dictionary of National Biography.
'The Mills Grenade. The Mysterious Mr Mills'. Whitehall Gazette. 1919.

7, Arthur Road. Also known as Elm House, this was the home of William Bowater, wartime Lord Mayor of Birmingham from September 1914 to November 1915. He was Deputy Mayor when the war began but took over when Sir Ernest Martineau took up his military role with the Warwicks. He was the initiator of the formation of the three City Battalions of the Royal Warwickshire Regiment, the 'Birmingham Pals' and visited them in their training camps and, with the Bishop of Birmingham, at the front in 1915. He also became the Honorary Colonel of the 1st City Battalion. As Lord Mayor he was an active promoter of the Prince of Wales National Relief Fund which raised £168000 through a Citizens' Committee. He acted as chairman of the City's Parliamentary Recruiting Committee and played a prominent part in enlistments via the Derby Scheme. He greeted the King at New Street Station in July 1915 when the royal visit took place over two days.

At the beginning of 1916 he was knighted for his wartime services and in July 1916 he was made an honorary freeman of the City and presented with a silver casket containing the scroll. He served on the City Council for 33 years having been first elected in 1896. In 1914 he was the Alderman for St Mary's Ward and also a Justice of the Peace. At that time he served on the Finance, General Purposes and Tramway Committees and was also a governor of King Edward's School and President of the Birmingham Boy Scouts and the Dental Hospital.

He was born on October 21 1855 at Kidsgrove, Staffordshire, the son of William Bowater, later a dentist but at that time a 'homeopathic chemist' and Anne who was born in West Bromwich. His father, who arrived in Birmingham in 1861 and lived at 207, Broad Street, but died in 1879; his mother died in 1889. He was educated at King Edward's School in 1868-70 and was articled to his father as a dentist at the age of seventeen. Later in life he remembered attending the unveiling of the Joseph Sturge statue at Five Ways when seven years old and hearing Mayor George Dixon read the Riot Act during the Murphy Riots in 1867. In 1879 he married Sarah Westwood, the daughter of John Westwood who kept the Woodman in Easy Row. His dental practice was at 207, Broad Street, now Brannigan's Bar; he was living there in 1881. By 1891 he had moved into a house at 7, Portland Road, Edgbaston. There was now a son, William, born 1881 and a daughter, Fanny, born in 1884. By 1901 he had moved to 7, Arthur Road, Edgbaston; his son was now a dental student. William Bowater was also a freemason and a keen cyclist and swimmer.

Before joining the City Council in 1896 he was a member of the Board of Guardians and was an active Conservative until his first mayoralty. He became Lord Mayor between 1909 and 1912 and skilfully handled the delicate negotiations which led to the major extension of the city in 1911. Lady Sarah Bowater also became an important part of the wartime story because she promoted the Lady Mayoress' Depot which provided comforts for the serving men on a very large scale. For this work she was recognised with an OBE in 1918. In 1920 the Bowaters appear to have been living at Fulford Hall, Hockley Heath. His wartime work concluded with his publication of the 'Birmingham City Battalions Book of Honour' in the same year. Sir William Bowater died suddenly at Birmingham on May 30 1932; he was survived by his wife, a son and a daughter.

'Edgbastonia'. November 1914. Library of Birmingham.

The house was on the corner of Arthur Road and Carpenter Road and has now been redeveloped and the site of a tall block of flats called 'Warwick Crest'.

44, Islington Row, near Five Ways. This house became the HQ of the Birmingham War Refugees Committee. Elizabeth Cadbury chaired the Allocation Committee and Norman Birkett was the overall Secretary. It was loaned on September 3 1914 and the first party of Belgian refugees (50) arrived on the following day. Here needs were assessed before suitable accommodation was found. The first Committee report wrote about No 44 "crowded to overflowing with refugees of all kinds – men, women and children – with their pitiful little bundles, representing all their worldly goods". A Lost Relatives Bureau operated. Across the road three houses were given to the use of the Committee; one was used for the reception of clothing. There were some early difficulties over whether Catholic children might go to Protestant homes, the Committee having to deny rumours that children had arrived mutilated and advising against the 'misguided hospitality of giving beer'. However, gifts of tobacco were fine. By mid-October 1914 about 1500 refugees had arrived and branch reception homes had been opened at 59, Bath Street, Temple House nearby, 36 and 37 Duchess Road, Edgbaston, Erdington Abbey, Harborne Hall and Moor Green House. The Friends Institute in Moseley Road coped with 400 although its use was short-lived. Many were housed in private homes. One notable October arrival was Hippolyte Tyncke, who had trained the European boxing champion, Georges Carpentier.

Church and street collections were held and Aston Villa gave the proceeds of a match. Around Bath Street poorer residents responded to 'pound' days by giving groceries in weight each week. On November 14 1914 3000 collectors were on the streets selling 300000 tokens which consisted of a medallion with the words 'Birmingham support for Belgian refugees' and a ribbon in their national colours. By January 1915 2580 refugees had been received. The majority were women and children. Most of the 8-900 men were skilled and were absorbed into the gun, ammunition and saddler trades. 250 men had not been found employment as they were "chiefly artists, sculptors, advocates and foreign correspondence clerks". However men aged from 18-25 (later 16-41) were required to enrol in the Belgian Army from March 1915. Hosts were also reminded that all Belgians had to register with the authorities as 'aliens' or they were liable.

Many refugees attended an event in the Town Hall in March 1916 when Princess Napoleon, daughter of the late King Leopold, visited Birmingham in order to open a Belgian art exhibition at the Royal Society of Artists in New Street. Amongst them were a few disabled soldiers, priests and nuns. The Princess also visited 23, Beaufort Road, Edgbaston, where several Belgian families were staying. She was received by Mrs Shakespeare who in May 1918 was one of six Birmingham ladies honoured by Queen Elizabeth of Belgium. In October 1916 Jules Fagard, President of the Belgian Workers' Association in the city, expressed concern about isolated cases of ill treatment by local people. He pointed out that Belgian males in the streets were not shirkers and were either unfit, discharged or did important munitions work. One man who had been verbally attacked had four brothers and three brothers-in-law in the Belgian Army. Amongst the accusations were others of a 'stealing their jobs' theme and that returning soldiers would be denied a job. Fagard pointed out that the latter point was ridiculous as all Belgians wished to go home after the war. Indeed a month later the War Refugee Committee reported that most refugees were now self-supporting.

Overall 4560 Belgian refugees came to Birmingham. The Birmingham Evening Despatch ran a column in Flemish. Those running homes were given advice on Flemish diet e.g. the refugees were coffee not tea drinkers. In February 14 1916 a Belgian school was opened. There was a Belgian club – Le Cercle Belge. A speech by a Belgian priest was quoted in a War Refugee Committee report… "He drew attention to the colours of the Belgian flag – black, red and yellow. Black is typical of the terrible days through which our Country is passing and the depth of sorrow into which we have been plunged; red is the blood that has been shed: but golden is the kindness of the British people and never can Belgians forget the generosity and warmth of their reception".

Birmingham War Refugee Fund cuttings 1914-1918. Archives and Heritage, Library of Birmingham. 78pp

Now all buildings have been demolished as part of the Middle Ring Road.

19, Carpenter Road. Became a Belgian refugee Maternity Home early in the war. Thirty Belgian children were born in the first few months of their arrival. It was financed by Geraldine Cadbury, the wife of Barrow who had given Uffculme for war use. Early in the war she had prepared temporary quarters for several hundred refugees at the Friends' Institute in Moseley Road.

The house no longer exists and flats have been built on the site which is on the corner of Wheeley's Lane and Carpenter Road.

Edgbaston High School, Westbourne Road. There is a blue plaque to Neville Chamberlain who lived on the site in a house called 'Westbourne' from 1911-40. He became Birmingham's wartime Lord Mayor and Director of National Service, a post to which he could bring his understanding of manpower issues in Birmingham. Early in the war his businesses prospered from wartime demand and, after only four years on the City Council, he was being spoken of as a future Lord Mayor. One business was Hoskins which made ambulance beds. He wrote at the time that "I hate the idea of making profits out of the war when so many are giving their lives and limbs". Neville was aware of the impact of the war on the political and social order. In February 1916 he wrote of "State Socialism, the sinking of the old party divisions, the new position of women and the altered relations between employers and employed". He resigned in frustration from his national post after a year – there were too many obstacles in his path. He could not easily go back to the City Council so looked towards a future election to the House of Commons.
'The Chamberlain Litany – letters within a governing family from Empire to Appeasement'. Peter Marsh. 2010.

20, Westfield Road, Edgbaston. This was given as the address of Brigadier-General Sir John Barnsley and his wife, Lady Ellen Barnsley, by CWGC in the entry on the death of his son, Captain Thomas Kenneth Barnsley, on July 31 1917 in the 1/Coldstream Guards near Ypres at the age of 25. Sir John followed his own father who was a leading Birmingham building contractor in Ryland Street; the firm was established by his grandfather. The firm employed between 500 and 1000 workers at different times. He began at the age of seventeen and served a three year apprenticeship in the carpenter's shop. His father had previously lived at 12, Greenland Crescent, Edgbaston before his death in 1891. Sir John, yet to be knighted, was living at 'Earlfield', Westfield Road in 1911 with his three sons, a daughter and three servants. He was born in Broad Street in 1858, educated at King Edward's School from 1872-3 and became a staunch Wesleyan. He had held offices within the Church and was well known as preacher. In 1882 he married Ellen Rutherford. In March 1914 he was adopted at the Liberal candidate for the Edgbaston Division; he was already a magistrate and was also committed to education, local hospitals, temperance (he was a lifelong teetotaller) and the housing of the poor.

He had joined the Volunteers in 1883 and had commanded the 1/5 Warwicks when the Territorials were created in 1908. He retired in March 1914 and was knighted three months later in the King's Birthday Honours for his services to the Territorial Movement. When the war broke out he helped to raise the three battalions of the Birmingham Pals and became the first CO of the first of them when they trained in Sutton Park. He also raised a reserve battalion of the 1/5 Royal Warwicks – the 2/5 Territorials. He then became the city's Chief Recruiting Officer. From May 1915 to spring 1916 he commanded 183 Brigade of 61st Division before they went to France, which consisted of four reserve battalions of Warwicks Territorials. He then returned to recruiting work in Birmingham until going to France where he became area commandant of the St Quentin district. He was there until early 1918 when illness led to a return home.

His brother, Robert (1886-1968) later became a Major General in the RAMC and acted as Honorary Surgeon to the King during the Second World War. In the postwar general election he fought the Birmingham Edgbaston parliamentary seat for the Liberals but was not elected. Sir John's firm built the Hall of Memory after the war. He was one of the guests at the Council House luncheon attended by the Prince of Wales which followed the laying of the foundation stone in June 1923. The firm had earlier built the Council House, the Art Gallery and the General Hospital and many schools, churches and chapels. After the war he took a great interest in the newly formed British Legion.

Sir John died on January 19 1926 at his home at 16, St Augustine's Road, Edgbaston and was buried in Key Hill Cemetery after a funeral where the attendees reflected his life's work. He had been a businessman, magistrate, politician, soldier and social worker. Local newspaper headlines reported his death as 'Notable Birmingham Public Worker', 'Man who raised the City Battalions', 'A great Citizen' and 'Man who Gave of his Best'. At his funeral at the Islington Wesleyan Church one of the ministers referred to him as a 'distinguished citizen, a great man and one of God's good men'.

The house still exists on the corner of Augustus Road and Westfield Road.

Birmingham Biography 1924-6. Library of Birmingham. A collection of newspaper cuttings following his death.

2, Pakenham Road, Edgbaston. This was the family home of Captain Henry Lynn Shaw who was killed in action in the 10/Warwicks on July 3 1916 at the age of 44. Sparkhill born he had attended King Edward's School in the 1880s and served in the Volunteers and the Territorials as an officer. He was the senior partner in the firm of Henry Shaw and Sons, nail and chain manufacturers, of Birchall Street. He had married Grace in 1906 and by 1911 there were two sons and a daughter at Pakenham Road. He was called up from the reserve of officers when the war broke out and he was one of six city councillors who served in the Great War, three of whom were killed. He was returned for St Martin's and Deritend Ward as a Liberal Unionist in a by-election in July 1914 so his political participation was brief.

After a spell on recruiting duty at Curzon Hall he joined the Royal Warwicks and went to the front. He left a widow, Grace, and four children. Both his brothers served in the Northumberland Fusiliers. He was buried in Bapaume Post Military Cemetery, Albert, France. On May 27 1918 a memorial service was held at St George's Church, Edgbaston, for his two younger brothers both killed in action in the Northumberland Fusiliers on October 26 1917. Lieutenant Philip Shaw had been the senior partner in the family firm and had joined the Artists' Rifles in 1915 aged 38. His other brother was Second Lieutenant J.H Shaw who had fought in the Boer War and afterwards became a farmer in South Africa. He fought in German South West Africa under General Botha but then returned to England. Both are commemorated on the Tyne Cot memorial. Their parents were living at Budleigh Salterton, Devon, after the war.

The house still exists on the opposite side of the road from St James Church and the former vicarage.
Birmingham Post July 8 1916.

83, Harborne Road, Edgbaston. A blue plaque on the wall commemorates the home of Austen Chamberlain M.P. He was the son of Joseph and half-brother of Neville. He served as Secretary of State for India 1915-17 and joined the War Cabinet in April 1918. As a young man he had spent a year at the University of Berlin, knew the German language and Otto von Bismarck. In 1911 the house was the home of George Henry Branson, aged 70, and his wife, Susan. He was living on 'private means'. There was also an unmarried daughter and three servants. Austen Chamberlain had been shunted to the political sidelines during the war. He served under Lloyd George but distrusted him – 'he doesn't know how to run straight'. His sister Beatrice established the French Wounded Emergency Fund; she died of flu eight days after the armistice.

The house still exists at the 'Highfield Road' end of Harborne Road and has a blue plaque commemorating Austen Chamberlain.

57, Wellington Road, Edgbaston. This was the home of Councillor Harrison Barrow J.P. He was due to succeed Ernest Martineau as Mayor in

November 1914 but as a Quaker and a pacifist felt it was impossible to take up the position. He wrote that "it seems obvious that the duties of the Lord Mayor in the immediate future must include those of a military character… I do not consider that I can conscientiously fulfil such duties in a manner which the peculiar conditions would probably demand". His wife Ethel, also a Quaker, supported his decision. He was born in Birmingham in 1868 and his father was Richard Cadbury Barrow, Mayor in 1888-9 when Birmingham became a city, and owners of Barrows Stores in Corporation Street, the leading grocery and provisions firm. Harrison joined the firm in 1886 and soon became a partner. His father died in 1894 and he became managing director.

In 1911, while there, J.R.R Tolkien and three friends, Rob Gilson, Geoffrey Smith and Christopher Wiseman, formed a semi-secret society which they called the "T.C.B.S.", the initials standing for "Tea Club and Barrovian Society", alluding to their fondness for drinking tea in Barrow's Stores near King Edward's School. In 1898 Barrow was elected to the City Council as a Liberal for Ladywood ward. From 1904-11 he was councillor for Deritend which then became St Martin's and Deritend. In 1907 he married Ethel who was born in Wales. In 1911 the married couple at Wellington Road were looked after by four servants, including a housekeeper, parlour maid, cook and housemaid. On the eve of the war he was Chairman of the Tramways Committee.

He remained active on the City Council despite his attitude to the war. He became chairman of the Birmingham Citizens' Committee which made payment of allowances to soldier's dependents and civilians who lost their jobs because of the war. He also helped form the Birmingham Citizens' Society. Barrow also joined the Union of Democratic Control, was active in the Society of Friends nationally and played a leading role in the Friends Service Committee which helped conscientious objectors. In this capacity he became involved in 1918 in a trial, with two others, which resulted in a challenge to censorship under the Defence of the Realm Act. The case began with a Friends Service Committee leaflet entitled 'A Challenge to Militarism' highlighting 500 conscientious objectors who had been denied exemption, were drafted into the army, refused orders and were then imprisoned with hard labour. The majority accepted conditional release for work under 'semi-penal' conditions in Home Office settlements. The leaflet took up the cause of about a 1000 men who would not accept this option and received repeated sentences. The argument was that this was unjust and harmful and represented an 'evil spirit of intolerance and fear'. The leaflet ended with extracts from prison letters and court martial statements. The trial arose because the Official Press Bureau, the censor, believed the leaflet had broken new DORA (Defence of the Realm Act) rules from the autumn of 1917 as it had not been submitted for censorship. This was rule 27c. When issued the Society of Friends had criticised it and would ignore it by standing for 'spiritual liberty'. Over 70000 copies of the leaflet were printed and distributed.

In February 1918 two women were arrested for giving out the leaflets outside Central Hall, Westminster. After investigation the trial was held at Guildhall Police Court on May 23 of Barrow and two other members of the Friends Committee, Edith Ellis and Arthur Watts. Rule 27c stated that there should have been a named author; Barrow named all thirty members of the Committee as collective authors. The court made clear it could only try those charged who accepted they had broken the rule but saw the issue as one of principle. Harrison Barrow stated that "we feel bound to protest… with a deep sense of responsibility and urgent desire for the highest well-being of the nation, the religious liberties of which have been and are a priceless possession… We believe it is essential under certain circumstances, when there are vital principles at stake, for us to obey what we believe to be the guiding hand of God rather than regulations made by the Government".

The magistrate sentenced the two men to six months and Edith Ellis for three months, having refused the alternative of a fine. An appeal failed. Barrow was sent to Pentonville. Ironically between the two trials he received a letter proposing him for an OBE because of his work for the Birmingham War Pensions Committee. He refused it and also resigned from the City Council. He was removed from the Bench. His stand found some strong support but also hostility. The Birmingham Post noted his 'peculiar views'. In December 1918 he left prison and the Birmingham branch of the UDC (Union of Democratic Control) held a 'welcome'. He lost a Council election as a Labour candidate in 1920 but was elected for All Saints ward in 1922 despite attacks on his patriotism by the Conservative candidate. Out of the Council in 1925-6 he was then elected for Duddeston and Nechells ward, became an alderman and served until retirement in 1949 when he was given the freedom of the city. He died in 1953.

The house no longer exists and another house was built on the same site. In1965 the Barrows store in Corporation Street was sold to the Fitch Lovell Keymarkets group which closed in 1973. The building was later taken over by Courts Furniture.

'Harrison Barrow, His Stand for Principle and his Civic Role'. John Stewart. Birmingham Historian Issue 23, October 2002.

Cannon Hill Park. On October 14 1917 the Duke of Connaught inspected airmen and other volunteers in the Park. In May 1918 concerts had been held in the New Pavilion as part of the Civic Recreation League. The climax of Win the War Day was held in the park on September 21 1918. Colonel Hart had a key role in organising the event. There were two assembly points for the procession – Harborne Road and Hagley Road; the latter for the exhibits on lorries. The route included Broad Street, Edmund Street, the Council House, Colmore Row, Old Square, Corporation Street, New Street, Paradise Street, Suffolk Street, Bristol Street and Bristol Road. It was led by a tank followed by the band of the 10th Hussars, naval ratings, troops, ex-soldiers, members of Women's War Organisations, boy scouts and the exhibits. The troops included Royal Warwicks, Belgians and colonials as well as 1200 men from the 3rd Battalion of the 335th US infantry. Works' bands would lead their lorries. These included Austin, BSA and Wolseley. During the day there were kite balloons at the Park and aeroplane fly pasts. One highlight was the presentation by the Lord Mayor of an address to Sergeant Finch VC.

13, Charlotte Road. Was the home and studio of Joseph Edward Southall, painter and leading Birmingham pacifist. He was Chairman of Birmingham ILP (Independent Labour Party) during the war and campaigned against conscription; the Birmingham Tribunal recognised 87 conscientious objectors. He was living in this house in 1901 with his widowed mother, Eliza, and two servants. He was described as an 'artist and designer'. In 1911 he was married and at the same house according to the census. He was born into a Quaker family in Nottingham on August 23 1861. His father died a year later so he moved with his mother to her mother's house at Edgbaston. He attended Friends' Schools at Ackworth and Bootham, York, where he was taught watercolour painting. From 1878 he spent four years in the offices of Birmingham's great architectural partnership of Martin and Chamberlain. He studied art at evening classes and read Ruskin and Morris and therefore identified with the Arts and Crafts Movement. In 1883 he made his second trip abroad, this time to Italy for thirteen weeks, where he admired the Italian Primitives, particularly frescoes. On his return he began to experiment with painting 'in tempera' i.e. using egg yolk rather than oil.

He became a close friend of Arthur Garstin at the Birmingham School of Art; Arthur taught there from 1885 to 1903 and then became headmaster of the Vittoria Street School of Jewellery and Silversmithing. He was now

Joseph Edward Southall in 1913, artist and anti-war campaigner

living at 13, Charlotte Road which had belonged to his uncle, George Baker. Baker showed some of Southall's Italian trip drawings to Ruskin who was impressed. Two further visits to Italy followed and he also found encouragement from Edward Burne-Jones. By 1897 he was established as one of the foremost tempera painters in the country. On June 23 1903 he married his cousin, Anna Elizabeth Baker known as 'Bessie' (1859-1947). In the new century he was at the height of his powers and exhibited his work at home and abroad. The high point was probably his one man show at the Galeries Georges Petit in Paris in 1910. His subjects were mythological, romantic, religious, landscape and portrait. Some pieces took up to two years to complete. He produced a fresco which is now on the main staircase of Birmingham Museum and Art Gallery entitled 'Corporation Street, Birmingham', in March 1914.

For a long time he had been a Liberal in politics but with the outbreak of war he soon became Chairman of the Birmingham branch of the Independent Labour Party, a post he held until 1931. He chaired the Birmingham Auxiliary of the Peace Society and was joint Vice-President of the Birmingham and District Passive Resistance League. Painting now took second place to his anti-war activism as a propagandist and assiduous attendee at tribunals and public meetings. His attitudes were often expressed through powerful, poignant and acerbic cartoons in pamphlets and radical newspapers. In the interwar years Southall made annual visits to France, Italy, Cornwall and Suffolk. In 1928 his friend Arthur Gaskin died. The Royal Academy Winter Exhibition of Italian painting in 1930 gave a boost to tempera work. He was still active politically and attended ILP annual conferences. In a meeting at the Town Hall in May 1920 he moved a motion deploring Poland's attack on Russia and congratulating the dockers who had stopped the Jolly George from taking arms to the Poles. In the following month he joined protests against a lack of action against General Dyer following the Amritsar Massacre.

At the 1922 ILP conference he moved a motion of sympathy with the Bolsheviks in their anti-imperialist struggles. In September 1927 he caused a national sensation at the annual conference of the Left Wing Movement by suggesting that the Birmingham Labour Party, where he was still a Vice-President, was being taken over by employers of labour who had originally been Liberals. Harrison Barrow was one of those criticised. He later supported the Aid Spain movement. In the spring of 1937 he made his last trip to Italy but fell ill later that year and needed major surgery from which he never fully recovered. He still promoted peace. He still painted and his last work was almost finished when he died of heart failure on November 6 1944; this was a memorial portrait of the Bradford MP, Frederick William Jowett, a founder of the ILP. He was buried in the Friends section of Witton Cemetery. At his funeral his cousin, Evelyn Sturge, spoke of his "great love of truth and of his willingness to be unpopular in the cause of truth and of his care for the downtrodden and for justice". George Breeze in his DNB entry recognised that "in his life Southall brought together the gathered stillness of a Quaker meeting, the jewelled calm of tempera painting and the peace sought by pacifism". He left an estate valued at nearly £14000.

See his Oxford Dictionary of National Biography entry written by George Breeze and the Victorian Web article by Peyton Skipwith.

His house at 13, Charlotte Road still exists and has a blue plaque commemorating Joseph Southall.

39, Augustus Road, Edgbaston.

39, Augustus Road, Edgbaston. In 1911 this was the home of Lieutenant Colonel Ernest Martineau, who in 1914 gave up the Lord Mayoralty to join his Territorial regiment, and Margaret his wife. He was born in Birmingham on February 23 1861 and attended Trinity College, Cambridge. In 1882 he was apprenticed to the firm of Ryland, Martineau and Co, solicitors. During the Boer War he was closely involved in the equipment of volunteer detachments sent to South Africa. In 1911 his unmarried sister, Clara, 36, was also at the house and there were two children, Wilfred, 21, a student, and Violet, 12, still at school. There were six servants. He had married Margaret Kenrick in May 1888 and the family were at the same address in 1901. Bernard Gaston Martineau, aged 5, was also in the family home as well as eight servants. In 1906 he acted as Joseph Chamberlain's election agent in Birmingham West and he fulfilled the same role in 1910. Martineau led the 1/6th Warwicks, based at Thorp Street, to Essex early in the war where they intensified training and acted as part of the defence of London.

On March 23 1915 they arrived in France. They received their induction around Neuve Eglise and Dranouter and then began trench rotations in front of Le Plus Douve Farm south of Messines. They had recently moved to the area of Ploegsteert Wood when Colonel Martineau was forced to leave for home sick on May 11. He did not return. The hardships of trench conditions did not suit a 54 year old whose health was impaired. After two weeks in a base hospital he was given command of a provisional battalion at home. In November 1916 he resigned this command to resume his profession and return to the City Council as an alderman. He was now placed on the reserve of officers. Just before his return to the Council he had visited his wounded son in Devon; this was Lieutenant Bernard Gaston Martineau, subaltern in the Royal Warwicks. His other son was now Lieutenant, later Captain, Wilfred Martineau who was able to take a week's leave for his wedding at Harborne Old Church in February 1916. He was serving in his father's battalion and later joined 4th Army Signal School; he also received the MC and was mentioned in despatches. After the war Ernest Martineau lived at 30, Rotton Park Road. At the end of 1916 Ernest Martineau took over command of the 3rd Battalion of the Warwickshire Volunteer Regiment. After the war he had moved to 'Ellerslie', 43, Augustus Road. In July 1938 he was honoured as a Freeman of the City. His wife died in 1943. He retired as 'Father of the City Council' in 1945 after 44 years continuous membership. He died on November 28 1951; at that time he was living at 64, Augustus Road. His son Wilfred Martineau was Lord Mayor of Birmingham in 1940-1.

Birmingham Biography 1951. Library of Birmingham.

There has been a great deal of redevelopment in Augustus Road with many closes built off the road. The house no longer exists and the site itself is too difficult to find.

Courtlands, Edgbaston. This is the home which CWGC gives for the parents of Second Lieutenant Henry Lionel Field, 1/6th Royal Warwicks who was killed on July 1 1916 aged 22. He lies buried in Serre Road No 2 Cemetery on the Somme. He was born in May 1894, came from Edgbaston and was the grandson of Jesse Collings. He had attended Marlborough School and the Birmingham School of Art. He wrote poetry and was also an artist. His 'Poems and Drawings' between 1912 and 1916 can be found today in the Library of Birmingham. At first he thought little of his poetry but during his service life it became very important to him. In a letter to his sister he wrote…

> "Fancy me writing poetry! Always before I used to laugh at the idea and say 'Never, never would I be such a fool!'. But it's like this when you can't draw you must write, when you can't write you must sing, when you can't sing you must act? And when you can't do any of these you must fall in love!...so you see I can't help myself."

'XXVI. I.C.F France, April 1916' has the opening verse of…..

> 'Sweet are the plains of France where the Lent lilies blow,
> Yet sweeter far the woods and fields I know.
> Fair is the land where the lark sings at dawn,
> Yet fairer far the land where I was born.'

'Poems and Drawings'. H.L Field. Cornish Brothers. 1917. Library of Birmingham.

The family home is probably now the site of Courtlands Close.

Blythe Court, Norfolk Road, Edgbaston. This was the home in 1913 of Harry Gilbert Barling, one of the city's leading medical men. He was at that time a surgeon at 87, Cornwall Street, Vice-Chancellor and Professor of Surgery at Birmingham University, surgeon at the General Hospital and the Birmingham and Midland Free Hospital for Sick Children and President of the Birmingham Medical Institute. He was also a city magistrate. Born in Gloucestershire in 1855, the son of a farmer and vet, he graduated at St Bartholomew's Hospital in London in 1879 after attending a boarding school at Weston, near Bath. He then came to Birmingham to work in the General Hospital as a pathologist and then a surgeon. In 1885 he married Katherine Jaffray, the daughter of a bank manager. In 1901 and 1911 his family were living at 35, Augustus Road, Edgbaston. He drew up the scheme for rebuilding the General Hospital which was completed in 1897. In June 1908 he successfully performed an operation for appendicitis on Dr Gore, the Bishop of Birmingham.

After the outbreak of war he joined the army as a Medical Officer and became a colonel. He was consulting surgeon for Southern Command. From October 1916 to August 1917 he served in France as a consulting surgeon. During the war he was also involved in the setting up of the Rubery and Hollymoor war hospitals. He had also been involved in the raising of the 1st South Midland Mounted Brigade Field Ambulance. In 1919 he was knighted. He died at 6, Manor Road, Edgbaston in 1940.

Edith was one of his two daughters. She worked as a nursing administrator during the war and ran two hospitals for officers in the city. She was awarded the MBE for her work. She had been born in Edgbaston in 1888.

In 1913 Gilbert, his preferred name, had a nephew, Seymour Barling, who was an assistant surgeon at the General Hospital and had his own premises at 81, Edmund Street. His home was also in Edgbaston at 6, Vicarage Road. His father, Frank, was Gilbert's brother and in 1891 was managing a tramway depot at Hackney, London. By 1911 he was a retired poultry farmer at Dunton House, Curdworth. He was also a Territorial medical officer as a major commanding the 2nd South Midland Field Ambulance at the Great Brook Street barracks. He took them to France and became a colonel. He raised some concern by performing abdominal operations which were usually performed further behind the lines. Later in the war he became a base surgeon. In 1919 he co-edited with Major John Morrison 'A Manual of War Surgery'. He personally wrote chapters on the 'Organisation of Surgical Work in Base Hospitals' and 'Wounds of the Chest'. He had a distinguished post-war career and from 1931 to 1946 was Professor of Surgery at Birmingham University. He died in 1960.

Gilbert Barling in the Oxford Dictionary of National Biography. L.G Parsons. 2004

3.

Aston/Witton/Lozells/ Nechell/Duddeston

Villa Park. A former Aston Lower Grounds building in 1914 was shared as the Drill Hall of the 1/8th Royal Warwicks and the club. On August 8 1916 Private William 'Willie' Gerrish, aged 27, was killed on the Somme serving in the 17/Middlesex Regiment which was better known as the Footballers' Battalion. His legs had been shattered by a shell and he was smoking a cigarette when picked up by stretcher bearers; he died soon afterwards at the age of 27. He had played for the club between 1909 and 1912 and scored 18 goals in 59 appearances as an inside forward and won a League Championship medal in 1909-10 when he was the top scorer. He is commemorated on the Thiepval Memorial. He was one of the first to join the Battalion. In February 1915 he saved another man's life through a blood transfusion when hospitalised in 1915. The Birmingham Weekly Post on September 9 1916 referred to him as "a player of a type the public likes to see".

Private Tommy Barber had scored Villa's only and headed goal in the 1913 F.A Cup Final against Sunderland at the Crystal Palace. He played and scored for the 17/Middlesex at St Andrews on October 30 1915 in a match which aimed to raise a reserve battalion to what was to become two Footballers' Battalions. He took part in a three man patrol towards ZZ Trench at Guillemont on the Somme on August 7 1916. Not long afterwards he was seriously wounded by gunshot in his leg. He was sent to a hospital at Aberdeen and later in the war worked in a Glasgow munitions factory. He developed pleurisy – doctors said he would never play again but he played for Crystal Palace and Walsall and other clubs. He died in Nuneaton in 1925 from TB.

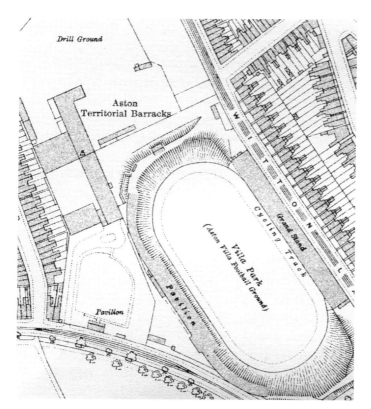

Villa Park in 1913 and the drill hall of the 1/8th Warwicks in a building shared with the club

Birmingham born Lance Corporal Walter Kimberley died at his home in Clifton Road, Aston, on April 22 1917. He was given a military funeral at Witton Cemetery. He had played for Villa, Coventry, after he left Villa in 1912, and Walsall. When war broke out was called up as a reservist and went soon after to France in the 5th Coldstream Guards where he was taken prisoner and sent to Doelberitz camp, Germany. In Germany he contracted TB and, as a result, was part of a POW exchange in August 1916. On April 2 1917 there was a benefit match for him at Villa Park between Ordnance Accessories Company and GEC.

The only current Villa player to die in the war was the promising Henry Arthur Dobson, 1st Battalion, North Staffordshire Regiment. He was born in 1892 or 1893 at Chesterton, Staffordshire as one of seven children of a coalminer. He himself in 1911 was a 19 year old 'taker off underground' and was living with his family at 26, Hodgkinson Street, Chesterton. As a private he died of wounds on March 29 1918 and was buried in Premont British Cemetery. He was a promising half back but only played seven games for Aston Villa. For example he made his debut at Villa Park against Blackburn Rovers in a 1-1 draw in February 1913 when other players were injured.

Tommy Barber also played that day. He had joined the club in August 1912 from Audley, North Staffs.

Three other current players were wounded – Harry Hampton was gassed, Frank Moss senior suffered a knee wound but survived to captain England and Tom Weston was injured in March 1918. Sam Hardy RN and Gunner James Stephenson also saw action. Other former players served e.g. RSM Joe Windmill MC DCM, a half back, who was gassed and wounded. He came from Brierley Hill and attended Saltley College and became a teacher. He played in Villa's 1905 Cup winning side. He later gave up top level football because of difficulty in combining teaching and football. His DCM was gazetted on April 17 1918. There was a novel event at Villa Park on Saturday June 8 1918 when a noisy crowd of 8000 watched a baseball match between the Americans and the Canadians. The former won 23-6. The losers were short of practice and, being connected with the Records Office, have not the same facilities for play as their rivals. The proceeds went to military charities.

'When the Whistle Blows: The Footballers' Battalion in the Great War'. Andrew Riddoch and John Kemp. Haynes. 2008.

'The Aston Villa Chronicles 1874-1924', John Lerwill. Volume 1. Aston Villa. 2009. Pages 343-4.

Birmingham Weekly Post June 15 1918.

Birmingham Weekly Post April 28 1917. (Kimberley)

Birmingham Weekly Post June 2 1917. (Windmill)

Aston Church dedicated to Saints Peter and Paul. Near the entrance to the churchyard stands a memorial to the 1/8th Royal Warwicks, who were based at a drill hall at nearby Villa Park, with lists of places where they saw action. It was unveiled on November 11 1920. There is at least seven CWGC headstones around the church. Two were men who died post-war. Private Eggar of the 5/Worcs died on May 1 1920 aged 26. He came from Nechells and there was an epitaph on the headstone which reads 'Gone but not forgotten by wife Cora and daughter Florrie'. Lance Corporal Lloyd died on September 29 1920 and had served in the Mounted Military Police. There is a special memorial stone dedicated to Alfred Wilcox VC – Aston born and served in the Ox and Bucks Light Infantry. He won the VC on September 12 1918.

Inside the church there is the main Aston war memorial with over 600 names. There is also a memorial plaque to Colonel Walter Robert Ludlow who was instrumental in raising and commanding what became the 1/8th Territorial battalion. In particular he persuaded Birmingham businessmen to support the new force as time off from work was necessary. He had been born in Aston in 1857 and was a partner with William Briscoe in a firm of surveyors, auctioneers, estate agents and valuers at 19, Temple Street although in 1913 he was living at Lovelace Hill, Solihull. His son, Stratford Walter Ludlow, was a captain in 'C' company of the battalion when he was killed on the first day of the Somme. Captain Ludlow is commemorated in Knowle Soldiers' Chapel and Solihull Church. In March 1918 his father, now a Brigadier General, went to the Somme to try to find his son's grave and later wrote a moving account of his mission. Aston Church still holds a 'Somme Sunday' to commemorated the 250 men from 1/8th battalion who were killed on July 1 1916.

Wilton Street, Lozells, off Lozells Road.
Lance Corporal Alfred Wilcox was born here in a back to back house on December 16 1884. He attended Burlington Street School, Aston and is recorded with his family at 23 Court, 7 House, Clifton Road, Aston in 1891. He was one of nine children; his three eldest siblings were already at work as a warehouse girl, machinist and wood turner. His father, William, was a 'jeweller' and his mother, Sarah, like her husband was Birmingham born. By 1901 he was working as a jeweller himself. The family were now a short distance away at 79, Tower Road, Aston and there were four further additions to the family. In 1911 he was boarding with a Birmingham family at 37, Ferndale Road, Leytonstone in East London; he was now described as a 'diamond mounter' as was the head of the household, Albert James. The family were at 79, Tower Road, Aston. On September 6 1913 he married Ellen Clarke at St John's, Perry Barr. A daughter, Doris, was born before he joined the army and a son, Leonard, in 1916.

Still in Leytonstone he joined the Royal Bucks Hussars on March 25 1915; his Birmingham family moved to 86, Little Green Lane, Small Heath. He was subsequently attached to the 2/4th Ox and Bucks and went with them to France in December 1917. In April 1918 he was promoted to lance corporal. He was awarded the VC as a result of an attack on Junction Post near Laventie, France, on September 12 1918. His company were under fire from German machine guns as they began their task to cut their wire and locate the posts. His section were badly hit and sheltered in a shell hole as he cut the wire. The citation then continued "On his own initiative with four men he rushed ahead to the nearest enemy gun, bombed it, killed the gunner and put the gun out of action. Being then attacked by an enemy bombing party Corporal Wilcox picked up enemy bombs and led his party against the next gun, finally capturing and destroying it. Although left with only one man he continued bombing and captured a third gun. He again bombed up the trench, captured a fourth gun, and then rejoined his platoon. Corporal Wilcox displayed in this series of successful individual enterprises exceptional valour, judgement and initiative". He expanded on these events in later interviews. "If I hadn't been after 'em they'd have been after me and I used more language than the British Army ever learnt".

On November 2 1918 he was badly wounded by machine gun fire in an attack on St Hubert, being hit twice in the ankle and four times in the leg. He was sent to the Sunderland War Hospital where he heard the news of his VC. He returned to Birmingham on December 19 still only able to walk on crutches. On February 22 1919 he was given a civic reception by Lord Mayor Brooks in Victoria Square. He told the crowd "After all is said and done we have only done our duty to our King and Country and women folk left behind". Alfred was discharged on May 2 1919 and received the VC at Buckingham Palace on November 26. He attended the Buckingham Palace VC party on June 26 1920 and was present with Arthur Vickers at the stone laying for the Hall of Memory on June 12 1923. With other ex-servicemen he was presented to the Prince of Wales at Quinton when the latter opened the new Birmingham to Wolverhampton Road. He was then President of the Birmingham County British Legion. On November 9 1929 he was present at the House of Lords VC dinner. He was at Westminster Abbey in 1936 at a service to commemorate the sixteenth anniversary of the Ypres League. In 1939, by now separated from his wife, he returned to Birmingham from London and became a publican at the Trafalgar Hotel in Moseley from 1940 to 1945. He then moved to the Old Engine in Hockley. From 1950 he was at the Prince Arthur in Small Heath where he died on March 30 1954. He was buried at Aston Church on April 3 where a memorial stone to his achievement now stands. In 1999 his VC medal group was bought by Lord Ashcroft.

'beyondtheschool' website.

Half of Wilton Street south of Lozells Road no longer exists. The northern portion has been redeveloped. According to the 1891 census 363 people lived in the street; half in court housing. Clifton Road and Tower Road were both affected by the building of the Aston Expressway.

Plaque to Arthur Vickers VC at Junction 6 Industrial Park, Witton (Witton Business Park). On September 25 1915 he won the VC for a brave action on the first day of the Battle of Loos in France whilst serving

in the 2nd Battalion of the Royal Warwickshire Regiment. They were attacking a German position known as the Quarries. When the initial attack was held up on the wire Private Vickers distinguished himself by cutting a lane through the wire for which he received the Victoria Cross. The citation read…."During an attack by his battalion on the German front line trenches, Private Vickers, on his own initiative, and with the utmost bravery, went forward in front of his own company under very heavy shell, rifle and machine-gun fire and cut the wires which were holding up a great part of the battalion. Although it was broad daylight at the time, he carried out this work standing up. His gallant action contributed largely to the success of the assault".

On his arrival back in Birmingham on November 27 he was greeted by his sister, uncle and friends at New Street Station. Vickers soon elaborated himself on the events to local reporters…"It was a good battle until we came up against the barbed wire. We began our advance at 6.28 a.m. We were in a ploughed field and it was raining heavily. When the order 'Turn out Wire-cutters' was given I was standing well in front of the other fellows. I dashed forward at once. I saw my officer fall. I shouted to the others to take cover. Then I went on and cut the wires. I made two gaps and our chaps were able to get through them… The other chaps, especially Serjeant Pountenay and Corporal Bryan, are brave men, Bryan is a Birmingham man. Pountenay, I believe, belongs to Coventry….We always sing – any old song that comes to mind – when we come out of the trenches or are passing through a village or town, everybody knows when the Warwicks are about". In a letter to his sister he added the extra detail that he needed both hands to use the wire-cutters so 'slung' his rifle.

He was born on February 2 1882 at 7 Court, Woodcock Street, Aston, the son of John and Amy Vickers. John was a brass strip caster. In 1901 Arthur had four brothers (all but one older) and two sisters (both younger). Between 1890-5 he attended Dartmouth Street School. He became an enthusiastic amateur boxer and worked for James Beresford and Sons, Cato Street, Birmingham, who manufactured railway carriage furniture. He played for the works football team. On May 29 1902 Arthur joined the Royal Warwickshire Regiment which he served until 1908 when he left the army to work for GEC, Witton, Birmingham. In 1914 he re-enlisted after five rejections – he was only 5 feet 2 inches tall and less than 8 stone. At that time he lived in Park Road, Aston, and worked for a firm of brass casters. On May 4 1915 he joined the 2nd Battalion in France. On September 25 1915 he committed the brave action at Loos for which he received the VC. In

November of the same year he was awarded the Croix de Guerre avec palm. He was promoted to Lance Corporal and then came the news of the VC award.

On November 27 1915 he arrived in Birmingham on leave and received a warm welcome and became a subject of civic pride. He was nicknamed the 'midget VC' and lauded by family, friends, neighbours, Dartmouth Street School, the Lord Mayor (Neville Chamberlain), Curzon Street recruiting office, where he joined up and the regimental depot at Budbrooke, near Warwick. On December 6 1915 he left Birmingham for France thus missing the special public civic event in Victoria Square five days later. On March 4 1916 he received the VC from King George V at Buckingham Palace. Three days later there was a civic reception in Birmingham in lieu of the one he had missed. He returned to France and was promoted to Serjeant.

In 1920 he lived for two years with his sister's family in Aston. In the same year on June 26 Arthur Vickers attended the Garden Party at Buckingham Palace for VC recipients. On November 11 he was a member of the Honour Guard for the burial of the unknown soldier in Westminster Abbey. On October 1 1921 he was a guest at the unveiling of the regimental memorial at St Mary's, Warwick; he carried the roll of honour on a cushion in the procession.

On April 29 1922 he married Lily Price at Aston church. They lived in Villa Street, Lozells. In 1923 a son, Arthur, was born but died a month later. His father was then described as a carter. On November 9 1929 he attended the VC reunion dinner at the House of Lords and on October 23 1934 he was part of a Guard of Honour for the Prince of Wales visit to Birmingham. In 1935 Arthur was employed by Lucas as a millwright's mate. Around 1938 the family moved to Farm Street, Hockley. In the Second World War he served in a Home Guard unit but contracted TB and died on July 27 1944 at the City Hospital, West Heath, aged 62. He was buried in Witton Cemetery. His wife, Lily, died soon afterwards. His VC is with the Royal Fusiliers Museum, Warwick. In November 1998 a plaque in his honour was unveiled at Junction Six Industrial Park, Witton, the site of the former GEC factory. On November 13 2000 a headstone was placed on his grave.

'Arthur Vickers – The Midget VC' by Chris Sutton. Birmingham Historian Issue 28. Spring 2006. Pages 5-12.

1, Bloomsbury Street, Nechells. This was the home in 1891 of 17 year old Henry Clutterbuck who was the first officer killed in the First World War with strong Birmingham connections that we can be sure about. In 1891

James, his father, was an Inland Revenue officer, a job which had already taken him to Cornwall, where Henry and his brother were born and to Norfolk where his sister was born. Henry at that time was a clerk to a metal merchant. By 1911 James had retired to Hampton Lovett near Droitwich with his wife and daughter. Henry had attended Camp Hill Grammar School in the late 1880s and did not remain a clerk for very long as in July 1893 he joined the Coldstream Guards as a private. He quickly rose through the ranks and was commissioned into the Yorkshire Light Infantry in August 1900. He served throughout the Boer War.

From 1904 to 1909 he was adjutant to the Kings Own Malta Regiment and afterwards served in India where we find him on the 1911 census as a captain at Havelock Barracks at Lucknow in the Kings Own Royal Lancaster Regiment. By that time he had married South African born Cora Rajaela at Valetta in 1908. She was the daughter of the Netherlands consul-general in South Africa. Henry was supposed to have become garrison

Captain Henry Clutterbuck is in the middle of this photograph

adjutant at Borden in October 1914 but the outbreak of war led to his joining his regiment's 1st Battalion in France. On August 26 they were at Haucourt near Le Cateau helping to stop the German advance when he was killed. Newspaper reports suggest that he was killed in leading a dashing, brilliant bayonet charge which was 'just like Clutterbuck'. However, such reports are generally unreliable. There was a bayonet charge as he was mentioned in despatches after his death. The first newspaper report of his death on September 7 included reminiscences of an old school mate who detailed a joke he had played on a science master at Camp Hill.

De Ruvigny.

Birmingham Weekly Post September 8 and 9 1914.

Witton Municipal Cemetery, Moor Lane. With major war hospitals in the city it is not surprising that many men died at home from 'blighty' wounds or from illness without going to the front. This large cemetery holds 466 First World War burials with over 200 in three denominational plots. All those buried or in 'lost graves' are named on an impressive memorial wall of nine metal panels. Arthur Vickers VC was buried there in 1944 as well as

George Ravenhill, a Boer War VC, who also served in the Duke of Cornwall's Light Infantry during the First World War. Many of those who have their last resting place there were home service men of various kinds or the thirty-two aged twenty or under who were probably victims of an unhealthy society and the flu epidemic.

One hundred and eight were members of the Royal Warwickshire Regiment and 43 in the Worcesters. Twenty served in the Navy or Air Force. Six were in the Canadian Infantry although the four with nine addresses were sons of Birmingham families. Amongst the contemporary burials eight had been awarded medals – six Military Medals, a DCM and a DSO. There were very few officers and the man with the highest rank was Lieutenant Commander William Hallwright DSO who commanded HMS Q16 which was attacked on the surface by a U-boat 300 miles west of Ushant island off Brittany on April 21 1917. His ship was a 1250 ton sloop which appeared to be a merchant ship on its top decks but concealed naval guns below. He was killed by a shell splinter whilst in his lookout at the end of the bridge.

The DCM had been awarded to CSM Frederick Howells of Aston Church Road who died on the first day of 1919. He had served in the 22nd Battalion of the Tank Corps after leaving the North Staffordshire Regiment. The award entry was gazetted on November 15 1918 and stated that "he commanded his tank with great gallantry and skill, rendering invaluable service to the infantry, in spite of heavy mist and other difficulties. Although under intense artillery fire at almost point blank range he engaged the enemy infantry and accounted for large numbers and, finally, when his tank was hit and disabled, he blew it up before the enemy could seize it".

Of those commemorated in the Cemetery 212 died between 1919 and 1921. Twenty-seven of the total had served in the Royal Engineers including signals, inland waterways, docks and railways. Susan Gibson of the Women's Royal Air Force is the only woman listed and died eight days after the end of the war at the age of 38. Nine men had been members of the Royal Defence Corps, five of them in 'Protection Companies'; these were men too old for conscription.

Kynochs. Later called Imperial Metal Industries and originally known as the Lion Works. This was a major munitions works visited by the King on July 23 1915. It was his first visit of the final and second day of his visit to the city. He could not visit every part of the works as it was too big but he did, however, go into a number of departments selected with the object of giving him an idea of the various stages of manufacture and organisation of the

King George V at Kynochs on July 23 1915

factory. By that stage of the war output had been increased by 600%. He also met the 'principal officials', departmental managers and older workers.

At one stage the company was contracted to manufacture each week 25 million rifle cartridges, half a million cartridge clips, 110000 brass cases for 18 pounder field guns and 300 tons of cordite. To make one rifle cartridge took 102 different operations. The firm and its workforce was also heavily involved in the wider wartime community including municipal savings,

One of Kynoch's contributions to Win the War Day in September 1918

support for hospitals and events such as Win the War Day. IMI left the site in 2003 and part of the 220 acre site then became a business park.

GEC, Electric Avenue, Witton. The factory opened in 1902 as the first one by the company. The main focus of the factory, one of several in the GEC group, was in the manufacture of electrical plant for the production or utilisation of power. This meant generators, motors, rotary converters and switchgear; all under wartime Government contracts. The motor department was very busy equipping many munitions works e.g. 240 were supplied just to BSA. In the First World War GEC also made radios, signal lamps and arc lamp carbons for searchlights. Early in 1915 the company built an extension at Witton at its own expense to produce 3-pounder and 4.5 inch high explosive shells. Women were largely employed on the necessary processes. During the war the enlarged plant made an average of a million carbons a year.

A long list could be made of the plant and apparatus adapted or newly designed for all sorts of military and naval purposes – e.g portable ASC workshops, dynamo exploders, arc generators for wireless sets. GEC also had another Birmingham factory at the Ileene Works which before the war made electric light fittings, electric heating and cooking appliances, lamp holders, switches and many accessories. This range made it easily adaptable to war needs. Primers were made there in 1915 before any factory other than ammunition works. Later quantities of suspension gear and directional gear for submarine detection were produced. The main works led the way in the

Female capstan lathe operator makes shell cases at GEC, Witton, in 1916

district for the manufacture of pressed aircraft parts and in the liquid brazing of them.

'Story of GEC'. Adam Gowans Whyte. Ernest Benn. 1930. Library of Birmingham.

Later demolished and now the site of a business park from 1995.

Aston Cross. HP sauce made its own contribution to the war effort. As male workers left to join up Samson and Edwin Moore, the owners, had to change employment practices and employ married women for the first time. They were able to control the huge workhorses and roll large casks of vinegar onto the drays. The new workers circumvented the no tea breaks rule by smuggling in bottles of tea hidden in their pockets and heating them on the factory steam pipes. Large government orders arrived for supplies of vinegar and sauce for the troops. Many front line soldiers claimed that HP sauce was the only thing that made an unvarying diet of bully beef and maconochie palatable. HP sauce bottles turn up in archaeological excavations of the Western Front trenches.

The factory was demolished when Heinz moved production to Holland. It is now the site of East End Foods cash and carry warehouse.

St Mary's, corner of Aston Road North and Avenue Road, Aston Brook. Aston Brook was the name of the area around Aston Cross. On Saturday November 11 1916 the Bishop of Birmingham unveiled the war shrine on the church wall. There were two lists of names surmounted by a crucifix with a canopy eleven feet high. The smaller one numbered 38 and noted the names of those who had made the 'supreme sacrifice'. The larger list had nearly 300 names of soldiers and sailors from the parish who were serving. There was an indication to show whether a man was wounded or a POW.

Birmingham Weekly Post November 18 1916.

The church was demolished c1969 to make way for the Aston Expressway.

Great Brook Street Barracks, Nechells. This had several uses, one was as an artillery base. For 'Big Guns Week' in Victoria Square in October 1918 it provided a 9.2 howitzer, a 6 inch naval gun, an 8 inch howitzer, a sixty pounder, a 4.5 howitzer and an 18 pounder. The 1st South Midland Territorial Field Ambulance Unit was also based there. The barracks was demolished by the Corporation in 1936 and made way for maisonettes. The barracks

Great Brook Street barracks in 1918

were originally built in 1793 following the Birmingham riots. The main building facing Great Brook Street was three storeys high and there were two-storey blocks down the east and west sides.

The now residential site is bordered by roads which have the names Barrack Street and Great Brook Street.

Nechells Gas Works. At the beginning of the war Dr W.B Davidson investigated the extraction of toluene, a constituent of TNT, from coal gas. The extraction plant there started work on June 1 1915 – the first in the country. A temporary electric power station was built during the war to provide additional power to munitions works; it was operational early in 1916. This was situated just to the north of the Aston-Stechford railway line and to the east of the River Rea and the Birmingham and Warwick Junction Canal. The temporary power station closed in 1936 and all trace has disappeared under the Nechells Parkway road scheme. The 'Birmingham Gas Works' produced over 9000 tons of TNT, lyddite etc which could fill 25-30 million 18 pounder shells).

Dyson Hall, Park Street, Aston. The Hall provided recreational activities for women war workers under the Birmingham Civic Recreation League. It was built in 1897 as a mission hall 'served by the clergy' of Aston Church.

24, Lozells Road, Six Ways, Aston. This is the post-war address which was given to the Imperial War Graves Commission by Julia Mannock, the mother of Major Edward 'Mick' Mannock VC, one of Britain's top air aces of the war. In 1918 and 1919 she had lived at 15, Witton Road, Six Ways and 96, Ettington Road, Aston. In 1916 she had lived at 10, Bruce Street and 159, Divis Street, Belfast. His father in 1919 was at 29, Siebert Street, Westcombe Park, Blackheath, London.

Mannock was shot down whilst on patrol on July 26 1918 at the age of 31. His body was never recovered and he is commemorated on the air memorial at the Arras Memorial. Born in Ireland he was working as a telephone engineer in Turkey in 1914 and was interned but was repatriated in 1915 when he became ill. He joined the RFC in 1916 and by March 1918 was flight commander of the new 74 Squadron. He soon left to command 85 Squadron. He had an obsessive fear of being shot down in flames and carried a loaded pistol in his cockpit for such an eventuality. He was highly regarded as a tactician, patrol leader and combat pilot with a cardinal rule of "Always above, seldom on the same level, never underneath". His posthumous Victoria Cross mentioned seven separate actions in the weeks before his death and concluded… "This highly distinguished officer, during the whole of his career in the RAF, was an outstanding example of fearless courage, remarkable skill, devotion to duty and self-sacrifice, which has never been surpassed".

'Mannock: The Life and Death of Major Edward Mannock VC, DSO, MC, RAF'. Norman Franks and Andy Saunders. Grub Street. 2008.

Mount Street, Duddeston. Lance Corporal William Amey VC was born here on March 5 1881. His father, Charles, was a railway carriage fitter. He was one of seven children, four brothers and two sisters. In 1891 the family were living at 47, Stuart Street, Nechells. By 1911 they were at 58, Stella Street, Nechells but his mother, Elizabeth, was now a widow. William was recorded as a chandelier maker. In 1914 he was employed by Messrs Veritys Ltd, electrical engineers, at the Plume and Victoria Works, Aston. In May 1915 he joined the 1/8th Royal Warwickshire Regiment based at Aston and went to France in early 1916. He was soon promoted to lance corporal and at some point was awarded the Military Medal.

He served on the Somme, at 3rd Ypres and in Italy. On November 4 1918 his battalion was involved in an attack towards Landrecies, France. His unit was held up by fire from the direction of Faubourg Soyeres. Amey lost contact with his own company and so attached himself to another. Unaided he attacked a fortified chateau which was holding up the advance. When assistance arrived the battalion reached a canal lock and were able to cross. Later that day the Germans retreated from Landrecies. His VC citation published in January 1919 stated that "during the attack on Landrecies, when owing to fog, many hostile machine guns nests were missed by the leading troops. On his own initiative he led his section against a machine gun nest, under heavy fire, drove the garrison into a neighbouring farm, and finally captured about 50 prisoners and several machine guns. Later, single-handed, and under heavy fire, he attacked a machine gun post in a farmhouse, killed two of the garrison and drove the remainder into a cellar until assistance arrived. Subsequently, single-handed, he rushed a strongly held post, capturing 20 prisoners. He displayed throughout the day the highest degree of valour and determination".

He left his battalion at Cambrai on December 14 to return for Christmas leave in 1918 but then found he needed an operation and became a patient at the Dudley Road Hospital when he learned of the VC award in a telegram from Colonel Whitehouse. He was decorated with his VC at Buckingham Palace on February 22 1919. He left the army that year with the rank of corporal. His younger brother had served with the Worcesters in Meso-potamia. His mother was still at Stella Street but he moved to Leamington Spa after the war and died in hospital there on May 28 1940. He was buried in All Saints Cemetery and given a full military funeral. He had worked in business as an agent. In 1920 he attended the VC Garden Party at Buckingham Palace and in 1929 the House of Lords dinner. He was a prominent member of the Leamington British Legion. His widow, Evelyn, remarried and after the death of her second husband, sold William's VC. In 1963 his medals were sold to the Friends of the Warwickshire Regiment for £600 and are now at the Fusiliers Museum at Warwick.

'VCs of the First World War. The Final Days 1918'. Gerald Gliddon. Sutton. 2000.

Globe Inn, Manchester Street. Off Newtown Row to the east. This was given by a local newspaper as the address of Edward Barry, who with his colleague, Edgar Hounsell, were survivors of the sinking of the Lusitania on May 7 1915 when the liner was torpedoed by a German submarine off the Irish coast. Hounsell was a Birmingham film renter of the Midland Exclusive Film Company of John Bright Street and also managed the Imperial Picture Palace, West Bromwich. Barry was a representative of the firm. The men were returning from a business trip to America where they hoped to set up a new company, the Anglo-American Film Distributing

Company with a headquarters in London. Barry recounted his experiences to the Birmingham Daily Post on May 9. He only had a few cuts and gashes as a result of making contact with floating wreckage. He and his friends, including Hounsell, had just finished dinner and ordered coffee when there was a dull thud. He said to Hounsell that he thought it was a torpedo. The ship began to list. The two men went to their cabins and put on life jackets and helped women and children to do the same. Stewards were directing everybody to the boats and Barry started cutting the cords of the tarpaulin covers over the boats.

He decided he had to jump into the water. When he surfaced he saw heartrending scenes and heard screams. As a strong swimmer he was able to make for a capsized boat. Exhausted he reached it and joined some men, a steward, an American lady who had lost her husband and an injured lady. They moved to an upright boat and there turned out to be 47 who could be saved. He was picked up by a patrol boat at about 7 p.m nearly five hours after the torpedo struck. Navy rum was welcome. They landed at Queenstown where they were kindly received. On the night of May 8 he and Hounsell were able to get a fast mail boat to England.

Edgar Hounsell told his story to the Post a day after Barry. He stated that everybody thought that the German warning given before the Lusitania sailed from New York on May 1 was a German bluff. He also said that the warning telegrams sent to passengers before boarding only went to Americans. When hit all the plates and dishes rolled off the table and confusion followed. After picking up his life jacket he reached the upper deck and found that most of the boats had already gone. Boats on one side could not be launched anyway because of the increasing list. Standing on the deck became impossible. To avoid suction he jumped off the stern but was dragged down with the ship. As the liner sank it turned to one side and Hounsell was released to the surface at a fast pace. He clung to a piece of timber for an hour and was then able to hold on to an overturned boat. One of three men on it helped him until they were able to take over a canvas sided collapsible boat. They were able to rescue other people until a trawler, the 'Brock', came at 6 p.m. and they, in turn, were rescued.

Hounsell was bringing back 'show copies' of five recent films which went down with the liner. The 1911 census shows him staying at the Temperance Hotel, Newcastle upon Tyne, and working as a 'bioscope entertainer'. He was born in Portsmouth and was then 28 years old. The following week Barry appeared at a recruiting meeting at the Rookery Road Picture House and stirred the audience with the recital of his exciting experiences.

There were other Birmingham survivors of the Lusitania. They included Mr J.S Arter of St Agnes Road, Moseley, and Mr H.F.H Ehrhardt of Woodbourne Road, Edgbaston. There was also Mr and Mrs J.J Frankum of 55, Webster Street, Aston, who were saved with their son but lost two other children. Mr J.L Harris of 280, Belgrave Road and Mr Maitland Kempson of 365, Hagley Road, were also saved. Kempson was a director of a Kidderminster firm and had been on a business trip to Canada and the USA. He was returning with three friends and they had ignored the warning from the German Embassy in New York. He jumped about thirty feet into the sea from the listing ship. He helped pull other people into boats and was later rescued by the 'Bluebell', a fishing boat. He stated that "We saw hundreds of bodies of dead men and women. Their heads were under water but their bodies were kept afloat by the lifebelts. The scenes were ghastly, too awful to describe". On the 'Bluebell' some of the women were hysterical because they had lost their children. They arrived at the Cunard pier at Queenstown at 10.30 p.m. and two hours later he bought the last suit of ready-made clothes in the town. One of his friends was drowned and the other two were saved.

Mrs A.T Wakefield survived. Her mother, Mrs Smith, lived at 14, Reddings Road, Moseley, and her brother-in-law lived at Chantry Road, also in Moseley. Mrs Wakefield had formerly been a mistress at Camp Hill Grammar School and had left to go to Honolulu to be married. Later her husband had died so she was returning to Britain. She was in hospital at Queenstown after rescue.

John Lewis Harris was missing. He had been a butcher on the Lusitania for eighteen months and had previously lived in Birmingham with his brother and worked at the Central Meat Market in Bradford Street. William Parkes was also saved. He lived at 1 back, 4, Chapel Lane, Selly Oak and had worked in Toronto as a sugar refiner for over five years. He was returning to rejoin his wife. He was smoking on deck when the torpedo struck and spent three hours in the water. Someone else with Birmingham connections was Mr S.L.B Lines of Toronto who was saved with his wife. He was the manager of the Canadian branch of the Birmingham firm of the Chamberlain and Hookham Electric Meter Company of 4, New Bartholomew Street. He was travelling to England on business and his wife wanted to work for the Red Cross. They were parted when the ship went down and met again at the Queen's Hotel, Queenstown.

On Saturday May 8 there was a 'largely attended' recruiting meeting in Victoria Square. Major Hall-Edwards made a typical speech on the subject and began by saying that it was "almost a disgrace that it should be necessary at this stage of the Empire's crisis they should have to go there to persuade people to do their duty". The duty of men was to enlist unless they were skilled workmen in munitions. "If the loss of the Lusitania did not make their blood boil and make them feel they ought to offer their services he did not know what would". It was a 'dastardly act'. Canon Willink, the Rector of Birmingham, followed. "It was not war, it was murder". "We were not the people to squeal if fair warfare went against us but we were confronted with horrors that seemed unthinkable and unspeakable".

The Globe Inn is still a pub in Manchester Street.
Birmingham Daily Post, May 1915.

King Edward VI Grammar School, Frederick Road, Aston.
The school still occupies the same site as it did when opened in 1883. It has an impressive memorial board to the 128 'Old Eds' killed in the First World War and among over 700 who served. The rank and regiment/unit are listed with the names. In February 1918 the school published a list of 536 'old boys' still serving. Seventy had been wounded and some of them discharged. A further eighty-two had been killed, died of wounds or died and three were missing in action. Four men were known prisoners of war. On March 31 1919 a meeting at the school promoted by Joseph Manton, the headmaster, and Bill Bailey resolved to raise money for the main school memorial, to fund the education of the children of those killed or disabled and to buy a playing field as a memorial to the Old Boys who had not returned. The new ground at Sunny Bank Avenue, Perry Common, was dedicated on December 10 1927, a date shown on a memorial stone at the site.

The examples which follow reflect the range of wartime service and stand for all those named on the memorial. Second Lieutenant Eric Newton Marson was killed, aged 20, as part of the 9th Warwicks assault on Sari Bair above Anzac Cove at Gallipoli which had begun the previous day. He was one of 94 men killed that day from his unit. In 1911 he had been a schoolboy and lived at Belgrave Cottage, 188, Villa Street, Aston, with his father, William, the manager of a silversmiths, his mother, Annie, and two brothers; the household had one servant. When he left school Eric went to Birmingham University and joined the OTC where he probably met Bill Slim who was to serve in the same battalion. Marson was commissioned early in the war and joined battalion officers who Slim later described as University men or Ceylon tea planters or 'odds like me and Marsden' (he meant Marson).

Slim's papers referred to a 'dugout major' who indulged in unpleasant sarcasm about 'temporary gentlemen' in his company whose social polish was somewhat lacking. Although not named this was likely to have been about Eric Marson who, he also noted, died after being hit a third time during the assault. He is commemorated on the Helles Memorial and the University of Birmingham War Memorial.

Second Lieutenant Lawrence Kay is also named on the Handsworth Grammar School memorial but had also attended the Aston School where he was school captain. He is described under the entry for the former. Corporal Edward Minahan has a private headstone in the churchyard of St Barnabas, Erdington and is described under that entry. Second Lieutenant Conrade Jacot died in an air crash at Castle Bromwich airfield and had been described under Curdworth churchyard. Captain Robert Phillips has been noted under his home at Hill Top, West Bromwich.

Lieutenant Ralph Howell Davies also served in the 9th Warwicks and was killed on April 9 1916, aged 24, when the battalion had moved to Mesopotamia and, in particular, the failed attack on the strong Turkish position at Sannaiyat as part of an attempt to relieve Kut. He was Birmingham born and had attended the school from 1898 to 1906. In 1911 he was an insurance clerk living with his widowed mother and seven siblings at 236, Kingsbury Road, Erdington. He played rugby for the Old Eds before the war and initially joined the cavalry before achieving a commission in the 9th Warwicks. He later became the battalion transport officer. His brother, Evan, was a medical student in 1911 and later joined the RAMC but was taken prisoner early in the war. Another brother, Second Lieutenant John Hickman Davies, also named on the memorial, was killed in the 2nd Warwicks attack on Judge Copse on October 9 1917 during the Third Battle of Ypres. He was 22. John is buried in Buttes New British Cemetery, Polygon Wood. He had originally joined the 1st Birmingham Pals. After the war his mother was living at 29, Wood End Road, Erdington.

Captain Alfred Claude Douglas Dingley, aged 25, was also killed in Mesopotamia on April 19 1916 when his 7th/North Staffs battalion joined a 39 Brigade assault on Turkish lines around Kut; the siege of the town could not be broken. He was leading 'A' and 'B' companies when he was killed. In 1911 he was living with his family at 79, Lodge Road, Hockley and worked as a gilt jewellers warehouse assistant. His brother, Philip, had the same occupation and they probably both worked for their father, Alfred, who was a silver chain maker. The firm was listed in 1913 at the same address and was described as 'Dingley, Hegmann and Co', probably serving the Mexican market. Captain Dingley is commemorated on the Basra Memorial. Post-war his parents were living at 'Imbros', Welford-on-Avon. The house appears to have been named after the island six miles west of the Gallipoli coast and an important staging post for 1915 operations.

We do not know a great deal about Lieutenant James Gerald Fussell who was killed on the first day of the Somme, aged 23, whilst serving with the 1/8th Warwicks, a Territorial battalion. He was one of 230 deaths during the failed attack on the Heidenkopf strongpoint on the Somme. His last words are believed to be 'Come on boys, come on the 8th Warwicks'. We do not know whether he joined pre-war but if he did the drill hall was the other side of Aston Park from his old school in a former Aston Lower grounds building shared with Aston Villa. This could be the case as he became a subaltern as early as September 24 1914. He is commemorated on the Thiepval Memorial.

The Clutterbuck brothers were one of the sets of siblings on the memorial. In 1911 Norman Eckstein and Arthur Stanley were aged 16 and 14 respectively and were living with their parents at 63, Hall Road, Handsworth. Their father was a diamond merchant and manufacturing jeweller with premises at 28A, Frederick Street. In a 1913 directory he was described as a diamond mounter. There was also a younger brother and sister and one servant. Arthur was still at school and Norman was noted as having the same occupation as his father. Post-war the parents were living at 'Sandwell', 45, Handsworth Wood Road. Second Lieutenant Arthur Clutterbuck was killed first on July 14 1916 whilst serving with the 8th Worcesters on the Somme; he achieved this rank in October 1915. He was buried in Sucrerie Military Cemetery at Colincamps. Lieutenant Norman Clutterbuck was killed on April 24 1917 whilst serving in the same battalion. He had probably been commissioned into it from one of Birmingham Pals battalions in May 1915. He is buried in Templeux-le-Guerard British Cemetery, east of Peronne, and died in the operations which followed the German retreat to the Hindenburg Line.

Second Lieutenant Ivan Pinson, aged 21, was shot down as an observer on May 4 1917 whilst on a reconnaissance mission of new German airfields around Tournai. He was buried in Halluin Communal Cemetery close to the French-Belgian border. The pilot of his Sopwith Strutter 1½ was Lieutenant Valentine Adams, who had come from Australia to join the RFC, and they were part of a flight of nine aircraft from 70 Squadron when they were attacked by Jasta 8. Adams was forced to land behind the German lines after being hit in the petrol tank. Pinson fired a coloured light to show that they would be forced down and they were seen to glide to the ground. They landed at 'Trois Tetus' near Linselle, 25 kilometres north of Lille. Five witnesses who were on the ground when the plane landed and were interviewed by French policemen later gave statements which reached the Red Cross in Geneva. They reported that some German soldiers camped at a nearby farm made for the scene. Adams pulled Pinson out of the aircraft and then set it on fire. As the German soldiers arrived they began shooting at Adams and he fell on his knees with his hands raised; they continued to fire until he was dead. Pinson was taken to a hospital and died the next day, a day later than acknowledged by CWGC. Both men had survived 'Bloody April' 1917 when there were severe losses during the Battle of Arras. 70 squadron was commanded by Major Arthur Tedder who became an Air Marshall during the Second World War. In 1916 70 squadron was the first to be equipped with the Sopwith 1½ Strutter. All Pinson's family were born in Willenhall, near Walsall, but in 1911 were living at Rosemary Hill Road, Streetly. His father was a lock manufacturer. There were five children and one servant. Ivan's older brother, Raymond, was a medical student. Ivan himself was at the time of the census a student cadet on the School Ship Conway at Rock Ferry on the River Mersey. This was a naval training school. As he is listed on the Tettenhall College roll of honour at Wolverhampton it is likely that he attended the College after the Aston school before joining the Conway. For reasons unknown he did not join the Navy when the war broke out but enlisted in the South Staffs Regiment before transfer to the RFC.

Captain Thomas Sidney Wathes, aged 28, was killed in the disastrous Anglo-Australian attack at Fromelles on July 19 1916. He was serving in the 2/6th Warwicks, the second line Territorials and was one of 104 deaths in his battalion. After King Edward's at Aston he went up to Wadham College, Oxford, where he joined the OTC. He left a widow, Doris, whom he had married in 1913. He had joined in September 1914 and was rapidly promoted. In 1911 he was living with his widowed mother, two brothers and a servant, at 52, Park Hill, Moseley and was working as a dairyman's assistant. After the war his mother, who had 'private means' was living at 66, Cambridge Road, Kings Heath.

Serjeant Percy Ketteringham had probably left the school before the others previously described as he was born in Handsworth on May 6 1884. He had worked as a 'traveller' before enlisting for twelve years in the Royal Marine Artillery in Birmingham on July 24 1905. He stood almost six feet tall and his next of kin was noted as his father, Harry, at 19, Stamford Road, Handsworth. He trained as a gunner and saw short periods of service on land

and on naval ships called Goliath, Edgar and Agamemnon. HMS Edgar was a cruiser and the first and third named were pre-Dreadnought battleships. His last ship before continuous land service was HMS Triumph, a similar battleship, from January 12 1911 to May 10 1912. At the time of the 1911 census Percy's ship was at Valetta, Malta, as part of the Mediterranean Fleet. At the same time his parents were still at the Stamford Road address with his brother and sister and two servants. His father was a Superintendent of Registration. In February 1914 Percy was promoted to corporal. On March 26 1915 he joined the RMA No 5 Howitzer Brigade and remained with them in action in the field until he was killed on November 9 1917 having achieved the rank of serjeant. His brigade consisted of twelve huge 15 inch siege howitzers which had a range of 10795 yards and fired a 1400 pound shell. One howitzer required three steam tractors to move it and had a crew of sixty men. Percy is buried in Steenkerke Belgian Military Cemetery which is some distance behind the front near Veurne. His unit had been supporting the Second Battle of Passchendaele from October 26-November 10 1917.

Private Frederick Horatio Homer was killed on June 1 1918, aged 18, whilst serving in the 2nd Wiltshires during the Allied withdrawals in the 1918 Battle of the Aisne. His battalion was at Chambrecy between the Marne and Aisne rivers west of Rheims. The battalion had only recently joined 58 Brigade of 19th (Western) Division. On June the Germans successfully attacked the French on their left and the battalion found machine guns firing into the rear lines of the Wiltshires and enfilading battalion HQ. The battalion was forced to withdraw and dig into a new position. Eight other men were killed that day. He is commemorated on the Soissons Memorial. In 1911 Frederick was still at the grammar school and was living with his parents, Frederick and Maria, at 'Penrhyn', 68, Gravelly Hill. His father was a gun finisher with premises at 8, Vesey Street.

Albert Gordon Burt had emigrated to Australia in 1912 sailing from London to Melbourne on the 'Orama' of the Orient Line. He was described as a 'student' aged 19. During wartime his home address was 4, Duke Street, Windsor, on the outskirts of Melbourne. He later became a state school teacher. He enlisted at Melbourne on August 7 1915 and embarked for overseas with the 15th Reinforcement on March 9 1916. After time with the 1st Light Horse Training Regiment in Egypt he landed at Marseilles on June 8. In France he joined the 1st Anzac Cyclists Battalion and was soon promoted to Serjeant. On October 14 he joined the 52nd Battalion of the 4th Australian Division in the field but a week later was transferred to the 1st ANZAC Intelligence Department; 1st ANZAC later became the Australian

Corps which commanded the five Australian Divisions in France. In February 1917 he joined its HQ as 'Intelligence Police'. He remained with them for the rest of the war. We can gain an insight into his duties from a report on accidental injuries on August 9 1917 when riding a motorcycle with an important message from HQ to the 1st Anzac Cyclists Battalion. On November 10 1917 he was sent to England after an injury to his right hand which was treated at a hospital at Cambridge. At the end of January 1918 he rejoined the HQ in France. In late August 1918 he was hospitalised at Rouen with dysentery. Either side of the Armistice he was granted leave in England. Back in France in January 1919 he was sent down the medical chain with debility. On February 13 he was admitted to St Dunstans in Fulham. A month later he entered the 3rd Australian Hospital at Dartford with a diagnosis of neurasthenia. He was granted extended leave in England without pay from June 3 to October 2 1919 because he had family in England. However, on July 10 he was admitted to Dartford with influenza. On August 28 he embarked for Australia on the HMAT Kanowna. After seven days at sea he was reported as lost overboard on September 4. A court of enquiry was held at sea. Seven witnesses gave evidence. He was still a medical case and Night Sister Donaldson was told he was missing at 1.30 a.m. Captain Wilton, the ward medical officer, stated that Burt was suffering from 'debility following influenza' which had led to 'mental dullness'. Another medical officer who had treated him at Dartford stated that Burt had been obsessed with the idea that he was becoming progressively weaker. The verdict was that he had fallen overboard 'whether accidentally or intentionally it is impossible to determine'. He is commemorated on the Hollybrook Memorial at Southampton, the Lichfield War Memorial and the both King Edward's memorials. His next of kin had been given as his mother at 21, Market Street, Lichfield and, if she had died, his sister Enid at the same address. He had been born in Lichfield in August 1893. In 1901 his father, Albert, was a boot dealer who employed others. In September 1908 the son joined the King Edward VI School at Stratford-upon-Avon as a boarder and was still there in 1911 as one of 22 boarders. His mother had been widowed and was at that time a landlady at Southsea. Albert won several prizes at Stratford and was active in sport. In 1910 he became a master at Kimbolton School at Kimbolton, Cambridgeshire. Whilst there he began to consider becoming a missionary and in 1912 sailed for Australia to train and study at St Columb's Hall at Wangaratta, Victoria. In July 1920 his mother wrote to the authorities in Australia for particulars of her son's war service "for a book in connection with his old school".

Albert's younger brother, Frank Eliot Burn, was also killed in the war whilst serving in France as a lieutenant with the 1/6th North Staffs on October 3 1918. He had also left the Aston school for Stratford and became a boarder a year later than his brother. He showed particular talent at photography, cricket and rugby. When he left he became a clerk for the National Provincial Bank at Walsall and then his native Lichfield. He attested on November 28 1915 and served in Dublin with the 2/6th North Staffs in the aftermath of the Easter Rising in 1916. He was promoted to lance corporal and then recommended for officer cadetship. He completed the course at Lichfield and was sent to France on April 7 1916 and joined the same battalion. On May 8 he was badly wounded in the left knee joint by a bullet and returned to England. In November 1917 he joined the 5th Reserve Battalion at Mablethorpe but it was not until April 1918 that he returned to France. He was given command of a company but was severely wounded once more and returned to England for two months in hospital. He was back in September as a lieutenant in the 1/6th Battalion and joined them at the end of the month for operations near St Quentin in which he was killed. He is also commemorated on both school memorials and the Lichfield War Memorial. He is buried in Busigny Communal Cemetery Extension, France, and had been awarded the Chevalier of the Order of the Crown of Belgium and the Croix de Guerre (Belgium).

The birth of Herbert Leslie Shillcock during the last three months of 1895 should have brought joy to his father to alleviate the shame of one of football's most famous events. On the night of September 11/12 that year his father's sports shop at 63 and 65, Newtown Row was broken into and the F.A Cup was stolen never to be seen again. It was on display after Aston Villa had beaten local rivals West Bromwich Albion 1-0 in that year's final. In 1901 Herbert was living with his parents and four brothers, four sisters and two servants at 200, Birchfield Road. In 1911, probably after leaving the Aston School, he was a pupil at the Rydal Mount College for Boys in Colwyn Bay. This was a Methodist boarding school. By the end of the war Herbert was a serjeant in the 100th Company of the Machine Gun Corps when he died of wounds on October 27 1918 and was buried in the St Sever Cemetery Extension, Rouen. After the war his parents were living at 47, Trinity Road, Aston.

'The Boys of Shakespeare's School in the First World War'. Richard Pearson. History Press. 2010.

Jim Perkins, the school archivist, has been helpful for this entry.

4.

Small Heath/Sparkbrook/ Sparkhill/Bordesley Green

Asda supermarket, Coventry Road. Built in 1994 on the site of an extension of the main BSA factory in nearby Armoury Road. It was a major centre for munitions production and was visited by the King on July 23 1915. Before the war it made 135 rifles each week. During the war this rose to 10000 (a short Lee Enfield had 131 parts) as well as 2000 Lewis guns weekly and aero parts in large quantities. Production included 12.5 million Lewis

A BSA float for Win the War Day September 1918. Factory canteens were a major improvement in working conditions produced by the war

gun magazine pans in a single year. The company made its own gauges, jigs, cutters, twist drills and other tools. The parts of the Lee Enfield rifle required 1250 different gauges to check accuracy during manufacture; the Lewis gun 2600. The first War Office order in August 1914 by telegram was for 500 military bicycles in 24 hours. This was achieved and they were taken away by special train. During the war the Cycle Department also made aero components – 150000 weekly. This included interrupter drive sets which synchronised between a propeller and a machine gun. During the war the workforce had risen from 3000 to 13000.

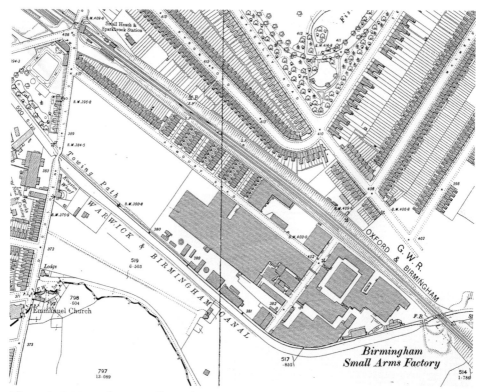

The main BSA works in Small Heath in 1904

St Andrews, Birmingham City Football Club. Friendly matches
were played there against the 17th Middlesex, the 'Footballers Battalion'. One match was on October 16 1915 in front of 15000 spectators; the match was drawn. Two weeks later there was another match – the Blues were two short so the Footballers' loaned them players. Private Tommy Barber of Villa played against the Blues as did the future Major Buckley. The Blues lost 3-2 and Barber scored. During the interval recruitment speeches were made and a hundred men joined up. A recruitment rally was addressed by Major John

Major Hall-Edwards addresses the crowd at St Andrews in 1914 and appeals for volunteers

Hall-Edwards RAMC. He was the chief of the medical staff at the Curzon Hall recruiting station and a distinguished Birmingham surgeon and radiographer.

'When the Whistle Blows: The Footballers' Battalion in the Great War'. Andrew Riddoch and John Kemp. Haynes. 2008.

Greenway Street. Here was the site of a wartime street shrine at the Coventry Road end. Many of these shrines were prominently erected on house walls in working class streets. Others included Walford Road, Sparkhill and in Small Heath others existed at St Andrews Road, Maxstoke Street, Watery Lane, Tilton Road, Garrison Lane and Herbert Road. Carl Chinn talked to David Cheshire from this area who remembered July 1 1936, the 20th anniversary of the Somme. David recollected… "our scout troop paraded at each of these memorials in turn where a short service was held in honour of the local men who were killed in this terrible event….as I remember…they all looked home-made and some even used jam jars to hold flowers. It is a great pity that all these were no doubt destroyed in the clearance of the old houses". There was also a memorial on a wall between houses in Saint Vincent Street, Ladywood.

'Brum and Brummies Volume 3'. Carl Chinn. Brewin. 2002.

Arthur Street. Near St Andrews, the site of another street shrine to the fallen long since disappeared.

Jenkins Street. A large centre for the Birmingham Civic Recreation League which provided recreational activities for female war workers to avoid undesirable influences in their leisure hours. It catered for nearly 2000 women and girls. The key organiser appears to be a Miss Irons. In January 1918 a Mens' Club was also opened there for 100 members. The scheme outline was presented to the Lord Mayor in September 1916 and highlighted three special problems arising from the war. There was a great influx of workers into the city. There was "nervous strain arising from unaccustomed work, long hours, anxiety etc felt by all classes of the community". Lastly there was the danger that "undesirable means of relaxation will be resorted to when no better alternatives exist". After approval an Executive Committee was set up and offices acquired at 10, Winchester House, Victoria Square. Amongst the Vice-Presidents were the Bishop of Birmingham, Colonel Gilbert Barling, Mrs George Cadbury, Mrs Neville Chamberlain and Sir Oliver Lodge. Mrs Harrison Barrow was the Honorary Secretary. Over time thirteen major centres were opened including the 'Conference Hall' in Jenkins Street. Existing organisations joined the scheme. A flyer from Jenkins Street shows the range of activities available every night except Friday and Sunday.

> Monday – dress-making, embroidery, Swedish drill, country dancing and singing
> Tuesday – dress-making, cookery, dramatic classes, Swedish drill and country dancing
> Wednesday – basket making, first aid, Literature class, drill
> Thursday – dancing class for beginners, Old English dancing, French class
> Saturday afternoon – hockey and netball matches at Farm Field
> Saturday evening – socials, dancing, entertainments, concerts, games etc. Male friends of members invited
> Sunday – tea talks etc, music, lantern lectures etc.

Civic Recreation League material – Library of Birmingham.

This is almost certainly the large redbrick building now called 'The Institute' and home to a number of community organisations.

Waverley Road Church. This had a Prussian born minister at the start of the war – the Reverend Gertrude von Petzold. She was the first woman ordained minister in England to win a full time appointment. She applied for naturalisation, having let her original application lapse whilst in America for two years, which was refused so she was deported from England to Switzerland on July 31 1915 via Tilbury. Her congregation had petitioned the Home Secretary to grant her naturalisation. Support from a privy councillor, a JP, a city councillor and the Mayor of Leicester carried no weight. As a committed internationalist she had promoted Anglo-German relations which did not stop an arson attack on her church. She had been in Britain since 1897 and was a graduate of a British university.

She was born in Thorn in East Prussia (now Torun, Poland) in 1876 as the daughter of an army officer of aristocratic descent. By the age of 18 she had passed the exams which qualified her to teach at a seminary but she wanted a higher education so came to Britain which she saw as a 'land of freedom'. She spent two years learning the language and teaching part-time before taking a degree at the University of St Andrews between 1895 and 1897, studying medicine at first before developing a calling to enter the ministry and switching to theology. She became a ministry student at Manchester College at Oxford in 1897 with a reference from St Andrews which described her as having a keen, clear intelligence as a fearless thinker desiring nothing but the truth. In her application for a bursary as an external exhibitioner she wrote that "I mean to settle as a minister in Great Britain, especially as there is not the least chance of my doing so in my own country". She did not become a regular student at Oxford until the autumn of 1901 having also completed a course in classical languages at Edinburgh University. The delay was caused by the college struggling to decide on a policy about accepting women students for the ministry. Life at Oxford was not easy and at first male students would not let her sit at the refectory table with them.

Would a congregation accept her as a minister? Her work as a guest preacher helped to pave the way. In September 1904 she overcame seven male competitors to become minister at Narborough Road Unitarian Church at Leicester which had a congregation of 150. She was an attractive young woman with a clear voice, a slight accent and a scholarly preaching style. She was 'modern in her ideas, theologically, socially and politically'. She set up a Sunday afternoon lecture series for men which featured prominent speakers on social reform topics. She was a strong supporter of the suffragettes; she later said that both Emily Wilding Davison and Jesus Christ had 'died for sinners'. In 1907 she spent two years in Iowa and Illinois, USA, working with radical Unitarian women ministers. Whilst there she lectured in Boston on the role of women in the early Christian Church.

Her second English ministry, on her return from Chicago in June 1911, was at Small Heath where she attracted large congregations. In her first year the congregation increased by 54 and continued to rise thereafter as she was a popular and inspirational speaker. In 1912 she conducted a service in a packed Town Hall in memory of George Dawson. When the war broke out she registered with the Birmingham Police on August 12 1914 as an 'enemy alien'. At that time she was living at 'Fairfield', Flint Green Road, Acocks Green, a home she shared with another German woman, Rosa Widmann, who was deported with her. Postwar she became a minister of the only two Free Churches in her native East Prussia, then took a doctorate and became Professor of English at Frankfurt University – another first in another country. She died near Frankfurt on March 14 1952. The congregation at Waverley dwindled over time and in 1966 the building was let for part of the week to local Sikhs who bought the building in the early 1980s.

Oxford DNB entry by Keith Gilley.

10, Sycamore Terrace, Wolseley Street. Joseph Paveley and his brothers can be regarded as a typical working class Birmingham family. He survived the war and was interviewed in old age. He became a gunner in the Royal Field Artillery and went to the front at some time after January 1916 after joining up as a volunteer in 1915. He saw out the war. In 1911 he was living at this address, aged 13 and at school. It was still the family home after the war. His father, George, was a porter in the Fruit Market and he had been married to his mother, Louisa, for twenty one years. Ten years earlier George had been a gas stoker. Also in the house was his older brother, Albert, 17 who was a 'lorry boy' for the Midland Railway. His younger brothers were Walter, 11, Thomas, 4, and Horace, 1. He also had a sister, Gertude, 7. The 1911 census states that there had been thirteen children in the family five of whom had died. His eldest brother, William, had already left home and, then aged 20, was a regular soldier in the Kings Royal Rifle Corps. He did not go to France with the 1st Battalion in the second week of the war but was there in 1915 and was killed on June 24 that year and is buried in Cambrin Military Cemetery, France. Another older brother, George, also served and became a sergeant in the 1/Kings Own Scottish Borderers and arrived in Gallipoli in April 1915.

Albert was also a regular and was in the 2/Kings Own Scottish Borderers when the war broke out. He went to the Western Front on April 29 1915 and later was commissioned into the East Kents before joining the RAF in 1918 as a second lieutenant. Walter, his younger brother, joined the 1/5 Warwicks in September 1916 at the age of 16 or 17. He later transferred to the 2/Berkshire Regiment and survived the war until discharge in 1919.

Joseph later described his background and military service. Interestingly in official records he is named as Jesse. Jesse attended Garrison Lane School, close to the family home, and left at the age of fourteen and went to work as a polisher. Before school he used to help his dad bag up three tons of potatoes from a lorry at Camp Hill Station. His next full time job was on a lorry for Randall Brothers and Parsons. Sometime after the war broke out he joined up at James Watt Street and then trained on 18 pounder field guns at Woolwich and Bournemouth. It snowed on his first night at Givenchy in France in 1916. He was on the Somme for the pre-battle bombardment of the German lines. On the field gun he did all the different tasks of the crew. Later in the war he transferred to trench mortars which fired 'toffee apple' bombs. As he did not smoke he gave his cigarette issue to his pals. Trench mortar work brought him nearer to the front line and on one occasion he was buried by a German shell and had to be dug out unharmed. He was wounded with shrapnel in the hand at Mont St Eloi and was disappointed to only reach Rouen for treatment rather than 'blighty'. He was sent up to the line to St Quentin with nine other men and a rifle as the Germans attacked in March 1918 but then rejoined the trench mortars.

At one point he met one of his brothers twice in Arras when he was 'doing a bit of volunteer running for the different batteries'; this was probably George. Jesse recounts a story of his only leave which coincided with his officer brother Albert also on leave. "I was an ordinary gunner – I wouldn't accept the stripe. I didn't want them. We were walking up the Bull Ring together and got to Moor Street and two redcaps pulled us up. First of all they got my brother – they choked him off for walking with me because I was a private. He said I was his brother. They said it doesn't matter a hang, you're an officer, you've no rights walking with a private. Then they looked at me; I'd got my top button undone. They said 'you've got your top button undone there you can report back to your unit at once'. He took my name and everything". Jesse stayed on leave and then went to London to join an army pal. They agreed to stay for three days beyond their leave. Jesse was confined to barracks for three days when he returned to the front.

Interview first published in the Newman Bulletin of local history source materials. 1970s.

Conway Road School.
This has an impressive war memorial which lists 'old boys' who served, including two killed. The school opened as a Birmingham Board school in 1900. The memorial lists 167 men by their service. Eighty were infantry, including 47 Royal Warwicks, 38 served in the artillery and 17 in the Navy. Two had served with the Canadians and two

with the Australians. Private Harry Wheeler Woods was in the 20th Canadian Battalion and had enlisted in Toronto in 1914. He was born in Hartlepool and his father lived at 3, Farm Road, Sparkbrook. He was a plumber by trade.

Private Percy Clarence Willday was in the Plymouth Battalion of the Royal Marine Light Infantry when killed at Gallipoli on June 31 1915. He was aged 19 and is commemorated on the Helles Memorial. Private Walter Rudland was discharged from the regulars just before the war but joined as a Kitchener volunteer early in the war and was killed serving in the 2nd Warwicks in the Battle of Neuve Chapelle on March 13 1915. He was born in Bath and his parents lived in Small Heath. He is commemorated on the Le Touret Memorial.

It is now Conway Primary School.

Sydenham Road and Fallows Road. On the border of Sparkbrook and Small Heath was the home of Alldays and Onions, an engineering company, who were involved in war work. On the eve of the war the company was based at the Matchless Works in Fallows Road and the nearby Great Western Works in Sydenham Road. The former works manufactured cars, motor cycles and cycles. The latter made a range of metal products – such as forges, hearths, anvils, vices, machine tools, fans and blowers. Its production was ideally suited to adaptation to war needs. The company built its own shell nosing furnace and a special riveting machine used to construct the tracks for tanks. Parts for shells were produced and additional drop stamping hammers were installed for their production. The company's portable forges were very useful for the army in the field. Field ambulances were also made. A serious fire in April 1915 swept through the Packing Case Department in Sydenham Road which was being used exclusively for the manufacture of wood drums used to transport barbed wire for the army. Like other companies new buildings were erected, including a new Machine Shop at Sydenham Road, completed at the end of 1915. A large area of land known as the Waverley Estate was acquired for a new factory to increase capacity off Oldknow Road, Small Heath, now the site of an Asda supermarket. This was known as the Waverley Works.

In April 1915 the firm prosecuted a Belgian refugee workman and mechanic called Victor Wolfs for breach of contract. He was then living at 28, Anderton Road, Sparkbrook. In December 1914 he had joined the firm and signed a six month contract at £2 per week. He left the firm without notice on March 9 1915 and joined Austin at Longbridge. He had been doing Government work and had been taught to work an intricate grinding machine. The firm claimed £5 in damages and stated that it had lost £28 because the machine had stood idle. The wages clerk testified that he had seen Wolfs sign the contract after it had been interpreted to him. He told the Victoria Law Court that he would go back if his wages were increased as he was supporting a wife and child in Liege. The magistrate gave him some weeks to return or he would receive a heavy fine.

'Alldays and Onions. A Brief History'. Norman Painting. Landmark. 2002.
Birmingham Daily Mail April 15 1915.

The Royal Small Arms Factory. Was taken over by BSA in 1906 – it was less than a mile from the main Small Heath works. Pre-war car body production was halted and rifle conversion taken up. Some Lewis machine gun parts were also made there. In 1916 900 people were employed.

Montgomery Street. Was the home of the Armourer Mills, where before the Great War the Lanchester Motor Company was based and built cars. One wartime order was for the construction of 450 aero engines of 100 h.p. for the Royal Aircraft Factory. The firm also made shells and some aircraft engines as well as the Lanchester armoured car. In 1915 36 armoured cars were delivered to the Royal Naval Air Service. Others were sent to Russia. The firm also ran the Alpha Works in Liverpool Street near the junction with Heath Mill Lane.

There is a blue plaque to commemorate the firm on the wall of the former factory.

54, Alfred Street, Sparkbrook. The 1911 census says that this was Balsall Heath. This was the family home of Private Richard Alfred Chinn, 9968, of the 2nd Battalion of the Coldstream Guards. Richard can stand for every ordinary Brummie who did their bit for King and Country. His proud grandson is Carl Chinn, a far from ordinary modern Brummie. His father was a blacksmith's striker. Richard survived the war and was an Old Contemptible, a pre-war regular. He arrived in France on August 13 1914 as a member of 4th (Guards) Brigade of 2nd Division. Five days later he wrote home… "We start this morning Tuesday for the front, sent out with rations and 120 rounds of ammunition each. Don't know where we are for just yet know later if we can. I don't think we will last long we are a happy

Battalion of men and that's what the Germans are not. England for ever". On August 23 the battalion moved into Belgium and soon were in retreat to the Marne and the Aisne with the rest of the B.E.F. His unit fought in the 1st Battle of Ypres in October 1914. After the battle he joined the Machine Gun section of his battalion. He spent Christmas in the trenches and afterwards was pleased that the Guards had not joined the truce. On January 4 1915 he wrote home to his mother – "we look like as if we had a cartload of mud tipped on us" and told how his officer had bought a concertina for his men so that "when we go in the barns we have a little concert". In February 1915 Richard Chinn was badly wounded in the knee joint in the La Bassee area. It was a 'blighty' wound and meant a spell in a Cardiff hospital.

'Brum and Brummies. Volume 4'. Carl Chinn. Brewin. 2005.

Corner of Ladypool Road and Colville Road. Here at the beginning of the war stood Mr Harry Styles' pork butcher's shop. On Saturday September 5 he was drinking in the parlour of the Clifton Inn on Clifton Road nearby and took "more drink than was good for him". He made some unpatriotic remarks about his own country, the British Army and observations 'very much in favour of the Kaiser and the German nation'. In the ensuing Police Court case, where he was charged with 'disturbing the peace' he is supposed to have said "I hope that every chap that has gone for a British soldier gets annihilated. I have got two sons and if I thought they were going

Police guard Harry Styles' pork butcher's shop in September 1914

to go for soldiers I would blow their brains out for England has caused it". News spread and this may not have been the first time he had made such remarks.

Just after 11 p.m. a large crowd gathered outside his shop and proceeded to wreck it by smashing the windows, throwing stones and also wheeling his trap into the street and breaking it up and then tried to set fire to it. The police found it hard to quell the riot and a sergeant was injured and constables were hit by stones. Styles' lawyer told the Court that he had business worries because of the war with a fall in takings which explained the drinking. He also had another shop 50-60 yards away where 'takings had fallen away to nothing'. People believed he was German or of German descent but he wished to point out that he was born of Herefordshire parents, both British. He had been in business there for 22 years. He also had no recollection of using the language attributed to him. He apologised. The case was adjourned for six months and Styles had to pay costs.

The building is now the 'Lahore Village' restaurant/takeaway. It can be identified by brickwork patterns.

Birmingham Daily Post, September 7 and 25 1914.

86, Solihull Road, Sparkhill.
This was the home of Private Wilfred John Townsend who died on the last day of the war, November 11 1918. He was serving in the 2nd South Staffs and is buried in Solesmes British cemetery, France. His unit had taken part in the final advances of the war, including the Battle of the Selle, October 17-25 1918. The battalion was at Solesmes on November 3-4 and out of the line and it is highly likely that he died of influenza as he was not killed in action or from wounds. His Medal Index Card shows that he embarked on August 27 1914 without naming the destination and yet only shows the two basic war medals and not the 1914 Star. The main body of the 2nd South Staffs landed at Le Havre on August 13 1914. He was aged 29 and left a widow, Betsy Florence, at Sparkhill. He had been born in Cirencester and his father, Daniel, from Wiltshire, had married Harriet from Birmingham in about 1902. He was already living in the city a year earlier at a court dwelling in Bishop Street. In 1911 there were four young sons at 10 Court, 2 House, Coleman Street. Daniel was then labouring as a galvaniser. Wilfred was born in 1890 and is the product of Daniel's first marriage which also produced an older sister, Ethel.

Other Brummies also died on the last day of the war although, like Wilfred, none in combat. Private H.E Dixon was in the same battalion as

Wilfred. He died of wounds and was buried in the St Sever Cemetery Extension at Rouen. Aged 31 his father lived at 179, Montgomery Street, Sparkbrook. Corporal William James Hadley is buried in the same French cemetery after dying of wounds. He was serving in the 2/7th Warwicks having originally joined the Ox and Bucks Light Infantry. He was 28 and left a wife at 9, Musgrave Road, Winson Green. He held the Military Medal. Air Mechanic James Rollings has been described under Handsworth Cemetery. Two other men were buried locally. Able Seaman Harold Walter Smith, aged 24, of the Royal Naval Volunteer Reserve, is buried in Smethwick Old Churchyard. His wife, Gertrude Louisa, was left at 91, Esme Road, Sparkhill. He had died of the influenza in the Tidworth Military Hospital at 10.10 p.m. Private H.B Clarke was only 18 years old and was in the 4th Hampshires. He is named on the screen wall at Lodge Hill Cemetery.

Two Birmingham born men also died that day. Private C. Bennett, aged 20, was serving in the 3rd Liverpool Pals and died as German prisoner of war in Poland. He lies buried in the Poznan Old Garrison Cemetery. He was born at Aston. Able Seaman H.F Coysh, aged 24, was an Able Seaman in the Royal Naval Volunteer Reserve and was based in the anti-aircraft section of the training ship, HMS President V. He was buried in Islington Cemetery and his parents were then living at Crouch End, London.

Talfourd Street. Was the site of an impressive street shrine. There are thirty-two names and the shrine was probably established after the war as at least one death listed can be attributed to August 9 1918. The shrine was decorated with two Union Jacks above it, a suspended flower pot on each side, a flower wreath on each side and a flower box under the names. Above the names were the words 'Talfourd Street Heroes'. Some of the men listed can be identified and described.

Serjeant John Hurley served in the 9th Worcs and was killed at Gallipoli on August 10 1915 at the age of 31. His parents lived at 50, Talfourd Street but he lived with his wife, Emily, at 1 Court, 2 House, White Road, Sparkbrook. He is commemorated on the Helles Memorial. His brother was unfit for service and worked at the Birmingham Metal Munition Factory at Saltley.

John and Charles Witsey were brothers and were both killed in the war. Charles was a private in the 1st Worcs and died of severe wounds on November 6 1916, aged 26, and was buried at Etaples Military Cemetery, France. He had been called up from the reserve at the beginning of the war. John, 23, was a private in the 1/5th South Staffs and was killed on August 9

1918 and buried in Fouquiers churchyard, France. He was a 1914 volunteer. The brothers lived at 36, Talfourd Street. In 1911 their family was at 482, Garrison Lane, where their father, Henry, was a gas works labourer. At that time Charles was already a soldier and John was a chain driller. They had three sisters and a brother.

Private William Henry Aizlewood was also a regular soldier and was killed early in the war on August 25 1914 serving in the 1st Duke of Cornwall's Light Infantry. He is commemorated on the La Ferte-sous-Jouarre Memorial in France. His wife, Fanny, had remarried by the time that the Imperial War Graves Commission collected information after the war but was still living at 1, back of 42, Talfourd Street.

Private John Aubrey Price died of wounds at Gallipoli on August 7 1915 and is also commemorated on the Helles Memorial. He was serving in the 9th Warwicks as they attacked Hill Q and Chunuk Bair above Anzac Cove. He had lived with his sister at Ash Cottage, Talfourd Street.

Private George Nutt left a wife and five children at 6 back, 37, Talfourd Street. His widow had to wait about ten months for a confirmed report of the death of her husband who was missing whilst serving in the 2nd Warwicks during their attack on Bullecourt on May 4 1917. He is commemorated on the Arras Memorial.

Some research here by Tony Woolley via the Birmingham History Forum.

5.
Saltley/Washwood Heath/ Ward End

Metropolitan Carriage. Wagon and Finance Co at Saltley. This firm was the base for the South Midland Royal Garrison Artillery who landed at Le Havre in March 1915. This was the 204 Battery, Medium Field Artillery who had their own Territorial drill hall there. The unit was commanded by Major Greg, a director of the firm. The works was visited by the King on July 23 1915. The YMCA established a canteen there.

National Shell Factory, Washwood Heath. Also called the Midland Works. Construction began in June 1915 and output began in February 1916. It made 18 pounder and 4.5 inch shell. The exact location of this factory is not clear.

The Electric and Ordnance Accessories Co. Ltd, Drews Lane. Was an offshoot of Vickers and produced millions of fuses as well as anti-aircraft shells and cases and naval and field gun cases. At first there was no canteen for the works so there used to be a huge marquee outside which sold cakes and other things to the munition workers.

36, Tilton Road Small Heath. One hundred and thirty women were listed in the Birmingham volume of the National Roll of the Great War published in the 1920s. Most were listed as 'special war workers' with thirty-five at a Handsworth address and forty-one a Small Heath address. Such women worked in the manufacture of shells, small arms ammunition, hand grenades, aeroplanes, tanks and gas respirators. They worked as machinists, lathe operators, gaugers and welders. Martha Underwood of 27, Belmont

Road, Handsworth, a married woman, was in charge of 200 girls at the Handsworth carriage works. The two female members of the Gillett family at 36, Tilton Road can stand for all those women who worked in the Birmingham munitions industry.

Emily Gillett seems to have already worked at Messrs Abrams, Washwood Heath, when the war broke out and spent the whole war in the manufacture of fuses for bombs. Her younger sister, Lilian, did the same. They were living in the same house in 1911 with their parents, John and Amy. John was a labourer in a brickyard. Their daughters were 16 and 13 years of age in 1914. Their older brother, William Henry, born in 1894, was a regular soldier in peacetime as a gunner in the Royal Field Artillery after working in a tube works. He went to the front in 1914 and was killed on March 15 1917 whilst serving in 129 Battery of 42nd Brigade. He is buried in the main Arras CWGC cemetery. Another brother worked in the same factory as his sisters from 1916 as he was unfit for military service. He packed explosives.

'The National Roll of the Great War 1914-1918'. Section VI. Birmingham. Naval and Military Press reprint, 2006.

Wolseley Motors Ltd at Adderley Park. Was transformed from a car factory into a shell and fuse factory and also made motor transport, including ambulances and tracks; all for the War Office. In January 1915 the company acquired a site of nearly eight acres in Bordesley Green Road, about 250 yards south of the Adderley Park works. The new factory built there, with its large Construction shed and Timber Store, was specifically for the production of aircraft. In 1916 there was a massive expansion of the Aero Site with extensions and new buildings. The latter included an Automatic Machine Shop. Four more acres were acquired in 1917 and a canteen was erected there. It could seat 288 people. Wolseley made nearly 4500 aero engines and spares equivalent to another 1500 as well as nearly 700 aircraft. Many of these were SE5a's. The de Havilland designed BE2c reconnaissance planes were also made. They also made 850 wings and tailplanes, 6000 propellers and over 1000 gun mountings and telescopic sights.

In early 1915 there were major changes in the East Works to convert part of it into a Shell Shop. Over a thousand machine tools were installed. One area became a Girls' mess Room and Toilet with a Matron's Room to meet the needs of the new workforce. The King made a sort visit to the works on July 23 1915. The Wolseley Works Band and a section from the 6th Warwicks accompanied him from the Britannia Works in Arden Road to the Main Office entrance where he was met by three directors. He was then introduced to the Chief Engineer and others and signed the visitor's book before moving across the Bordesley Green Road to the East Works entrance. He then toured the Shell Shop. He also visited the Aero Engine Assembly Shop. The King then left on the royal train which was standing in the works siding. Early in the war men not in uniform could be given a white feather in the street. Some men were key workers in engineering so the company gave them a Works Certificate which read "This is to Certify that the Bearer… is in the employ of Wolseley Motors Ltd of Adderley Park, Birmingham, and that his services are required by this firm in order to enable them to carry out fully and promptly the requirements of the British Government for the supply of War Material". It was signed by Alec McCormack, director.

'The Real Wolseley Adderley Park Works 1901-26'. Norman Painting. Landmark. 2002.

23, Ronald Road, Saltley. This was the home of Thomas Turrall in 1911 who went on to win the Victoria Cross on the Somme on July 3 1916. In 1911 he was a house painter and paper hanger, aged 24, and Hay Mills born. He was living with his parents William, a carter, and Louisa. In the house there were also two brothers, four sisters and two step brothers. Thomas was the second eldest and Violet, the youngest, aged four. In 1901 the family had lived at 2/44 Back, Baker Street, Aston where his father then worked as a bricklayer's labourer. His father had married Louisa in 1896 after the death of his first wife. By late 1916 his home was with his parents at 23, Oakley Road, Small Heath and his father worked at the BSA, Small Heath, as a labourer.

Thomas was born on July 5 1886 at Speedwell Road, Hay Mills and attended Dixon Road School. In 1913 he married Mary Mansell and a daughter, Lilian, was born on May 25 1914. The new family moved to Wroxton Road, Yardley and Thomas went to work for the Council. With work short in the winter of 1914 he joined the 10/Worcesters in December that year. He left for France in the summer of 1915. In December 1915 he learned that his wife had died aged 26. He was unable to attend the funeral. In July 1916 he was freed from the guard room to take part in his battalion's attack at La Boiselle on the Somme. In the early hours of July 3 he committed the deed which resulted in the award of the Victoria Cross….

"During a bombing attack by a small party against the enemy the officer in charge was badly wounded, and the party, having penetrated the position to a great depth, was compelled eventually to retire. Private Turrall remained with the wounded officer for three hours under continuous and very heavy fire from machine guns and bombs and, notwithstanding that both himself and the officer were at one time completely cut off from our troops, he held to his ground with determination and finally carried the officer into our lines after our counter-attacks had made this possible".

The officer was Lieutenant Richard Jennings who died soon after rescue but not before leaving an account of what had happened. Turrall had dragged him into a shell hole and began to dress his wounds, including a shattered leg, using a trench tool as a splint and his puttees as bandages. With the officer unconscious Turrall feigned death as Germans approached. Afterwards Turrall wrote to Jennings' mother in Gloucestershire. Later in the battle he was presented to the King in France. His parents also received a congratulatory letter from Neville Chamberlain, the Lord Mayor. Thomas Turrall received the VC from the King on December 31 1916. In June 1919 he was feted by about 2000 people at Victoria Park, Small Heath when Colonel Leo Amery M.P presented him with £250 in war certificates and a gold watch.

Thomas Turrall stayed on active service until the end of the war and was demobilised in April 1919 and then returned to Birmingham to take up his pre-war occupation. A testimonial match was played for him at St Andrews on May 10 1919 between the Birmingham Colts and the Birmingham Works FA. He remarried in 1920 to Daisy Davis. Turrall attended the Buckingham Palace party for VC holders on June 26 1920 and the House of Lords dinner on November 9 1929. He was part of the Guard of Honour when the Prince of Wales visited Birmingham on October 23 1934. He continued to attend VC events after the Second World War including the medal's centenary parade in Hyde Park on June 26 1956. He also regularly attended regimental functions. He was always proud of his status as a VC and it is probably true that he used to sign his cheques 'Tom Turrall VC'. From at least 1932 he probably lived with Daisy at 44, Arcot Road, Hall Green. In 1962 he sold his medal to the Worcestershire Regiment for £500. Thomas died on February 21 1964 in Selly Oak Hospital. He was given a military funeral a week later at Robin Hood Cemetery, Solihull. In 2006 a local man, Len Copsey, cleaned the headstone.

The terraced family home in Ronald Road still exists.

St Peter's College, Saltley. This teacher training college hosted the pre-war 'B' company of the 1/8 Royal Warwicks. Before the war a new armoury was built and a miniature range opened. Captain A.A Trowell was in command. The College inevitably lost many of its students who had been part-time soldiers at the outbreak of war. There were 109 students in 1915, some having transferred from other colleges. When the Derby scheme was brought in, only men medically unfit for war service were eligible for a training course so all Church training students were sent to Battersea and the War Office occupied the buildings for the rest of the war. The College re-opened on September 23 1919. The fate of some Saltley men is known. On the night of 18-19 April 1915, when the 1/8th were in the line for only their third day, two Germans on a scouting patrol tried to get through the British wire in a wood near Wulverghem in Belgium. Private Bernard Shiel, at an 'A' company listening post, grabbed Private Georg Lofolmr of the 5th Bavarian Regiment who was then sent to Brigade HQ in handcuffs. Shiel received the DCM because of the danger presented in April 1915 as one of his comrades – Private Wilfred Rainsford – was killed by the other German. Sheil came from Leamington where he had been a pupil teacher at Shrubland Street School before attending Saltley College, where he had joined the Territorials. He was one of the first former Saltley College students to fall and later became a sergeant. In 1914 he had been teaching at Holy Trinity School, Birchfield. He is commemorated on the Birmingham Education Committee memorial and lies buried in Serre Road Cemetery No 2 on the Somme where he was killed on the first day although regarded until April 1917 as missing in action.

Lieutenant Frederick Wareham, aged 25, was also killed on the first day of the Somme. He came from Malvern Link in Worcestershire and had attended Saltley College before the war and then became a schoolmaster at St Matthew's Boys School, Westminster, London. He had initially joined the 1/12 London Regiment (the Rangers) before obtaining a commission into the Warwicks in June 1915. Also killed at that time was Second Lieutenant Francis Freeman who had attended Saltley College after Evesham Grammar School and was also working in London in 1914. He came from Bengeworth, near Evesham. Several of those killed on July 1 had attended Saltley College which trained teachers. Corporal Harold Apthorpe, 23, was headmaster of a Bedford school when war broke out. Private Robert Stanton, also 23, came from Evesham.

Serjeant Oliver Summers, aged 25, came from Studley and was teaching in Birmingham in 1914. He had been awarded the DCM which appeared in the London Gazette ten days before his death. This was for recovering a wounded comrade under heavy fire. He had played cricket for Coughton and hockey for Studley. Private George Farmer, 29, was on the staff of the college; Australian born he lived in Tamworth. The college memorial to those who fell is made up of two tablets in St Saviour's Church, Saltley. There are 42 names on each.

The College closed in 1978.

6.

Moseley/Balsall Heath/ Highgate/Kings Heath

Moseley School today was formerly Spring Hill Wesleyan College. In 1914 the building became the training centre for the 3rd City Battalion, the 16th Royal Warwicks, with some men billeted in private houses nearby as the College could not accommodate all the men. An empty large house opposite the College, Windermere, was used as officers' quarters. Their first Commanding Officer, Colonel Lewis, had been with Kitchener in the Sudan. He came from Salford Priors so took up residence at the Plough and Harrow Hotel. The battalion left for Malvern and Yorkshire in 1915 and went to France in November that year. The building was later used after the war as a rehabilitation centre for ex-servicemen.

Highbury Hall. Joseph Chamberlain's home given over as a VAD hospital by Austen Chamberlain; Joseph had died just before the outbreak of war. It gradually specialised in neurological cases. It opened on May 28 1915 and received some support from employees of Kynochs. Additional buildings were erected in the grounds. In 1917 Austen Chamberlain gave all of Highbury to trustees. A postcard has survived showing two Canadian soldiers at Highbury at Christmas 1917 – Sergeant G.West and Sergeant E.M Tessier.

The latter, Ernest Medland Tessier, was born in 1887 at St John's, Newfoundland, and attested on November 10 1914. In peacetime he was a clerk. He was serving in the 15th Canadians who had been subject to the first use of gas in April 1915. They were one of the three battalions of the 48th Highlanders of Canada. In 1916 Mrs A.F Parker was the VAD commandant at Highbury.

Uffculme, Queensbridge Road. Was built in 1891 and had been the home of Richard Cadbury until his death in 1899 and his wife, Emma, until 1906 . It became a hospital used for the rehabilitation of limbless soldiers on September 10 1918 when 32 men were transferred from Dudley Road. Its first patients as an auxiliary war hospital of the 1st Southern General arrived on December 7 1916; the hospital was run by the Friends Ambulance Unit. It rose from an initial 80 beds to 200. Expansion was made possible by, firstly, equipping the tea rooms in the grounds as wards in 1917, and then, the following year, erecting large marquees on the lawn in the front of the house. Matron Catell, who had served with the Friends Ambulance Unit in France, managed the nurses, typically 3-4 sisters and 7-10 VADs. There were over 30 orderlies.

Some staff had served on the Hospital Ship Clenart Castle until disbanded but not on its final fatal voyage. Dr Austin Priestman was the chief medical officer. He had been the assistant school medical officer for Bradford. From December 1917 to September 1918 1854 patients were admitted and 101 operations were performed. The first wartime use of the house was as a hostel for Belgian refugees, then for 50 children from the slums of Birmingham whose fathers had joined the army. Then until November 1916 it was used by Belgian families. By the end of the war it was a limb fitting centre for six Midland counties. On September 10 1918 the first batch of new patients arrived – 32 one-legged cases. When open 242 discharged men were treated. In February 1919 it became a home for disabled ex-servicemen. The building was given by Mr and Mrs Barrow Cadbury. There is a plaque at the house which commemorates its wider use.

'The Friends Ambulance Unit 1914-1919. A Record'. Meaburn Tatham and James Miles. Library of Birmingham.

The house still survives as the 'Uffculme Centre' and is used for functions, conferences and training. It is open to the public on certain open days each year.

Moor Green House. Was given by Sir John Holder and opened on July 3 1916. It provided 40 beds as an extension of the Highbury VAD Hospital. It was generously supported by Kynoch workers. On June 6 1917 it opened as an auxiliary of the 1st Southern General Hospital for officers. Initially it had been a hostel for the families of Belgian refugees.

The house was demolished in 1927 to make way for offices for Pitmaston having been purchased by the Britannic Assurance Company in 1920.

171-5 Moseley Road. This was the family home of Hilda Moss who was living there in 1911 at the age of five. In old age, having retired as a school teacher to Sutton Coldfield, she wrote down her life story with about twenty pages devoted to childhood wartime memories. She was the only child and daughter of Wilfred Alfred Moss and Marguerite who were married in 1905. He was a manufacturer of edge tools in the city which his daughter called the 'Works'. Mr Peglat was the manager. Hilda described how a shipment of spades and tools were sent to a customer in Brussels and then news came that the Germans had taken the Belgian capital. "The seaside spades intended for Belgian children had been lost beyond trace". Before the outbreak of war Hilda felt she was living a sheltered life and was cared for by a nurse; there was another servant in the household. Hilda remembered the Territorials leaving for their camp at Rhyl. Nearby houses were taken over for Belgian refugees with red, yellow and black flags in the front garden. Also nearby was the Reception Centre at the Friends Institute. As an eight year she was frightened that the Germans would land in England and arrive at Birmingham. "We were going to be like the Belgians, having to run away and leave everything and I should lose all my toys". These feelings were intensified when she heard that Scarborough had been bombarded.

The family used to go to Sutton Coldfield each summer and in 1915 her father met a shop proprietor on the Moseley Road who had joined one of the two City Battalions in huts in Sutton Park. He showed them around the camp. At home war economy for patriotic reasons meant margarine rather than butter. Early in 1916 Hilda fell ill with pneumonia and a young nurse came to look after her while she was housebound. The same girl later tended the badly injured Lady Mayoress of Walsall from the Zeppelin attack on January 31 1916. Hilda began to keep a diary. On June 12 1916, Whit Monday, she wrote "There are few people having a holiday today because we want munitions for the War….but our workpeople are having a holiday on Monday and Tuesday just the same". As the war progressed there were problems relating to food; queues, potato shortages, Bird's Egg Substitute. the reduced standard of bread. There were power failures on the trams. A pantomime song became popular relating to making comforts for the troops – 'Sister Susie's sewing shirts for soldiers'. Hilda's school adopted a soldier and everyone gave a penny a week to pay for his food parcels. She also remembered Canon George Tredennick of Christ Church, Sparkbrook (1860-1942), who took the streets near her school as a special constable. At Hilda's school there were two Russian boarders who were the children of the Russian consul in Brussels and an English mother. The children boarded with Miss Jones, Hilda's teacher.

The elder one, a boy, won a scholarship to King Edward's. At school fuel shortages led to the end of Saturday lessons and lengthened weekday lessons. In her diary she recorded details of the April 12/13 1918 Zeppelin raid. "Mother heard the first explosion but thought it was the wind and went to sleep. Daddy called her; we drew the blind and saw bright, rose-coloured lights in the sky. They turned out to be 'star lights' thrown by the Germans to see where they were. I heard a dull boom, perhaps it was anti-aircraft guns. Cousin Nina saw the zeppelin and the star lights falling from it". Days later Hilda was out walking with her mother and went to look at a bomb crater in a field at Hall Green. On another day "we saw one in a field at Shirley, that one full of water and yellow from the clay soil. The bomb had fallen on soft ground and on the main road, three fields away, a row of shops had their windows shattered". In May 1918 she wrote in her diary "The Zeppelin warning at Greet was practised today; at school we heard it very faintly". On June 29 she recorded a new danger but the wrong conclusion – "A new kind of influenza has broken out in which people became suddenly very weak, in some cases losing the power of their limbs. They have intense headaches and pains in their backs. It is not dangerous but very miserable and infectious".

During the summer of 1918 she was pleased to hear of French and American success "but the wicked munition workers want to take the chance of victory from our fingers by striking again…..They should be sent into the army and made to fight". She knew about Win the War Day on September 21 because of leaflets picked up from her garden and dropped from an aeroplane. She attended some of the events in Cannon Hill Park, including going up in a balloon for 10s/6d. Armistice Day stood out in her memory. Miss Jones told Hilda's class when the news became official. The boys stood on the seats clapping and cheering. At home her mother comforted her charwoman who had broken down because she was a war widow. Later in the day the family went into the city via a Bradford Street transformed with flags and fireworks. They prayed in St Martin's. Celebrations lasted days and included an Illuminated Tramcar which displayed Allied flags and coloured lettering with the names of the victorious generals, Haig and Foch. During the post-war election she attended political meetings with her father who supported John Dennis, the Coalition candidate for Deritend, and was a member of his committee. She remembered the jingle…

> "Vote, vote for Dennis, and make the Germans pay, Vote, vote for Dennis and sweep the slums away, Vote, vote for Dennis, and speed the brighter day, When the boys come marching home."

Dennis was easily elected. On December 12 1918 Hilda went with her father to the ceremony at St Philip's for the handing over of the colours of the 1/6th Royal Warwicks.

'Memory Lane'. Hilda Moss. Library of Birmingham.

2, Amesbury Road. This was the family home in 1911 of five Alabaster brothers who all attended King Edward's School and served in the First World War. Four survived and one was killed. Their father, Arthur, was a manufacturing goldsmith and jeweller and part of a partnership called Alabaster and Wilson at 11, Legge Lane in the Jewellery Quarter. There were six children, all Moseley born, and two servants in the household.

The eldest son was Arthur Stanley Alabaster who was born in 1885 and attended King Edward's from 1898 to 1902. By 1911 he was 'assisting' in the business. He was a pre-war Territorial and held the rank of Lieutenant in what became the 1/5th Warwicks battalion in 1910. His unit was mobilised at the beginning of the war and by October he was a temporary captain. He went to France later than his battalion in 1915 and joined No 1 Entrenching Battalion for three months when they were constructing strongpoints in a rear line near Ypres. In November 1915 he joined 1/5 on the Somme at the northern end of what became the 1916 battlefield. During one of the many actions in the Somme battle he received the Military Cross. On July 8 he sat on the court martial panel of Private Arthur Earp for quitting his post. Although the sentence was death by firing squad the panel recommended mercy. This was not accepted by the Commander in Chief and Earp was shot on July 22. Charles Carrington mentions Arthur Alabaster, his company commander, in one of his memoirs where he stated that the latter would "engage a machine gun with his single rifle and silence it by accurate shooting". He spent the winter of 1916/17 near Peronne and took part in the German withdrawal to the Hindenburg Line. On April 18 1917 he left for a senior officer's course at Aldershot and when he returned in July was attached to the 1/7th Warwicks. During the 3rd Battle of Ypres that year he was second in command. He went with the 1/7th battalion to Italy in November 1917 and ended the war there with the rank of major.

Frederick Clifford Alabaster was the unfortunate brother who did not survive the war. He was born in 1887 and attended King Edward's from 1899-1905. Like Arthur he was assisting in his father's business in 1911. He was gazetted as a second lieutenant in the same battalion as Arthur in July 1915 and went to France in January 1916 to join 'C' company. He was severely wounded in Alsace Trench at Hebuterne on the Somme on June 25

1916 and died of wounds in London on August 25 1916. He was buried in Brandwood End Cemetery.

George Herbert Alabaster was the middle brother. He was born in 1889 and attended King Edward's from 1902-7. In 1911 he was a medical student. He was successful and in 1913 was a house physician at the Queens Hospital in Bath Row. Unsurprisingly he was a RAMC lieutenant in France in June 1915 with 83 Field Ambulance and then became attached to 19th Brigade, Royal Field Artillery. At some point in 1916 he was at Aldershot and became a captain before going to Salonika to work at No 36 General Hospital inland at Vertekop where he stayed for the rest of the war.

James Wilfred Alabaster was born in 1890 and attended King Edward's from 1904-8. In 1911 he was an articled accountant. James joined as a private in August 1914 and was in the 2/Ox and Bucks Light Infantry. They went to France in August and he appears to have joined them in November that year. In February 1915 he was invalided home. In May he was commissioned into the 13th Warwicks, a reserve battalion, as a second lieutenant. He was then with the 11th Warwicks and was wounded on the Somme in July 1916. At some point he returned and was one of five officers wounded in an attack along the Arras-Cambrai Road on April 10 1917, the second day of the Battle of Arras. He was promoted to lieutenant in October 1916 but never returned to active service. He later joined the Ministry of Munitions as A.D.M.A and in June 1918 became Sectional D.M.A.

Edward Beric Alabaster was the youngest brother. He was born in 1894 and was at King Edward's School from 1906-11. He was also a medic. He joined up in October 1914 as a 'dresser' and was soon serving with Lady Paget's combined Serbian Relief Fund and St John's Ambulance Unit at a military hospital at Skopje in Macedonia. He probably became a POW when Skopje fell to the Bulgarians on October 22 1915 although his unit was allowed to continue to tend the wounded. Lady Paget arrived back in England, after her release, in April 1916, and Edward Alabaster was probably also released because he later served as a RAMC lieutenant in Mesopotamia from August 1916 to April 1919. Here he served with a River Sick Convoy Unit, was in medical charge of various paddle steamers, served at the 3rd British General Hospital, Basra, a field ambulance at Uqbah and a CCS at Hit on the River Euphrates north of Baghdad.

The house still exists but is now divided into seven apartments. There is still a firm of Alabaster and Wilson at 11, Legge Lane.

See Sherborne Street, Ladywood for Private Arthur Earp.

'Service Record of King Edward's School, Birmingham during the War 1914-1919'. Cornish Brothers. 1920.

1911 census.

Moseley Church of England School, School Road. Two teachers joined up early in the war – one, Mr Harvey, was later to be Captain Harvey of the Army Service Corps. Both returned to teach at the school in 1919. Harvey had received permission in April 1914 for a fortnight's training on the Isle of Wight in a Territorial machine gun section. In 1915 the boys sent over 1000 cigarettes to the wounded soldiers at Bournbrook, the 1st Southern General. A number of former pupils came back to the school. Henry Cox presented an aeroplane propeller. Sergeant F. Chatham MM of the Canadian Highlanders left a souvenir – a German soldier's identity disk. Corporal H. Gardner visited; he had survived the retreat from Mons in 1914. On November 11 1918 a signal was given during playtime that the Armistice had been signed. The children cheered lustily and the Master gave a talk on the significance of the news. The children then sang 'God Save the King' and the Doxology.

'The Moseley Church of England National School History 1828-1969'. Fred Price. Moseley Society. 1998. Library of Birmingham.

The school is now in different premises in Oxford Road. The original site is now occupied by retirement flats.

52, Anderton Park Road. In the summer of 1916 this became the family home of Kees and Beatrice Boeke. Beatrice is perhaps better known by her maiden name – Cadbury. She was born at Moseley Hall on April 28 1884, the daughter of Richard and Emma Cadbury. For a long time the Quaker Cadbury Brothers meant Beatrice's father and his younger brother, George, the sons of John Cadbury. In 1891 Richard's family moved into Uffculme. Beatrice attended a Froebel kindergarten and from 1895 Edgbaston High School for Girls. Tragedy struck in 1899 when her father died in Jerusalem during a family trip. From 1901-3 Beatrice boarded at the Mount School in York, a strictly Quaker School. In 1903 she passed the examination for Westfield College, London but in 1905 she returned home to care for her mother followed by a world tour a year later. However pleasure turned to tragedy in May 1907 when her mother died in the Pacific as the result of a fall.

When she returned she moved into the house called 'Tennessee' which her sister Helen had built with her American husband in the grounds of

Uffculme. In 1910 after another foreign trip she decided to become involved in Quaker mission work. She joined the Friends Foreign Mission Association and became a member of its Candidates Committee. She joined others to interview for the headship of a boys school in Syria. One of those interviewed was Cornelis Boeke from Holland – known as 'Kees'. He was successful and had to spend a year in missionary training at Woodbrooke on the Bristol Road, formerly the home of Beatrice's Uncle George. A romance began and an engagement followed after six weeks. He went out to Syria and returned for their wedding on December 19 1911 at the Friends Meeting House in Bull Street. In 1912 the newlyweds were at the school at Brummana, Syria. In November 1912 their first daughter, Helen, was born.

When the war broke out the family returned to England. A foretaste of the future came when they were not allowed off the ship at Southampton because their papers were Dutch and they had to get official papers at London. They returned to 'Tennessee' and a new daughter in November that year. In 1915 Kees became secretary of the new Birmingham branch of the Fellowship of Reconciliation (FOR) which opposed the war on Christian grounds and was against conscription. Barrow Cadbury, the half-brother of Beatrice, donated £500. Kees enrolled on a teacher training course at Birmingham University. He made national contacts through the FOR and was asked to travel to Germany to make contact with German anti-war campaigners. He left in July 1915 and travelled via Holland in order to see his mother. At a holiday cottage in North Wales a month later Beatrice was interviewed by a policeman about Kees and his visit. His letters from Holland had been opened by the censor. Kees returned in September having met significant German pacifists. A month later he began to teach at 'The Woodruffs', a private school. In January 1916 a third daughter was born.

Around the same time Kees was forced to resign after parent's protested about his teaching of scripture, particularly the Sermon on the Mount. That year Beatrice began to question her lavish lifestyle at 'Tennessee' paid for by significant dividends from her Cadbury shares. That summer the family moved into 52, Anderton Park Road, Moseley. Around this time Beatrice offered help to the Friends' War Victims' Committee which supported the wives and children of 'enemy aliens'. In December that year Kees was preaching regularly every week outside a munitions factory. He told the crowd "Love your enemies, do good to those who hate you. The Germans are our brothers. Let the soldiers throw down their arms and refuse to fight and join in the brotherhood of man". He was observed by two special constables who were making notes. When a drunken soldier picked up a chair and shook it at Kees, accusing him of being a traitor, the constables stepped up and moved him on as things were becoming 'disorderly'. He still continued to speak on street corners and Beatrice gave out leaflets. In June 1917 a fourth daughter arrived. In January 1918 the family went to Neath in South Wales for a short time to spread their message. It was not successful as many people thought that he was German. He was arrested for obstruction and just avoided Swansea prison.

However, whilst still in Wales, he received a summons to appear at Birmingham Law Courts on February 17 1918 under the Defence of the Realm Act. The charge was that "he had made statements likely to interfere with the success of His Majesty's forces and prejudice their recruiting and discipline". In court he was alleged to have said at Sparkhill – the Germans are our brothers; man was not made to kill man; the quickest way to end war would be for all soldiers to lay down their arms. A constable witness admitted that Kees had been speaking at an ordinary religious gathering. Lord Ilkeston, the magistrate ruled that he should pay a fine of £50 or face 41 days prison. So he was sent to Winson Green prison. The event which got him into trouble was held at the corner of Showell Green Lane and Eileen Road, Sparkhill with about one hundred people present on December 23 1917. A local newspaper called Kees the 'dangerous Dutchman'. The prosecutor said he was a propagandist for the 'peace at any price party'. There was a sting in the tail. The magistrate recommended the immediate deportation of Kees to Holland. His friends and allies lobbied the Home Secretary to no avail. Kees was transferred to Wormwood Scrubs where he learned that he was suspected of being a German spy. On April 9 Beatrice travelled to London to find that he had been deported on the previous day to Rotterdam. She had to wait until July for permission to travel incognito with her children on a convoy to Holland.

In September the family took over a large villa at Bilthoven, near Utrecht. After the war the couple resumed their peace work and organised international conferences at their home as well as street preaching in Utrecht. The latter brought conflict with the authorities and a short prison sentence for both of them. At the beginning of the 1920s Beatrice began to feel guilty about her dividend income from Cadburys of about £3000 per annum. She decided to give her shares to the Bournville workers much to the dismay of her Cadbury relatives. She wrote to them and stated that "the great war and its appalling consequences have led us to believe that the private holding of capital...lies at the root of nearly all the social and economic trouble in the world today". After protracted discussions the Boeke Trust was created in

May 1922 on behalf of the Bournville Works Council. Difficult times lay ahead, including German occupation from 1939-45. Kees died in 1966. Beatrice died in Holland on February 13 1976, aged 91. Their names are recognised on the 'Righteous Among the Nations' wall at the Yad Vashem Museum in Jerusalem for sheltering Jewish children in the Second World War.

The house still exists in Anderton Park Road.

'Beatrice. The Cadbury heiress who gave away her fortune'. Fiona Joseph. Foxwell Press. 2012.

Birmingham Daily Mail February 22 1918.

Sorrento in Wake Green Road. Was converted into a hospital for military paraplegic cases and, later, a hospital for discharged soldiers. The large house was built by the rich philanthropist, William Adams, who was born in 1857. He had been a director of the Refuge Assurance Company. He was a Primitive Methodist and had stood unsuccessfully for Parliament as a Liberal. He died in 1911 and his wife and family moved a year later to Abingdon Lodge, 62, Wake Green Road.

In 1929 Sorrento became a Maternity Hospital with twenty-one beds. The site has since been redeveloped for flats.

In St Mary's Row. Nearby there was probably a hostel which was established by the YWCA for women and girls who came to the city for war work. It was opened in December 1915. The YWCA also had a hostel in Saltley which could accommodate 500 for the same reason opened on May 18 1917 by Princess Louise.

St Mary's Church, St Mary's Row. In 1916 a window was erected in the South Aisle in memory of Second Lieutenant Douglas Greenaway of the 14th Battalion of the Worcestershire Regiment who was killed in action at Gallipoli on October 17 1915 at the age of 24. His parents lived at 64, Greenhill Road, Moseley. He is also commemorated on the Azmak Cemetery memorial at Suvla. As early as January 1918 it was decided that the parish war memorial should be a new Church Hall and the Calvary now standing in the churchyard.

There is a wooden memorial board which lists 98 names by year of death and "whose names are also inscribed on the Memorial Calvary" in the churchyard. An example has been chosen from each year. Bombardier Nigel

Hurle was killed in the 1st Battle of Ypres on October 24 1914, aged 26, whilst serving in 60th Battery, Royal Field Artillery. He is commemorated on the Menin Gate. He had lived at 88, Trafalgar Road, Moseley. Lance Corporal William Drummond, 22, probably died of wounds on January 27 as he was buried in Boulogne Eastern Cemetery. He was serving in the London Scottish, the first Territorials to go to France. Captain Thomas Wathes, 28, was killed at the Battle of Fromelles on July 19 1916 in the 2/6th Royal Warwicks. He had attended Wadham College, Oxford University, and his mother lived in Cambridge Road, Kings Heath. He is commemorated on the Ploegsteert Memorial. Lieutenant Thomas Mitton, 20, was killed on Christmas Eve 1917 on the staff of GHQ Signals. His parents lived at 'Abbotsford', Wake Green Road, Moseley. Corporal Howard Mortiboys, 19, also died of wounds on October 9 1918 in the 1/Duke of Cornwall's Light Infantry and lies buried in the St Sever Cemetery at Rouen. He had attended King Edward's at Camp Hill and his parents lived in 'Clarendon House', 94, Trafalgar Road, Moseley. Also named on the memorial is F.C Alabaster who is documented elsewhere in this study.

In addition there are four individual memorials on the walls of the church. There is a stone inscription to Private John Jennens Belsey of the 26/ Royal Fusiliers which includes the words 'This bay was faced with stone by his sister'. He was killed on the Somme between October 7 and 10 1916. He is buried in the AIF Burial Ground, Flers. His parents lived in Moseley. There is also a wooden plaque to the Reverend James Leitch Cappell, aged 41, who was an army chaplain attached to the 1/9th Royal Scots when he was killed on January 23 1918. He died of wounds in hospital and was buried at Le Havre. He wife, Alice, was living at Blackburn. He is on the memorial because he was curate of St Mary's from 1912-1915 before he joined up. In 1904 he had been a curate at Berkswich, near Stafford, and he is also on the war memorial there. He was Perthshire born and had qualified at Glasgow University in 1898. The third memorial is to Lieutenant John William Hudson, 20, who was killed near Fonquevillers on the Somme on November 30 1915 whilst serving in the 1/5th Warwicks. His parents lived at 'Meerend', 60, Salisbury Road, Moseley.

The final example is the window erected in the South Aisle in memory of Second Lieutenant Douglas Greenaway of the 14th Battalion of the Worcestershire Regiment who was killed in action at Gallipoli on October 17 1915 at the age of 24. His parents lived at 64, Greenhill Road, Moseley. He is also commemorated on the Azmak Cemetery memorial at Suvla. He also has a brass plaque adjacent to the window. As early as January 1918 it was decided that the parish war memorial should be a new Church Hall and the Calvary now standing in the churchyard.

30, Brighton Road. In 1901 this was the family home of Charles James Simmons, aged 7, better known as Jim. He was living there with his father, James Henry, a house decorator born in Birmingham in 1867 and mother, May Jane, born in Bow, London in 1873. Charles was the eldest with four siblings – Ellen, 6 ,George, 4, Harold, 1 , and William who had just been born. Three more arrived later, Frederick, Norman and Edward. His grandfather, Charles Russell, 55, also a house decorator, was also there. He received a Board school education at Clifton Road. He left school at 14 and became a Post Office messenger. He was also a Sunday School teacher at the Greet Primitive Methodist Mission. On the 1911 census Jim is recorded as an 18 year old private in the Worcestershire Regiment at the Norton Barracks with a service number of 413. He had joined the 5th (Special Reserve) Battalion in January of that year not quite 18 years of age. He signed on for six months service and six years in the reserve which involved a month in camp each year. He joined the Army Temperance Association at the depot and found a local Primitive Methodist Chapel.

He returned to civilian life because of his interests in religion and politics despite his colour sergeant's advice for him to become a regular. He later attended the annual camp at Croome Park, Worcester and joined his battalion at Tregantle Fort, Plymouth, when mobilised for war. On January 12 1915 he left for France and the 2nd/Worcesters at Festubert. He left with considerable doubts about the war having read ILP and UDC literature since the outbreak of war as well as the 'Labour Leader', 'Forward' and 'Weekly Herald'. He had also written openly as a soldier to Birmingham newspapers. He wrote in his diary just before leaving "I am off to the front and, in a way I am glad, for though I have come to oppose all war I am no coward and wish to prove it".

On March 17 1915 Simmons was wounded by a German shell, was hospitalised but returned in time for 'going over the top' at Richbourg on May 15 during the failed Battle of Festubert. He spent five nights in a shell-hole in No Man's Land on the wrong side of the German wire. He was sent to hospital at Rouen and then to a Red Cross hospital at Stacksteads in the Rossendale valley of Lancashire. From there he went to the convalescent hospital at nearby Bacup. Whilst there he preached at every chapel in the valley. On his way back to Birmingham he called at the office of Labour Leader in Manchester and had a long talk with Fenner Brockway. This paper had published some of his letters from the trenches. On August 19 1915 he married Beatrice Roberts at Solihull Register Office but soon returned to Norton Barracks. In his service record his wife's address was given as 14, Richmond Road, Olton and his father was at Ivy Cottage, Hamstead Road, Handsworth.

At the end of October 1915 he sailed for Gallipoli and joined 29th Division at Suvla Bay. After evacuation a long stay in Egypt followed. Here he held 'discussion groups on the origins of the war and the principles of a just peace most nights'. One day his company commander sent for him to tell him that a letter to Councillor J.W. Kneeshaw in Birmingham had been destroyed for 'its subversive matter'. The letter was about plans for conscription. When questioned by the CO he told him that "you've only bought my body not my mind". The CO tried to get the Brigade Medical Officer to remove him without success and stated that he was 'a danger to the discipline of the Regiment' and 'his officers consider him mentally unbalanced' but he was still sent to a Cairo hospital 'officially suffering from rheumatism'.

Eventually he landed back in France with the 3rd Battalion. Here he became friends with six other kindred spirits – the 'Khaki Pals (Active Service) Branch of the ILP'. They used to meet in a YMCA hut. At Vimy Ridge in 1917 he was wounded again with a shattered ankle and a bullet lodged in the sole of the foot. After a spell in a hospital at Etaples he went to No 2 London General Hospital, Chelsea, arriving on June 8 1917. After months of trying to save the limb on December 19 the lower third of his leg was amputated. During his stay at the hospital he met many political and trade union figures, particularly Ramsay MacDonald, who enabled him to make many visits to the House of Commons. He spent a lot of time reading socialist books. Eventually he was allowed to go home to Birmingham whilst still waiting for an artificial limb. Here he preached in chapels and attended political meetings.

He took on the organisation of the Midlands Workers and Soldiers Councils Conference for August 18 1917 which was to welcome the Russian Revolution following the Leeds Convention on June 3. 220 delegates were promised. However, a senior Birmingham police officer served him a notice which banned the conference under Defence of the Realm regulations. Afterwards Simmons became active throughout the Midlands in the 'Peace by Negotiation Campaign' being billed as 'Private Jim Simmons with a Message from the Trenches'. His main message was 'No Patched Up Peace'. Plain clothes police took notes at his open-air meetings. He denounced 'war profiteers, the armament sharks and the politicians'. "I had a special duty to speak for my inarticulate comrades who were still risking life and limb on the battlefield". On September 26 at Rochdale he was arrested by two military policemen and spent a night in the cells before escort to Chester Castle. His wife contacted Ramsay MacDonald who raised the matter in the House of Commons. He was then sent to military detention in Wallis Yard, London, where he was taken to Roehampton Hospital for the fitting of an artificial limb and then released under 'open arrest'. He prepared a court martial statement and sent copies to Ramsay MacDonald and the press. He stated he was a victim of 'British Prussianism', that the charge was under an obsolete order, and that he was there only because of his opinions.

He was eventually discharged from the army as unfit for further service on November 22 1917 and returned to Birmingham. He was awarded a Silver Wound Badge. He continued to campaign. In March 1918 he was detained at Nelson, Lancashire, and taken to York where he learned that he had incensed the military authorities by an attack on the use of Field Punishment No 1 – a kind of crucifixion. He was sentenced to three months 'with such hard labour as he is capable of performing'. At Armley Gaol, Leeds, he told the warder that his employment status was 'propagandist'. He picked oakum and sewed mailbags. He read and wrote on lavatory paper with a pencil hidden at the end of his 'stump'. He was released on June 12 1918. He returned to Birmingham and Beatrice and their two rooms and he became an organiser for the newly formed Birmingham ILP Federation. This included attendance at military tribunals to speak for conscientious objectors.

In the 1918 general election he acted as the election agent for the ILP candidate at Moseley. The candidate was Doctor Robert Dunstan, a young RAMC lieutenant, who had served in Mesopotamia and was soon to join the Communist Party. Post-war he was also active in the National Union of Ex-Servicemen which was later subsumed into the British Legion. He was also involved in the Labour churches movement. In 1921 he was elected to the City Council and served until 1931 and again from 1942-5. He became the Labour MP for Erdington from 1929-31 and for West Birmingham from 1945-50. Later he was MP for Brierley Hill from 1950 to 1959. He had also been active in political journalism and edited the Town Crier, the Birmingham Trades Council journal, from 1940-45. His wife, Beatrice, was also politically active and became an alderman on the City Council. There were four sons. He remarried in 1972 to Kate Showell.

'Soap Box Evangelist – Jim Simmons'. January, 1972.

Times obituary August 1975.

Friends Institute, 220, Moseley Road. This was built in 1899 at the expense of Richard Cadbury. The 'Friends' found room there to run Sunday School classes, hold meetings of clubs and other meetings. The large Hall could seat 2000 and there were thirty-seven classrooms and a gym. Its memorial board lists by year eighty names 'of our dear comrades'. The examples which follow are dedicated to all of them. Private William Fantham was aged 19 when he was killed on December 22 1914 serving in the 1st Coldstream Guards. His mother was living at 50, Newport Road, Balsall Heath and in 1911 he was with his widowed mother at 16, Muntz Street; he was a cycle fitter. He is also commemorated on the Le Touret memorial. Pioneer Alfred Harnaman was in 62nd Field Company, Royal Engineers, when he was killed on September 25 1915, aged 19. His parents lived at 42, Bordesley Green Road, Small Heath from at least 1911 when he was an office boy and the son of a house painter. He is commemorated on the Menin Gate at Ypres.

Lance Corporal Ernest Curbishley was killed on April 19 1916, aged 20, serving in the 2nd South Staffs. His parents lived at 3, Greenhill Avenue, School Road, Moseley and he is buried in Loos British Cemetery. In 1911 his family were living at 3, Mount Pleasant Grove, Camden Street, and he was noted as an errand boy for a jeweller; his father was an ivory artist. Private Edward Wilkins was killed on the Somme on July 20 1916, also aged 20, serving in the 8th Devons. He had lived at 69, Salop Street, Highgate from at least 1911 when he was recorded as a screw maker and the son of a Corporation ashman. Edward had no known grave and is commemorated on the Thiepval memorial. Private Lawrence Sykes was killed on the first day of the Third Battle of Ypres, July 31 1917, whilst serving in the 2nd Coldstream Guards. His wife, Maud, lived at 49, Vincent Street, Balsall Heath. In 1911 he was a cabinet maker and living at that address with his in-laws. He is commemorated on the Menin Gate. He was 37. Private Thomas Gaffey, a signaller aged 23, was killed in the same battle on August 22 1917. He was in the 1/5th Warwicks, which he had joined before the war, and is listed on the Tyne Cot Memorial. He had lived in a terrace in Lawrence Street and, before that, in 1911 was at 45, Gem Street where he was noted as a 'turner engineer'. As a boy he had been a boy scout. His father, Luke, had been the caretaker of Bishop Ryder's Church and Schools in Gem Street.

Private Joseph Frederick William Woodwiss was definitely a Quaker and died on October 29 1918 whilst serving with No 5 Ambulance Train, British Red Cross, as a member of the Friends' Ambulance Unit. He was twenty and came from 203, Grange Road, Kings Heath. In 1911 he was still at school, the son of Enos, a tridox maker. His brother of the same name was a chocolate worker. He is buried in Abbeville Communal Cemetery Extension.

The future of the building was in doubt in 2008 when it was being used by over forty organisations and groups.

Birmingham Tramways Department memorial. Wheelers Lane, Kings Heath. The memorial is not visible from the main road as it is just inside the drive of the 'Stadium'. Those killed are listed under the names of thirteen depots and departments. It is dedicated 'To the glorious memory of our comrades who during the Great War made the supreme sacrifice'.

The depots listed are Arthur Street; Bournbrook Cotteridge; Highgate Road; Hockley; Miller Street, Witton and Perry Barr; Moseley Road; Tennant Street; Rosebery Street; and Washwood Heath. There was also the Kyotts Lake Works, Head Office, Overhead Department and Permanent Way Department. One man has been chosen from each to represent the 234 listed. Private Harry Mavity lived at 59, Cheapside and had worked at Arthur Street, Small Heath. He was killed in the 1/8th Warwicks on the first day of the Somme and is also commemorated on the Thiepval Memorial. Driver James Bolstridge, aged 32, died on the May 4 1917 whilst serving in 661st Company of Horse Transport in the Army Service Corps. He probably did not see overseas service and is buried in St Nicholas churchyard, Kings Norton. He had worked at the Bournbrook/Cotteridge Depot. Private J. Beecher of the Highgate Road depot was a reservist called up at the start of the war because he was killed on September 16 1914 in the 1/Royal Scots Fusiliers during the Battle of the Aisne. He is buried at Vailly on the north bank of the river.

Private Bernard Balnaves, aged 25, of the Hockley Depot died on June 19 1918 whilst serving in the Royal Army Medical Corps. He is also commemorated on the screen wall in Key Hill Cemetery. Private Walter Curry, 25, had worked at the maintenance and repair works at Kyotts Lake, Sparkbrook. He was killed in the 10th Warwicks on July 3 1916 during their attack on La Boiselle on the Somme. He had also lived at Sparkbrook. He is also commemorated on the Thiepval Memorial. Serjeant Percy Weeks, aged 27, of the Witton/Perry Barr depots, was killed as a member of the 1st Warwicks on August 30 1918. He left a wife at 51, Church Vale, Handsworth. He is buried in Eterpigny British Cemetery in France. One of the few officers listed on the memorial was Captain Joseph Coley of the Head Office staff who lived in Pretoria Road, Bordesley Green. He was aged 21

One panel of the Tramways Memorial

when he was killed on March 22 1918 in the 4/Royal Fusiliers. He is also commemorated on the Arras Memorial.

Serjeant Arthur Ellesmere, aged 34, had worked in the Moseley Road Depot. He left a wife in Wordsworth Road, Small Heath. He was serving in 'E' company of the 1/8th Warwicks when he was killed in Belgium on May 29 1915. He is buried in La Plus Douve Farm Cemetery. He was shot in the head by a German sniper the day after his promotion to the rank of serjeant for his 'soldierly qualities' including his readiness to volunteer for any dangerous enterprise. Private George Snape, aged 20, had worked for the Overhead Department. He had joined the 3rd Birmingham Pals and was killed on July 27 1916 as a result of their attack on Morval on the Somme. He had lived in Station Road, Harborne and is also commemorated on the Thiepval Memorial. Corporal John Breeze of the Permanent Way Department was also killed on the Somme on July 6 1916 and also has his name on the Thiepval Memorial. He was serving in the 8th North Staffordshire Regiment.

Private Henry Buller, aged 32, probably did not see overseas service as he served in the 1st Garrison Battalion of the Worcesters. He died on August 9 1917 and is also commemorated on the screen wall in Yardley Cemetery. He had worked at the Tennant Street Garage and lived in Malmesbury Road, Small Heath. Private Charles Bonnard, aged 24, had been a driver at the Rosebery Road Depot and was killed on the day after Serjeant Ellesmere in the same battalion and is buried in the same cemetery in Belgium. He had lived in Balsall Heath and his wife Annie had pre-deceased him. Private R.H Wolvin, had been serving in the 25th Company of the Machine Gun Corps and was taken prisoner. He died on October 24 1918 and is buried in Hamburg Cemetery. He had worked at the Washwood Heath Depot.

69, Springfield Road. This was the family home of Lieutenant Leslie Glendower Humphries who was flying an RE8 over Glencorse Wood, near Ypres, when he was shot down and killed on September 16 1917. He was engaged in a photographic reconnaissance over the Anzac front from Abeele Aerodrome. His plane probably landed as his observer was only wounded. Before joining the RFC he had joined the Artists' Rifles. On June 4 1917 he was given his flying certificate at Thetford after flying a Maurice Farman bi-plane. He had been born in 1898 at Lichfield where his father owned a bakery. By 1913 his father had retired from business and was living in Kings Heath. Before joining up Leslie had worked at Lloyds Bank in Leamington Spa. He is buried in Hooge Crater Cemetery, Belgium.

Colmore Road Council School. This school, only opened in 1911, was taken over as a new section of the 1st Southern General Hospital. It was opened on October 5 1915 with a staff of two officers, a nursing staff of fifty-one and seventeen RAMC personnel. It opened with 225 beds. The first convoy of seventy two patients was admitted on the same day. The nursing staff were accommodated in old mansions at King's Heath House and Hazelwell Hall.

The Southern Cross No 14. February 1917. Library of Birmingham.

The school buildings are still part of Colmore Infant and Nursery School and Colmore Junior School.

7.

Jewellery Quarter/Hockley

W Stewart Turner and Harry Simpson set up a silversmithing business in 1912 at 12-16, Legge Lane. In 1914 they began to make patriotic souvenirs in silver such as badges and brooches. They were involved in 'send a lucky horseshoe pendant to your boy in the trenches'. This idea was started by a newspaper who offered to send one free of charge. It was free but the buyer had to send coupons from four penny journals and a stamp for postage. The first order was for 5000 and there was a staggering response. They probably finally made half a million. The two men were also commissioned in 1914 to make the dies for the chocolate boxes given by Princess Mary to the troops. For the design the Princess sat for Harry Simpson at Buckingham Palace.

The building now exists as separate business premises in Legge Lane.
'Jewellery Making in Birmingham 1750-1995'. Shena Mason. Phillimore. 1998.

30, Frederick Street. Manufacturing jewellery business managed by Carl Otto Valhinger. The firm's headquarters were at Pforzheim, Germany. Early in the war there was concern about 'trading with the enemy' but Carl needed silver bolts and rings, as well as some gold and silver wire. He continued to bring what he needed into Britain from Zurich in Switzerland until January 1915. The issue featured at Birmingham Police Court on July 29 1915 when Valhinger and Emily Haag, of Wellingborough, were accused of unlawfully obtaining between November 1 1914 and January 15 1915 2874 silver bolt rings, 250 metres of 9 carat gold wire and a large quantity of other goods. Valhinger was brought to court from Handforth internment camp. Also at the Police Court a week later evidence was submitted in the form of letters and a letter book from Frederick Street. They were remanded again.

The issue came to Birmingham Quarter Sessions on September 29 that year when the jury heard that the Zurich firm was Ernst Gideon Bek which had transferred its business with England from Pforzheim. Valhinger had not kept records and had diverted most of the work through the company's subsidiary at Wellingborough managed by Emil Haag, another German who had a Birmingham wife. After a lengthy deliberation by the jury Valhinger was sent to prison for two years and Haag to six months. By the time of the police investigation Valhinger had already been sent to the Handforth internment camp in Cheshire because he was an 'enemy alien' of military age; he was single and aged 42 at the time. He left Birmingham on May 27 1915. He had registered with the Birmingham Police on August 8 1914 and the aliens register shows that he came to Birmingham in February 1899 from Pforzheim. He was then living as a lodger at 46, Ivy Road, Handsworth. Valhinger was sentenced to two years in prison and Haag to six months.

The building still exists in Frederick Street.

'Trading with enemy' by Chris Upton. Birmingham Post March 16 1996.

Birmingham Daily Post July 30 and September 29 1915.

Bridge Street West. Here was the munitions factory of William Mills the designer of the Mills bomb or grenade. The firm manufactured this effective trench weapon with a largely female workforce. (see 14, Church

Mills munition workers at Bridge Street West in 1916

Road, Edgbaston, for William Mills) Sixty seven workers served during the war and two of this number were killed. One of them was Sergeant Observer W.H Gumbley who was with his pilot in a DH9 of 49 Squadron on a bombing operation when they were shot down in flames near Mons on October 30 1918. He was nineteen years old and lived in the street where the factory was located at No 263. He is buried in Mons Communal Cemetery.

244, Barr Street. Here was Joseph Hudson and Co, the famous whistle manufacturers, who moved into a new building there in 1909 from 13, Barr Street. During the war officers' whistles were made and blown as a signal to 'go over the top'. Some Sam Browne belts had a 'whistle pouch' on the cross strap in which the whistle could be inserted.

Whistles are still made today by Acme Whistles, the descendant company, with a headquarters in the Jewellery Quarter selling over five million a year. The Hudson building in Barr Street still exists with a prominent name of the firm displayed on the wall.

James Hinks, Crystal Lamp Works, Great Hampton Street. During the war the firm made mess tins, hand grenades and various shell components. It was closed in 1920 and the site was later taken over by Lucas. The present building on the site – Hampton Lofts – was the Lucas building.

Lucas of Little King Street and Great King Street. During the war the firm of Harry Lucas made electrical equipment such as batteries for aeroplanes, armoured cars, ambulances, cycle lamps and acetylene lamps for Douglas motor-cycles which carried machine guns. They did experimental work on searchlights. Vast quantities of repetition parts like shell fuse covers and rings were also made. They also made self-starters for tank engines. The company became a controlled establishment under the Ministry of Munitions. One of the earliest Government contracts was for the Aldis signalling lamp for the Royal Navy and airships. The lamp could be read from ten miles. Oliver Lucas, who had joined the RNAS Armoured Car section, designed a more effective infantry signalling lamp after his experience on the Somme; previous designs could be read by the Germans. His design was widely used by the British Army.

In 1916 magneto production moved there from Cheapside into new seven-storey buildings but was still run as a separate Thomson-Bennett concern which overall supplied 130000 magnetos during the war – more than half the total British number. Many were used on a variety of aircraft. Each Lucas worker who went off to war was given a parting gift by Harry Lucas. During the war the payroll had grown from about 600 to 4000 people of whom 1200 were employed by Thomson-Bennett. The cold storage room in the Birmingham Meat Market in Bradford Street was used to test a Lucas self-starter for a 240 h.p. Sunbeam engine for seaplanes flying at high altitude and in the Arctic.

The factory closed in 1987 and the land was sold to Birmingham Corporation.

Heaton Street. Was the site of another wartime street memorial.

49, Icknield Cottages, Icknield Street. This was the family home of Private Charles Hunt of the 1st Battalion, Royal Warwickshire Regiment, who returned to Birmingham from two years as a POW in September 1916. The newspaper report of his experiences speaks for itself.

Birmingham Soldier's Return Home
His Experiences as a Prisoner in Germany
Stories of Harsh Treatment Confirmed

"Amongst the English prisoners of war who have recently been restored to their own country is Lance Corporal Charles Hunt of the Royal Warwickshire Regiment, whose home is at 49, Icknield Cottages, Icknield Street, Hockley. He was serving with the colours at Shorncliffe when war broke out and went to France as a member of the first Expeditionary Force. He was wounded by a bullet in the right knee in the retreat from Mons and was an inmate of the hospital at St Quentin when he was taken prisoner on August 26 1914. Despite his injured knee, which was in splints, his captors made him walk two and a half miles to the station for entrainment to Germany. Thence he was despatched to a prison camp at Sennelager and this journey thither will, he says, never be effaced from his memory. It was a hideous nightmare. There were 38 of them in a cattle truck and they were without food and water for four days and night. In all there were about 270 prisoners who were thus treated.

On arrival there they slept three nights in the open and, despite the fact that the weather was bitterly cold, they were not given their greatcoats let alone blankets. He remained at Sennelager from September to November 1914 and was then removed to a camp at Guttersloh, where there were English, French and Russian prisoners. Though he was still troubled by the bullet wound in his knee he was able to do Red Cross work amongst the prisoners. The stories, he declares, concerning the conditions of life in the prison camps were not exaggerated. The food was very bad and the pittance daily served out was not sufficient to keep body and soul together and, but for the parcels sent from home,many men, in his opinion, would have starved to death. Their daily ration was a 4lb loaf between ten men and a few scraps of fish.

Asked whether the prisoners regularly received the parcels which were sent from home, Lance Corporal Hunt said they did except in cases where they were continually moved from camp to camp. He complained, however, that the Germans made a practice of opening all the tinned stuff and examining it before handing it over, consequently it had either to be eaten at once or it went bad. Subsequently he was moved to Mannheim where he was interned for several weeks and had to sleep on a wooden floor of a hut without any bedding. The prisoners were worked very hard and several who were sent to chemical works were rendered nearly blind. The treatment generally meted out to the prisoners was very harsh and he declares that he had seen men made to stand on a brick which was kicked from under their feet when they had been tied up to a tree and left with the weight of their bodies depending on the thongs for a considerable time, suffering excruciating agony. He himself had had two of his ribs broken whilst a prisoner.

Owing to his injuries and privations he became very ill and was amongst the first batch of men sent to Switzerland on the 12th of August 1916. He went to Interlaken and was delighted with his treatment there. Of Miss Simpkins, the matron of the hospital at Manor Farm, he speaks in the highest terms, describing her as 'one of the best'. His condition rapidly improved in Switzerland and, all things considered, Hunt looks fairly well, though owing to the want of proper treatment at the time he is still troubled by his knee and feels far from strong owing to his prison camp experiences in Germany."

Birmingham Daily Mail September 27 1916.

8.

Dudley Road/Winson Green/ Handsworth/Smethwick

The Poor Law Infirmary in Dudley Road. Now the City Hospital, was an offshoot of the University Hospital from May 1915 and was designated, on June 1 1917, the 2/1st Southern General Hospital. It also took twenty-two auxiliary hospitals under its wing. The hospital began its new status with 1650 beds. It had opened for patients on May 10 1915 when it was known as the 'Dudley section'. Convoys of wounded arrived via Soho Goods Station and Winson Green GWR Station. By 1916 it had 1560 beds. 267 convoys were received during the war. The total number of wounded and sick men admitted reached 53896. The main building consisted of a central corridor with eleven blocks of three storey buildings leading off it alternately right and left. The Nurses' Homes were at the end of the corridor; sisters took over the Infectious Hospital. RAMC men were housed in the laundry.

The hospital had four operating theatres. Some workhouse buildings were also taken over. The main administrator throughout was Lieutenant Colonel F.W Ellis. Matron Miss Thomas had been in charge of the infirmary nurses in peacetime and had the same role in wartime and became responsible for 277 nurses at the peak. One of the RAMC doctors, Major Reginald Tweedy, had been senior resident surgical officer and had joined from his practice in Kenilworth. He died at Newquay and Cordelia Leigh of Stoneleigh Abbey attended his memorial service at Kenilworth Parish Church on July 16 1917. Those attending included VAD hospitals from Birmingham. There were regular concerts to entertain the men and a YMCA hut was erected for this purpose in 1917. There were 268 deaths during the whole period, many of whom were influenza cases from soldiers on leave. Military funerals were held at Lodge Hill Cemetery. After the Armistice it became the Demobilisation Hospital for the Birmingham District with cases transferred from other hospitals. It closed in July 1919.

1 Back, 17 Aberdeen Street, Winson Green. In 1911 this was the home of Albert Gill and his wife Rosetta. He was a 'tube drawer press' who had been born in Birmingham. His wife came from Torquay. The street was adjacent to the Birmingham workhouse. On July 27 1916 he was a sergeant in the 1st Battalion of the King's Royal Rifle Corps which attacked Delville Wood on the Somme. He was killed but there was a subsequent award of a Victoria Cross for conspicuous bravery. The citation was published in the London Gazette on October 24 that year and stated "The enemy made a very strong counter-attack on the right flank of the battalion, and rushed the bombing post after killing all the company bombers. Serjeant Gill at once rallied the remnants of his platoon, none of whom were skilled bombers, and reorganised his defences, a most difficult and dangerous task, the trench being very shallow and much damaged. Soon afterwards the enemy nearly surrounded his men by creeping up through the thick undergrowth, and commenced sniping at about twenty yards range. Although it was almost certain death, Sergeant Gill stood boldly up in order to direct the fire of his men. He was killed almost at once, but not before he had shown his men where the enemy were, and thus enabled them to hold up their advance. By his supreme devotion to duty and self-sacrifice he saved a very dangerous situation". The Wood was captured later the same day. He now lies buried in Delville Wood Cemetery, Longueval.

Albert was born on September 8 1879, the son of Henry and Sophia Gill, at 83, Hospital Street, Hockley. The family soon moved to Dugdale Street, Hockley and then to 2/40 Cope Street in the same area. He attended Steward Street School in the street next to Cope Street; this was one of Birmingham's earliest Board schools opened in 1873. Soon after leaving school he joined the army. Part of his army career was spent in India. At some point he left the army and was employed by Messrs Earle, Bourne and Co Ltd of Heath Street, Birmingham. Around 1907 he joined the GPO and was employed as a 'town sorter' at the Head Post Office. Here he met his wife Rosetta; later they had two children who both died in early childhood. He then became a delivery postman at Key Hill, Hockley. By 1911 he appears to have changed jobs. As a reservist he was recalled to the colours at the outbreak of war as a private but was soon promoted to serjeant in 'A' company. He went to the front in 1915.

After his death and news of his VC his father told a newspaper "I knew Albert would do something of the sort, he was a good soldier and a real fighter". He was glad "it was as it is rather than have him returned to his father as a cripple". Neville Chamberlain, as Lord Mayor, wrote to Rosetta on behalf of the City Council. She was working for the GPO in Pinfold Street as a hand stamper at the time. She had already received a complimentary letter from Albert's company commander, Captain Stafford. Rosetta attended the investiture at Buckingham Palace on November 29 1916 and received the VC from George V. David Delderfield met Albert's niece in the 1990s and helped organise a re-dedication ceremony at the Hockley Delivery Office memorial in September 1999. His VC and other medals were bought at auction by the Michael Ashcroft Trust for £60000.

Pdf article on the internet written by David Delderfield.

There is a memorial to Albert and other postmen who died at Hockley PO Delivery office.

W and T Avery at the Soho Works. Was a major manufacturer of weighing machines. During the war the firm produced machines adapted for war work. In 1914 3000 people were employed there. By 1915 the buildings at the works covered 453000 square feet and had been expanded significantly since 1905. The most important extension was a shop in the southern part of the works for the assembly and testing of automatic scales of various types. The foundry had also been extended. In 1914 the Foundry was largely self-

Women workers from Avery in Mill Lane, Digbeth, on Win the War Day, 1918

sufficient with its own power station, iron and brass foundries, smithy (formerly the Mint), light and heavy machine and erecting shops, pattern-makers' shop and offices.

The Avery Museum booklet summarises the role of the works during the war as follows… "production included direct munitions such as mine sinkers and shell fuses, and press made components for a new seaplane were made at the Soho Foundry for the first time. A canteen was built at the south-east corner and a works hospital was opened. Changes in production methods led to the introduction of central facilities for hardening and heat treatment of components, and the increasing popularity of self-indicating scales brought about the building of an electro-plating shop. A planning department was also created. During this period the smithy had twelve steam hammers and employed forty blacksmiths. Many thousands of drop stampings and forgings were made – forged legs for Army trestle tables, gun-carriage parts, gun sights and ammunition boxes. A special beam scale was made to weigh twenty hundredweight shells, the largest of their kind, for use in the bombardment of the Dardanelles". They also made an Avery automatic weigher for the Ministry of Munitions which weighed high explosive shells at a rate of 30 tons per hour.

Edgbaston born Sir William Beilby Avery died in 1908 and his only son, Sir William Eric Thomas Avery, then 18, became the last member of the family to be associated with the business. He had been educated at Winchester and University College, Oxford. He became an acting major in the Army Service Corps during the First World War but died on November 20 1918 as a result of a chill caught during a channel crossing. On February 12 1919 the London Gazette printed an appeal for his creditors to come forward and stated that he was 'late of the Conservative Club, St James Street, Middlesex' and formerly of Oakley Court, Windsor. He had been awarded the Military Cross.

The Managing Director of Avery from 1913 was Gilbert (later Sir) Christopher Vyle. He was an engineer who had previously worked at the Post Office, overseas with the Colonial Office, and in Manchester and Birmingham. In 1913 he was living at 42, Cotton Lane, Moseley. During the war he organised the manufacture and design of aircraft for the Admiralty, Army and Air Force. He was a member of the Board No 4 area of the Ministry of Munitions. He was knighted in 1928 and died in 1933 aged 63.

The firm is now Avery Weigh Tronix.

Avery Museum booklets on the Internet.

Hawthorne Park, Hamstead Hall Road, Handsworth Wood.

This was the home in 1911 of Lieutenant Colonel William Charles Retallack who commanded the 1/5 Battalion of the Royal Warwickshire Regiment from September 1916. He had gone to the front with them in March 1915 as a captain. This was the Territorial unit which he had joined from its early days in 1908. He was awarded the Military Cross which was gazetted in January 1917. In August 1917 he was severely wounded in the Ypres Salient. His father, Mark Nicholls Retallack, Cornish born, was then the managing director of the Birmingham Railway Carriage and Wagon Company which made shells and 70 Handley Page O/400 bombers at a site on the Handsworth/Smethwick boundary next to Middlemore Road. They were flown from an aerodrome at Halford Lane, Smethwick. The works closed in 1963 and the company had existed since 1854.

Charles was born in Handsworth in 1883 and attended King Edward's School from 1892-7. He was living at 261, Birchfield Road, Six Ways in 1913 and practised as a dentist at 89, Cornwall Street in the city centre. He was also surgeon dentist to the Magdalen Home in Clarendon Road, Edgbaston and was involved as a demonstrator at the Birmingham Dental Hospital. His father had worked his way up in the firm; from a draughtsman in 1881 to works manager in 1891 and 1901. In his years as works manager the family were living at The Laurels, Middlemore Road, which was adjacent to the factory. The Colonel had left the army by June 1920 when he married Muriel Hunter-Jones in London. His address was then given as 32, Wellington Court, Knightsbridge. His parents were still at Hawthorne Park. In July 1946 his address was 14A, Hyde Park Gardens Mews when his eldest son, John, a Captain in the Welsh Guards, was married. That was still his address when his younger son, Timothy, married. He was still alive in November 1972 when his wife died. We do not know his date of death.

There is a Retallack Close in B66.

The site of the railway works is now the Middlemore industrial estate. Hawthorne Park no longer exists and the site developed for housing but there is still a road of that name near the site. It is to Hawthorne House on Hamstead Hall Road, which at one time was a public library and is now a private residence.

42, Nineveh Road, Handsworth.
This was the birthplace of Serjeant Norman Augustus Finch VC on December 26 1890, the son of John, a mail porter. In 1891 he was the youngest of seven. He went to Benson Road Board

School and Norton Street Council School; in 1901 the family, with one addition, were at the same address. As a lad he worked for the firm of H.W Ward and Co, engineers, in Lionel Street. He joined the Navy on January 11 1908 and received his basic training at Eastney. For the next four years he served on various ships and shore stations. In 1911 we find him on the April census at Hong Kong serving on HMS Minotaur as a gunner, Royal Marine Artillery. This was an armoured cruiser launched in 1906. In 1915 his parents were living at 115, Linwood Road, Handsworth but then moved to Stockport. Finch had three brothers who served; one in the naval air service, another was a lieutenant in the Lancashire Regiment and a third was an instructor gun layer. In June 1913 he was promoted to bombardier.

For the first two years of the war he served on the North Sea but then began to suffer from 'nerves' so was given a shore position. In March 1918 he joined the 4th Battalion of the Royal Marine Artillery. However, he was serving on HMS Inflexible when he later volunteered for the Zeebrugge Raid. He won the VC in this operation on April 22/23 1918 as a member of the Royal Marine Artillery on HMS Vindictive. The official account stated…

"Sergeant Finch was second in command of the pom-poms and Lewis guns in the foretop of the Vindictive under Lieutenant Charles B.B Rigby. At one period the Vindictive was being hit every few seconds, chiefly in the upper works, from which splinters caused many casualties. It was difficult to locate the guns which were doing the most damage but Lieutenant Rigby, Sergeant Finch and the Marines in the foretop kept up a continuous fire with pom-poms and Lewis guns, changing rapidly from one target to another, and thus keeping the enemy's fire down to some considerable extent. Unfortunately two heavy shells made direct hits on the foretop, which was completely exposed to enemy concentration of fire. All on the top were killed or disabled except Sergeant Finch who was, however, severely wounded; nevertheless he showed consummate bravery, remaining in his battered and exposed position. He once more got a Lewis gun into action and kept up a continuous fire, harassing the enemy on the mole until the foretop received another direct hit, the remainder of the armament being then completely put out of action. Before the top was destroyed Sergeant Finch had done invaluable work and by his bravery undoubtedly saved many lives. This very gallant serjeant of the RMA was selected by the 4th Battalion Royal Marines to receive the Victoria Cross."

Finch revealed in letters to his friends in Birmingham that he fired the shot which sank a submarine. After being knocked down and stunned during the operations he spent some time in Deal Hospital where he was visited by Admiral Keyes. Sergeant Finch received the VC from the King in the quadrangle at Buckingham Palace on July 31 1918. Seven other VCs were awarded at the same ceremony. On September 21 1918 he was presented with an engrossed and illuminated copy of a congratulatory resolution passed by the City Council. This was in Cannon Hill Park as part of 'Win the War Day'. A week later he was honoured by the residents of Handsworth in a very well attended ceremony at the bandstand in Handsworth Park. A wallet with war bonds worth £250 was presented in addition to another illuminated address. He had paraded down the Soho Road as part of the recognition. Flags flew in nearby streets and a message was read from Admiral Jellicoe. He told the crowd that 'I didn't run away and, if you have any idea what the firing top of a ship, is, you will understand why'.

After the war he became an instructor of Coast Defence Gunnery and in 1920 became a Colour Sergeant. On April 3 1919 he married Elizabeth Ross in Portsmouth. A son, Jack, arrived the same year. For the rest of his life his shore home was at Portsmouth. In December 1929 he retired as a Quarter-Master Sergeant. In 1931 he became a Yeoman of the Guard. He returned to serve in 1938 and probably spent most of the war as a storekeeper officer for a Royal Marine training brigade. He finally left the Navy at the end of the war. In 1964 he was made Divisional Sergeant-Major of HM Bodyguard of the Yeoman of the Guard.

He died at Portsmouth on March 15 1966. A memorial plaque was unveiled in April 1967 at St Andrews Church, Eastney, but was later moved to the chapel at Stonehouse Barracks, Plymouth. There is a road at Eastney named after him.

His house in Nineveh Road still exists off the Soho Road, Handsworth as part of a terrace.

St James Church, St James Road, Handsworth.

There is a full size bronze figure of Lieutenant Eric Goward Abbott of the 1/5 South Staffs. He was killed in action on March 14 1917 aged 24. He had lived at 'The Austins', Sandwell Road, Handsworth where his mother, Julie, still lived after the war. His father, Councillor E.T Abbott, had already died. In 1911 he was an 18 year old accountant living with a brother and a sister and their widowed mother, Julie, and widowed grandmother, Ann Smith, at The Austins; there were four servants. He is buried in Foncquevillers Military Cemetery on the Somme. In the church there is also a commemorative plaque from his brother and his grave marker.

There is also a metal plaque in memory of Captain John Theodore Spencer Weston, 3rd Warwicks attached to the 1st Berkshires. He was killed at Cuinchy on August 20 1915 aged 23. He had been awarded the Military Cross for gallant conduct 'notably at Richebourg'. He had been twice mentioned in despatches and is buried in Vielle-Chapelle New Military Cemetery, Lacoutre. His father was a doctor and lived at 'The Oaklands', Holyhead Road, Handsworth.

Lieutenant Frederick William Coverdale has a marble tablet in his memory. He was killed in action on July 17 1917, aged 26, whilst serving in the Royal Naval Reserve in the Aegean Sea. His ship was HMS Newmarket which was sunk by a torpedo from a German U-boat off Nikaria Island. Sixty-nine other men were lost. He left a wife, Marie, at 73, Somerset Road, Handsworth. He is also commemorated on the Portsmouth Naval Memorial.

There is also another marble tablet with two names erected by their 'brother scouts' at St James. Private Arthur Crook, 19, is buried at Handsworth St Mary Churchyard. His mother lived at 82, Wattville Road, Handsworth. He died of wounds on September 19 1918 whilst serving in the 1st Devons. The other 'scout' was Sidney Thomas Pickersgill. 3rd Birmingham Pals, who was killed in action on October 13 1918 at the age of 20. He is buried in Belle Vue British Cemetery, Briastre, France. His parents lived at 56, Woodland Road, Handsworth.

The church is also home to the main Handsworth war memorial with about 180 names. It has the words 'Death is swallowed up in victory'. The baptistery and porch were erected in their honour by the parishioners.
Help was provided for this section by Tony Woolley.

Handsworth Cemetery, Oxhill Road. This Corporation Cemetery opened in 1909 and contains 106 First World War graves or names listed on a screen wall. Fifty were post-war deaths. A variety of military formations are represented including twenty Royal Warwicks, ten artillery men, eight Royal Engineers, five RAF/RFC and four Navy. There are three Canadian infantrymen, two with Birmingham links and one from Quebec. Only two were officers. We know little about Captain Joseph Darby who died on June 27 1916 and intriguingly served in the Indian Military Works. Lieutenant Colonel Charles Sherwood Denniss died on December 8 1917 at the age of 57. He was a member of the Railway Staff Corps of the Royal Engineers and may have performed this role alongside working as a civilian in a senior role as a railway manager. He was born in 1860 as the son of a goods manager of the North East Railway at Hull. He joined the same company himself and also worked for the Great Western Railway before becoming Superintendent of the Central Division of the North East Railway in 1892. In 1895 he became general manager of Cambrian Railways based in mid-Wales. It is likely that he had some kind of military role before 1908 because the London Gazette confirmed his appointment to the Engineer and Railway Staff Corps from April 1 when the Territorial Force was formed. In 1911 he was living in Sherwood Park Road, Penarth, Cardiff, and was described as general manager of the 'Cardiff Railway'. After the war his wife, Edith, who he had married in 1890, lived at Lytham in Lancashire. He also left a daughter, Violet.

Air Mechanic 1st Class James Rollings of the RAF is listed on the screen wall. He died on Armistice Day in 1918, aged 28, leaving a wife Lily at 183, Newcombe Road, Handsworth. He was living there in 1911 with his widowed mother and was working as a millwright. He had been attached to the 5th Aeroplane Acceptance Park at Filton, Bristol. James was born in Handsworth. Serjeant Hubert Wragg died of sickness the day before the Armistice at the age of 33. He was serving in the 2nd/1st Kent Heavy Battery of the Royal Garrison Artillery. He was Bristol born and his parents were living near Hamilton, New Zealand. In 1911 Hubert was living at 43, Victoria Road, Handsworth and worked as a whip finisher.

Able Seaman Francis Hammond died on January 31 1918 at the age of 23. He was killed in an accident involving his submarine, HM Submarine K1, near May Island off the coast of the Outer Firth of Forth. The wreck is still below the sea at a depth of about 45 metres and is a protected site. A major, secret exercise was taking place, involving nine submarines and battleships from Rosyth thirteen miles off the coast, when HMS Courageous changed course to avoid two trawlers. Two submarines collided but K17 managed to turn away. Meanwhile HMS Fearless, a light cruiser leading the 12th Submarine Flotilla, was steaming towards the scene unaware of what had happened. It rammed into K17 and water rushed into the boat through the pierced pressure hell. The order was given to abandon ship and it sank within eight minutes. Eighteen men managed to escape through the hatch but in the confusion of the night the escorting destroyers ploughed through the area. Only nine men survived of the 59 man crew. A memorial cairn to the disaster was established in 2001 at Anstruther harbour, Fife.

Lance Corporal Sydney Claud Jones died of wounds in Stobhill Hospital, Glasgow, on April 19 1921. This was a particularly tragic case as he was wounded in the head on the Somme on July 27 1916. He was twenty-four years old and had served in the 3rd Birmingham Pals. He was wounded in their attack on Longueval and Delville Wood on a day when 59 men were killed.

He had been educated at Trinity School, Handsworth, and was an active boy scout. He then became a commercial clerk to a firm of jewellers although we cannot be sure that it was his father's firm of manufacturing jewellers in Warstone Lane. He joined up in September 1914. In 1911 he was living with his family at 108, Leonard Road, Handsworth and worked as an office boy. Sergeant W.J Grendon, who died on May 27 1921 at the age of 47, was the only medal winner buried in Handsworth Cemetery; he held the Military Medal. He served in the 1/6th Warwicks and post-war his wife was living near Rhyl in Flintshire. Private Fred Shale, was another victim of the Blyth drowning disaster of the 5th Reserve Battalion of the Warwicks on August 24 1917. He was given a military funeral. He had lived at 78, Mary Road, Handsworth. Private William Widdows, aged 22, died on January 3 1916 and is listed on the screen wall. He was serving in the 1st Warwicks and had been 'lying for seven months suffering from gas poisoning and gunshot wounds in the spine'. He had joined as a regular in 1912 and had been previously shot through the lung but had recovered to return to the front. He lived in Handsworth and his parents lived at 277, Heath Street, Winson Green.

114, Tew Park Road off Nineveh Road. This was the home of Annie Ham according to the National Roll of the Great War and the 1911 census. The vast majority of the 130 women listed in the Birmingham volume were munition workers. Annie can represent all those women who played other important roles during the war – e.g. tram conductresses, postwomen, forestry, WRAF, VAD, RASC motor driver and Land Army. She volunteered in November 1917, aged 23, for the newly formed Women's Army Auxiliary Corps, and was sent to France by the end of the year where she did special duties at Abbeville, Doullens, Etaples and Dieppe. In 1911 she had been a press worker and lived with her parents, Walter and Nellie; her father was a mounter in the jewellery trade. Her younger brother, Walter, worked in an office in 1911 and joined the Royal Warwickshire Regiment in 1914. He went to the front in 1915 and for two years was acted as a stretcher bearer although he was a company signaller when demobilised in 1919.

Drill Hall, Belgrave Terrace. Off Soho Road, this was the southern-most base of the 5/South Staffordshire Regiment, 'G' company. Before 1908 it housed the 1st Volunteer Battalion of the South Staffs. The building occupied the far end of this cul-de-sac.

The Drill Hall no longer exists but one row of terraced houses leading to the site still exist.

Handsworth Grammar School, Grove Lane. Like in other schools war led immediately to staffing problems. Two of the eleven assistant masters in 1914 joined up immediately and five others afterwards. Three replacements joined up as well. Gaps were filled by the local clergy and the employment of four lady teachers. These difficulties were against a background of increasing numbers; 240 in 1914 and 299 in 1918. In 1915 the school swimming sports were cancelled because Grove Lane baths had been taken over by a military unit. In 1916 a Belgian refugee joined the school and in 1917 senior boys began to cultivate allotments in Church Hill Road. The OTC became more important. Some boys spent their holidays working in local shell factories. An annual fruit-picking camp to Evesham in the summer holidays grew in scale from 1915. Every effort was made to contact every 'old boy' who was serving. They were encouraged to visit on leave and write to the school and contribute to 'The Bridge', the school magazine.

Mr C.C Thompson, an assistant, wrote a letter published in the Christmas 1914 edition. He was already at the front with the Inniskilling Fusiliers. He had received two bullets through the tail of his great coat. In his first night of a trench tour he was "wet up to the knees getting in.....You can have little idea how cold it is in a clay pit with a very muddy bottom...All one could do was snipe at the Germans and that this was of necessity limited almost entirely to the night. It was death to show one's head above the parapet in the daytime for more than one second. Of course one can look through a slit in an iron plate and fire through it". Bert Howse also wrote from a minesweeper in the North Sea published in the Midsummer 1917 edition. He had a picture postcard of the old school put up in his cabin. He was a telegraph operator. He went on... "it is not exactly appetising to see concentrated death pills floating by one's home".

About 500 former pupils served, 18 were highly decorated and 77 fell. The full record of all these men is kept in 'The Record of Service' illuminated roll of honour at the school and there is a memorial window and bronze memorial tablet to those who did not return. The window and the memorial tablet were dedicated by the Bishop Wakefield on July 15 1921. The sister of George Sharples, amongst those killed, gave a sum of money for an annual prize. He was killed on the first day of the Battle of Arras on April 9 1917, aged 25, whilst serving in 124th Siege Battery, RGA. His parents lived at 68, Hunter's Road, Handsworth. Second Lieutenant Dominic Roe Dathy O'Daly was killed by a bomb at the end of the Battle of the Somme on November 14 1916 at the age of 21. He was serving in the 7th Northumberland Fusiliers and is commemorated on the Thiepval Memorial. Handsworth born he had been School Captain and captain of football and athletics and has been described as a 'school hero'. Afterwards he went on to Exeter College, Oxford, in 1913 where he joined the OTC. He had hoped to become an Anglican priest. He was commissioned in August 1915 and had gone to France on August 14 1916. He had been the Lewis Gun officer and was in charge of a company when he was killed. He left a widow, Eleanor, and had only been married three months. He had a dedicated plaque at St Bartholomew's, Newbiggin by the Sea.

Private William Billington is buried in Jerusalem Cemetery. He was aged 21 and had lived at 11, Robert Road, Handsworth. He had also served in France, Salonika and Egypt in the London Regiment. Lieutenant Frederick Coverdale from 73, Somerset Road, had been lost at sea on July 17 1917 when his ship, HMS Newmarket, was torpedoed in the Aegean Sea. Lance Corporal Frank Newbery was with the 7th Battalion of the Australian Infantry when killed on October 4 1917. Two brothers can be identified. Greaser Allan Robathan is buried in Gamboa British Cemetery, Rio de Janeiro. He died on June 6 1915 whilst serving with the armed merchant cruiser HMS Oltranto and had probably seen action at the Battle of Coronel in 1914. His younger brother, Laurence, was a subaltern in the Leicestershire Regiment when killed on September 28 1917. His parents had moved to Teignmouth in Devon but had lived at Handsworth Wood. Serjeant Esmond Nicholls of the 2/8th Warwicks had lived at 44, Murdoch Road and had attended Birmingham University. He was killed on December 5 1916.

Private Leigh Butler of the 1st City Battalion had been in the school OTC but had left for King Edward's. He had joined up in September 1914 aged only 16. He was a first class shot, signaller and scout when killed on the Somme on July 21 1916. He had lived at 82, Wellington Road. Lance Corporal Arthur Dowler was in the same battalion and was killed two days later. He is also commemorated on the Electricity Supply Department memorial. He had lived at 137, Church Lane. The Kays were another set of brothers. The Reverend William Kay M.C was a chaplain with the 5th Dorsets when killed in France on April 5 1918. He had lived at 6, South Road. Second Lieutenant Laurence Kay studied German at Birmingham University and before the war was teaching at Great Yarmouth Grammar School. He was killed at Suvla, Gallipoli, on November 18 1915 with the 9th Warwicks. Their father was the headmaster of All Saints School, Hockley and lived at 16, Wretham Road, Handsworth. Lieutenant Roger Bowen was in the same battalion as Laurence Kay and was killed on September 1 1918 as part of Dunsterforce. He is commemorated on the Tehran Memorial.

One of the most interesting casualties was Corporal Chester Homer who died of wounds on June 15 1916, aged 21, near Arras whilst serving in the 2nd City Battalion. He was preparing for final examination as an articled surveyor when he joined up. The family lived at 'Hursley', 128, Hamstead Road. His father, James, was a city councillor and decided after the war to fund the Cannon Street Baptist Memorial Church which was built at the junction of Alfred Road with the Soho Road. The original church had been lost to the development of Corporation Street.

'Handsworth Grammar School 1862-1962'. Reverend J.J Walton and D.C Gregory. Library of Birmingham.

74, Cheshire Road, Smethwick.

74, Cheshire Road, Smethwick. This was the family home of Harold John Colley MM VC. He was born in Winston Street on May 26 1895 near the Cape Hill Brewery. His father was a pattern maker and later worked for Tangyes. Harold attended Dudley Road Council School and then went to work as a silver spinner in the Jewellery Quarter. In 1911 he was described as an errand boy for a silversmith. He was a keen member of the Smethwick Baptist Church and an enthusiastic cyclist, gymnast and cricketer. He joined the Army Cyclists Corps on September 1 1914 and became attached to the Duke of Cornwall's Light Infantry. Afterwards he became a despatch rider. On March 30 1917 he was wounded while digging out two men buried by a mortar bomb. He received a Certificate of Meritorious Conduct from the 17th Division commander. After recovery from his wound he was transferred to the 10th Lancashire Fusiliers. On June 4 1918 he was awarded the Military Medal for bravery at Beaumont Hamel. As a result he was promoted to Acting Sergeant.

His VC action took place at Martinpuich on the Somme on August 25 1918. His citation stated that "during a strong counter-attack Sergeant Colley's company was holding an advanced position with two platoons in advance and two in support. The forward platoons were ordered to hold on all at costs and Sergeant Colley went, without orders, to help these two platoons. He rallied the men, then formed a defensive flank and held it. Out of the two platoons only three men remained unwounded and the serjeant himself was dangerously wounded in the stomach and died on the same day. It was entirely due to his action that the enemy was prevented from breaking through". He was buried in Mailly Wood Cemetery. The news of his VC award reached his family before news of his death, including his brother who had been invalided out of the Warwicks in 1917.

Digital Ladywood.

62, Linwood Road, Handsworth. This was the home of Second Lieutenant Thomas Silver who was one of three Birmingham councillors to be killed on active service. He represented Soho Ward from 1913 as a Unionist and was an auctioneer and surveyor by profession with an office at 120, Soho Hill. He had previously served for several years on the Handsworth Urban District Council and was active in public and social movements. He was keen on horticulture and helped promote the success of the annual flower show in Handsworth Park. Thomas had also served on the Corporation Education and Tramways Committee before joining the Royal Garrison Artillery at the end of 1916, probably as a conscript in his late 30s. He was soon commissioned and was killed on April 16 1918 whilst serving in 80th Siege Battery. He lies buried in Wytschaete Military Cemetery. He left a wife, Florence, and three children. In 1901 he was living at 65, Grove Lane, Handsworth, one of nine children of Thomas H Silver, a grocer and provision merchant.

Birmingham Post April 26 1918.

Smethwick Heritage Centre website.

Cape Hill memorial, Smethwick. Of the brewery firm of Mitchells and Butlers. There are 132 names of those who were killed and had worked for the firm. The memorial was unveiled on Sunday October 1 1922. 1359 members of staff had served in the war. After three weeks of war the directors of the brewery announced that they would make up the wages to their standard weekly wages for any man who volunteered. They were already doing so for men recalled to the colours. Shortly afterwards they announced that new staff for their managed public houses would be over 35, married and employed as temporary staff because enlisted staff had promised employment when they returned. Under the Defence of the Realm Act it was an offence to treat a soldier or sailor 'with intent to make him drunk'. The firm issued posters as warnings to publicans and customers on this issue. Beer prices went up with a war duty and licensing hours were reduced. Beer strength was also reduced. In 1915 Lloyd George, the Chancellor, announced that 'We are fighting Austria, Germany and Drink'. There was a fear of excessive drinking amongst munitions workers.

The memorial itself is of limestone with inscriptions on granite tablets and is in front of the office block which used to be the fire station for the brewery. The memorial was restored and rededicated in 2006.

9.

Sutton Coldfield

War memorial in King Edward Square opposite the Town Hall.
This is a major memorial and lists 430 names. The memorial is impressive
in size and features a bronze figure of a British 'Tommy' on a granite pedestal.
It was unveiled on November 1 1922 and designed by Francis Doyle Jones, a
noted sculptor of the time. One and hundred and three of those named served
in various battalions of the Royal Warwickshire Regiment with seventeen
members of the 2nd Birmingham Pals.

Three of those named had attended Bishop Vesey Grammar and were
killed on the same day, Sunday June 4 1916, in the 2nd Birmingham Pals
when in the front line near Roclincourt north of Arras. At 4 p.m. there was
an intense German bombardment which lasted for three hours. At 9 p.m.
there was a further fifteen minutes of shelling followed by the explosion of
three large mines along the battalion front line. The craters still exist and were
christened Clarence, Cuthbert and Claud after a well known song performed
by the Whizzbangs, the Divisional Concert Party. A German infantry raid
followed but was stopped by British artillery. Amongst the 62 dead were
Private Edgar Bromwich, 26, his brother Lance Corporal Leslie Bromwich
and Lieutenant John Larkins, 22. All three are named on the memorial. The
brothers had joined up together on September 4 1914. Edgar had worked in
the family bakery and confectioners at 25, High Street, Sutton Coldfield and
Leslie was an articled chartered accountant in Colmore Row. Larkins had
been killed and buried in a blown in dugout. He had worked for his father
who was a wholesale milliner and draper in Livery Street, Birmingham. His
family home was Mayfield House in Penn's Lane. All three were buried in
the Faubourg D'Amiens Cemetery, Arras.

Sutton Park. Near the Wyndley entrance there is a plaque to commemorate the use of Park for the training of the 1st and 2nd City Battalions

165

Part of the hutted camp in Sutton Park of the 1st City Battalion, the Birmingham Pals

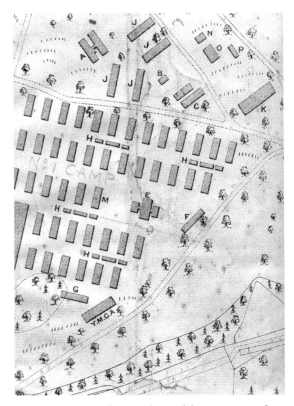

in 1914-1915. The words on the plaque state that "This tablet is erected to commemorate the occupation of this Park from 1914 to 1920 by H.M. Troops. The Park was placed at the disposal of H.M. Government entirely free. Over 50000 of H.M Troops occupied the various camps constructed. The Birmingham City Battalions of the Royal Warwickshire Regiment received their training here and were followed by other units. For a considerable period the camps were used for convalescent officers and men, and New Zealand Troops also were in occupation prior to their return home. The Council of the Royal Town received the thanks of the War Office for their patriotic action". The 'Crystal Palace' in the Park was the HQ of the 1st Battalion and the 2nd Battalion was based near Powell's Pool. YMCA huts were provided by Mrs John Feeney and the Birmingham Chamber of Commerce. Training included bayonet drill, trench digging, target practice and route marches. After the departure of the City Battalions to Yorkshire in mid-1915 the Park and Crystal Palace were used by New Zealand troops and convalescing soldiers from local military hospitals. Possibly 50,000 troops passed through the camps in the Park during the war. The Crystal Palace was demolished in 1962 and Clifton Road Youth Centre is now on the site.

Bishop Vesey Grammar School. Where the headmaster of 24 years was the father of Flight Lieutenant Alan Jerrard VC, 66 Squadron RAF. He won the VC for an action in Italy on March 30 1918 when flying a Sopwith Camel. He later became a prisoner of war and escaped. He died on May 14 1968 at Lyme Regis and was buried at Hillingdon, London. He was 20 years old when he won his VC, now displayed at the RAF Museum at Hendon. Captain William Earl Johns, the 'Biggles' writer, later described the VC action…

"On March 30 he was out on patrol with two other officers when he saw a hostile formation of five machines. He attacked at once with such determination that one fell in flames, although he had to follow it to within a hundred feet of the ground in order to complete its destruction. Glancing round he saw that he had descended near an enemy aerodrome from which no less than nineteen machines were preparing to take off, but instead of hurrying from such a dangerous vicinity, he turned and attacked the aerodrome and the hostile machines from a height of only fifty feet. He swooped on the first enemy machine to leave the ground and it crashed to destruction. But several of the other machines were soon in the air and, while he was fully occupied with them, he saw one of the pilots of his patrol was in difficulties. Without hesitation he raced to his assistance and, regardless of the streams of bullets that converged on him from all sides, he succeeded in driving the attackers away from his comrade, shooting one of them down out of control. This was his third victory within a few minutes. Fresh enemy machines continued to take off from the aerodrome but still this very brave pilot was undaunted and he attacked them one after another, only retreating – still engaging five enemy machines – when ordered to do so by his patrol leader. Although wounded, he turned repeatedly and attacked single-handedly the pursuing machines until he was finally overwhelmed by numbers and driven to the ground."

In 1911 13 year old Alan Jerrard was a boarder at Oundle School in Northamptonshire. He was born in 1898 at Ladywell, Middlesex.

A second former pupil from the school to win the VC was Charles George Bonner who attended the school between 1893 and 1898. He was born at Shuttington, Warwickshire, in 1884 and before the war was a master mariner. On August 8 1917 he was a First Lieutenant, Royal Naval Reserve on HMS Dunraven, a 'Q' or 'mystery' ship, when it was engaged by a German submarine in the Bay of Biscay. 'Q' ships were converted merchant ships concealing large deck guns. The citation began with "greater bravery than was shown by all officers and men on this occasion can hardly be conceived".

It also stated that he "was in the thick of the fighting and throughout the action his pluck and determination had a considerable influence on the crew". "Lieutenant Bonner, having been blown out of his control station by the first explosion of a depth charge due to shell fire, crawled back into the 4″ gun hatch with the gun's crew (6 men), were well aware that it was only a matter of time before the magazine and depth charges below them would explode, and they remained there until it happened. The gun was shifted bodily and the gun's crew were blown up in the air, one man being blown overboard, but fortunately none of them were killed and only four wounded". He survived and died in Edinburgh on February 7 1951, aged 67. After the war he had returned to the mercantile marine and became an expert in salvage. There is a headstone at St Mary's Church, Aldridge. Bishop Vesey Grammar School lists 64 former pupils on its Roll of Honour.

Times obituary of Bonner September 2 1951.

Boldmere Swimming Club memorial. It is now in the reception area of Wyndley Leisure Centre Swimming Baths. The Club was founded c1895 and after the Great War Benjamin Creswick, from Jockey Road, cast two small bronze figures – a tutor teaching a pupil to swim. This was 1921 and the memorial was erected as part of a drinking fountain at 'Hallets Field' and placed near the dam at Powell's Pool near the Boldmere entrance to Sutton Park. It was unveiled by the Mayor of Sutton Coldfield on October 19 1921.

Allerton, Lichfield Road. The house was opened as a VAD hospital on January 19 1916 and provided 54 beds.

'The Hollies', Four Oaks Road. This house opened as an extension of 'Allerton' VAD Hospital with 32 beds on October 6 1917. It was given by Mr Godrich. It was opposite one of the entrances to Sutton Park. The hospital closed in April 1919. At least 359 patients were treated including Canadian, American, Australian soldiers and two prisoners of war. Dr G.P Jerome was the medical officer and Miss Beatrice Cooper was the sister in charge. The VAD commandant was Beryl Ryland. She was a member of one of Birmingham's leading families and lived at Moxhull Hall in Holly Lane, Wishaw. Just before the war she gained some notoriety as a suffragette who attacked a painting in Birmingham Art Gallery.

St Winnow, 22, Ladywood Road, Four Oaks. This was the home late in his life of Arnold Horace Santo Waters VC. He was born in Plymouth on September 23 1886 and attended Hoe Grammar School there. His father was a minister for the United Methodist Free Church, the son of a miner. His parents were Cornish born and there were three siblings. By 1911 his father had died and his widowed mother had moved to Fulham. Arnold trained as an engineer at University Tutorial College, London, and by 1910 was working for the Birmingham consulting engineering firm of Wilcox and Raikes. Just before the war he was sent to work on projects in the South Wales valleys.

He joined the Royal Engineers as a second lieutenant in January 1915. Early in the war he had been in charge of engineering staff engaged in supervising the construction of new water supplies for troops on Salisbury Plain. He was awarded a MC in 1917 and a DSO in 1918. In early November 1918 he commanded 218th Field Company which was involved in bridging the Sambre-Oise Canal in France to assist the infantry. The bridge works came under German shell fire on November 4 and during the day Waters won the VC. His citation for 'conspicuous bravery and devotion to duty' stated that "From the outset the task (bridging) was under artillery and machine gun fire at close range, the bridge being damaged and the building party suffering severe casualties. Major Waters, hearing that all his officers had been killed or wounded, at once went forward and personally supervised the completion of the bridge, working on cork floats while under fire at point-blank range. So intense was the fire that it seemed impossible that he could escape being killed. The success of the operation was due entirely to his valour and example".

Arnold Waters was originally recommended for a bar to his DSO but the King, learning of the details, changed it to a VC. He was also given an illuminated address by the Mayor of Plymouth. He returned to his profession after the war and in 1920s ran his firm of AHS Waters and Partners which advised local authorities on water supply and sewage disposal. In April 1922 the British Legion journal published his article entitled 'Why am I a Member of the Legion?'. He gave four reasons – 'comradeship now can still be useful as it then was indispensable'; 'helps to remind us of those whose memory must live for ever'; 'our show with opportunities for doing some useful service to another less fortunate than himself'; 'it will be what we make it'. He also devoted himself to those disabled in the war; he acted as chairman of the Birmingham and Sutton Coldfield War Pensions Committee and was President of the Birmingham and Midland Limbless Ex-Servicemen's Association. In 1924 he married another Methodist, Gladys Barribau, with another sapper VC, Cecil Knox, as best man. During the Second World War he was Divisional Food Officer for the West Midlands. Post-war he became chairman of the South Staffordshire Waterworks Company and chairman of Sutton Coldfield magistrates. He was knighted in 1954. He died at his Four Oaks home on January 22 1981.

'VCs of the First World War. The Final Days 1918'. Gerald Gliddon. Sutton. 2000.

Times January 27 1981.

The red-brick house, built in 1901-2, is listed as a fine example of the work of the Edwardian architect, William Bidlake.

'Corris', Maney Hill Road.

'Corris', Maney Hill Road. In addition to Arthur Langley (see 31, Francis Road, Stechford) another former King Edward School pupil served at the Stratford Experimental Station, London, of the Royal Naval Air Service. Born in 1875 in Wednesbury, Thomas Slater Price had attended King Edward's School between 1887 and 1890. In 1891 his family were at 23, Stafford Street, Wednesbury, where his father Thomas, a schoolmaster, was head of a family of eight children. In 1892 he began a course at Mason College, the forerunner of Birmingham University, where he achieved a first class science degree in 1895. In the same year he became Priestley research scholar in Chemistry at the College before going on a year later to study under Professor Wilhelm Ostwald at the University of Leipzig. In 1898 he studied at Professor Arrhenius's laboratory at the Hogskola, Stockholm. Both these professors were eminent men and won Nobel prizes for Chemistry in 1909 and 1903 respectively. These experiences enabled him to achieve a doctorate at Mason College in 1900. He was at a new family home in Walsall Street, Wednesbury at the time of the 1901 census when he was described as a 'lecturer in Chemistry'. This was probably at the Birmingham Municipal Technical College in Suffolk Street because in 1903 he became head of the Chemistry Department there.

His tenure, which lasted until 1920, was interrupted by the war. In 1905 he married Florence, also from Wednesbury, and by 1911 they were living in Maney Hill Road, Sutton Coldfield, with two young children, his brother, brother-in-law and one servant. In December 1917 he held the rank of lieutenant commander in the Royal Naval Volunteer Reserve, having joined in 1916, and was based at Stratford, east London. He was in charge of the research laboratory and the Prussic Acid and Smoke Mixture Producing Plants. His work on chloro-sulphuric acid led to the production of the 'artificial fog' for the Zeebrugge Raid in April 1918. That year he was also the Admiralty Chemical representative on the Chemical Warfare Committee. For his war work he was awarded the OBE (military). By 1931 he was Professor of Chemistry at Heriot-Watt College, Edinburgh, from where he retired in 1940. He died on October 29 1949.

Obituary in 'Nature'. December 31 1949.

St John's Church, Walmley. In addition to the war memorial unveiled in December 1920 there is a reading desk and plaque commemorating the life of Second Lieutenant Henry Noel Francis Forge, aged 19, who was killed in action near Cambrai on November 20 1917 whilst serving in the 8th Bedfordshires. He was the son of the Vicar of Walmley, the Reverend John Francis Forge, and is buried in Villers-Plouich Communal Cemetery, France. Henry was born in Nottingham on December 31 1897. He attended Sutton Coldfield Grammar School from 1907-1911 and then Bedford Grammar until 1916. He joined a cadet officer battalion in Oxford and was commissioned into the 5/Bedfords in March 1917. He went to France that spring and was wounded on June 27 1917. He recovered in time for the opening of the Battle of Cambrai, the first battle to make effective use of tanks. He was killed during the attack on the Hindenburg Line on the opening day north of Villers-Plouich. In addition to his parents he left an 18 year old sister, Annie and a 14 year old brother, Eric. At the time of his death he was attached to the 6th Divisional sniping company.

77, Parade, Sutton Coldfield. This was the family home of Rose Elizabeth Kendall, a sister in the Queen Alexandra Imperial Military Nursing Service, who was drowned and missing when on the Hospital Ship Glenart Castle on February 26 1918 in the Bristol Channel. It was torpedoed by a German submarine. Also see the entry of Matron Katy Beaufoy who died in the same event. Rose was born in Yardley on January 24 1887, the daughter of Alfred and Elizabeth Kendall. He was a house painter. There were two older sisters, Beatrice and Ada. The family were living at 12, Talfourd Street, Bordesley in 1891 and 10, Dawson Street, Aston in 1901. She attended Somerville Road Council School, Small Heath and at the age of 14 was a sewing machinist.

From October 1908 she trained as a nurse in the Infirmary of what became in 1912 the Erdington Workhouse. She trained for three years and three months and then became a staff nurse and in January 1912 was promoted to sister. She held the same post in October 1914 when she applied to join the QAIMNS reserve. She lived in but her mother was at 77, Parade. She probably had begun war nursing in May 1915 and was at Wharncliffe

War Hospital, Sheffield in February 1917 when she signed a new agreement to conditions of service in the QAIMNS. She joined the Hospital Ship Glenart Castle at Liverpool on November 12 1917 the same date as Katy Beaufoy. They are both commemorated on the Hollybrook Memorial at Southampton.

Service file – National Archives WO399/4543.

Oscott College, Chester Road. This was and still is the Roman Catholic seminary of St Mary. Edward Ilsley (1838-1926), the first Roman Catholic archbishop of Birmingham, was based there during the First World War. On August 7 1914 he wrote to Canon Glancey that "the authorities are commandeering right and left – horses, motor cars etc….suppose we get an order one of these days to put up 50 or 60 wounded here. I fear we shall have to send the students to their homes". At the time there were 52 students training for the priesthood. At the beginning of the war he wrote to all diocesan clergy and forecast the horrors to come. "Within the past few days war has been declared involving this nation and nearly all the nations of Europe. The conflagration thus ignited is one of unparalleled magnitude involving loss of innumerable lives and inflicting untold suffering. Who can fail to see that such a war as this is a scourge in the hand of the Almighty for the chastisement of our sins?". In November he wrote to Bishop Amigo, Bishop of Southwark, stating that there were insufficient chaplains in the army and the navy. He wanted to do more 'effective' work. He went on "Our University buildings are being utilised as a Hospital and there are many wounded Belgian soldiers there – when it was first opened I called to see the Catholic patients and at the suggestion of the Colonel in charge I asked for War Office recognition for Father Keating, the priest of the local mission who was attending the Catholic soldiers. In a few days I received notice of his appointment".

About thirty Oscotian priests served at the front as chaplains but only Herbert Collins was killed. He was at Oscott from 1902 and was ordained there in 1908. He was killed on April 9 1917 whilst attached to the 9th Black Watch near Arras. He is buried in Cabaret-Rouge British Cemetery, Souchez. Ilsley also warmly welcomed the "exiled, homeless fugitives from Belgium who have lost their all because they refused to betray the truth and the right". Although some students left the seminary to join up numbers increased with the arrival of a number of Belgian refugee seminarians. In February 1916 he was writing to Bishop Amigo about the 'vain delusion' that the Midlands was safe from enemy aircraft. "We must….trust in Divine protection". This was a reference to the raid on Walsall, Wednesbury and Tipton which left 35 dead, including the Lady Mayoress of Walsall. In late 1915 Archbishop Ilsley moved to a new Archbishop's house called Lawnside in Norfolk Road, Edgbaston. Pugin's official residence near St Chad's was regarded as inadequate. However, now well into his 70s it did not suit him and within a year he had returned to Oscott.

The religious revival that war brought caused him to write as follows to Bishop Amigo on December 29 1916. "Our people have been very devout this Christmas, thronging the Altar in greater numbers than ever". At the end of the war he wrote to the clergy stating "The war is ended. Deo Gratias! He has heard our cry. He has given us the victory we asked for. There will be ample need of the divine assistance in the days that are before us". In October 1921 he addressed a meeting at Birmingham Town Hall and said that "The claim of the League of Nations to a fair trial is borne in upon the conscience of every right-thinking man by the strongest moral arguments. It is in our hands whether it succeeds or fails".

'Edward Ilsley, Archbishop of Birmingham'. Mary McInally. Continuum Publishing. 2001.

St Peter's, Maney Hill Road. The church dates from 1904 and a new parish was created soon afterwards. The memorial boards commemorate sixty-two fallen of the First World War and usually the names are listed under 'Parochial' and 'Non-Parochial'. The latter, twelve in number, refers to those from the parish who had moved away. Lance Serjeant Horace Edgar Shenton died of wounds at home on August 28 1917 as a result of 'poisoning' from a shrapnel wound. He had been serving in the 1st Birmingham Pals. He was 38 and had lived at 6, Manor Hill, Sutton. He was buried in Sutton Cemetery and is commemorated on the Sutton war memorial.

Serjeant D.W Tuffley died after the war on December 21 1918 as a result of sickness caused by gas. Born in Moreton in the Marsh he was aged forty and had also served in the 1st Birmingham Pals. He had worked for the Birmingham Electricity Supply Department before the war and is listed on their memorial. He left a wife, Ada, at 151, Coles Lane, Sutton. During his service he was mentioned in despatches and was awarded the Distinguished Conduct Medal. This was during the final phase of the war because it was announced in the London Gazette of September 3 1918. His 'conspicuous gallantry' came when he was in charge of the battalion transport "when he succeeded in conveying to the front line a very large quantity of ammunition which was badly needed at the time. It was necessary for his limbers to proceed along a road which was continuously shelled by the enemy, and it was largely due to his perseverance and courage that the ammunition got through". He is also buried in Sutton Cemetery.

Second Lieutenant Felix Lionel Townley was listed as non-Parochial probably because he had moved to Nottingham to work for GEC before the war. He did, however, join the 1st Birmingham Pals as a private in 1914 and, after several promotions, was commissioned into the same battalion in February 1917. He was born in May 1888 and had attended Borden Grammar School in Kent and then from 1904-6 attended Bishop Vesey Grammar School. He was killed during his battalion's attack on Polderhoek Chateau east of Ypres on October 26 1917. As the attack went forward the right flank, where Townley and his 'B' company were attacking, became exposed as the battalion on their flank had not made the same progress. He was killed with his servant, Private Frank Box, 19, alongside him. Felix is commemorated on the Tyne Cot Memorial and the Sutton Coldfield Memorial. Before moving to Nottingham Felix had worked as an electrical engineer for Veritys Limited at Plume Street, Aston. His parents were recorded by the CWGC as living at Simla in the Punjab. His brother, Captain Bertram Townley, died of influenza in Iran four days before the armistice whilst serving in the South Persia Rifles.

Stoker 1st Class Samuel Vyse was killed in the Battle of Jutland on June 1 1916 when his destroyer, HMS Tipperary, was sunk by fire from a German battleship with the loss of 185 men. The ship was leading the 4th Destroyer Flotilla in the night action at the time as the main German battle line escaped across the rear of the British fleet after the main battle on May 31. Vyse was aged 24 and had lived at 50, Newhall Street, Sutton. He is commemorated on the Portsmouth Naval Memorial and the Sutton Coldfield Memorial. It is interesting to note that his mother was Florence Nightingale Vyse.

Two 'Canadians' are listed on the St Peter's memorial and both had links with Holland Street, Sutton. When Private Howard Parker Cashmore was killed on June 9 1917 his wife, Beatrice, was living at No 25; his parents were in Wylde Green. He was born in May 1885. He had joined up in Saskatchewan in June 1915. This was probably at Moose Jaw. Before he left England he had already served three years with the Staffordshire Yeomanry whilst working as an electrical engineer. His 42nd Battalion in 3rd Canadian Division, known as the Royal Highlanders of Canada, took part in the famous attack on Vimy Ridge on April 9 1917 but Howard was killed later when his battalion was involved in a large scale night raid on the German line southwest of La Coulotte; 42nd Battalion provided nine officers and 420 men. Three battalions were involved so Howard was unlucky to be one of his battalion's five deaths.

Serjeant Bertram Clibbery left Liverpool for Montreal on November 1 1906. He was 24 years old, single and described as a 'labourer'. When he joined up at Edmonton on January 5 1915 he was noted as a storekeeper and his next of kin was his mother, Mary, at 5, Holland Street. During his time in the 49th Battalion he would have been involved in major Canadian actions at Vimy Ridge and Passchendaele in 1917 and the advances of the Battle of the Hundred Days in 1918. His battalion was in the same brigade as that of Howard Cashmore. Bertram survived the war but not the peace and died on February 18 1919 and is now also commemorated on the screen wall of Key Hill Cemetery. He is listed on the screen wall because originally his name was on a monument to his older brother, William, who died in 1912 but it became damaged and only a part which tells us that Bertram died in hospital and confirms that he served through the Great War. William in 1911 was a brewer's clerk.

Sutton Coldfield Congregational Church, Brassington Avenue.

The building was completed in 1880 and is now a United Reform Church. The road was then called Park Road. There is a memorial tablet with twenty-three names below a memorial window dedicated in 1920. The list was confined to actual members of the Church and Sunday School. CSM Ernest Aldridge was shot by a sniper on October 12 at Third Ypres at the age of 27 whilst serving in the 7th East Kents. He was born in Lichfield but attended Duke Street School at Maney and worked as a dining car attendant for the Midland Railway before enlisting at Canterbury on September 6 1914. He had lived at 13, Holland Street, Sutton but had married Emily Howard in September 1916 whilst at home recovering from a gunshot wound to the shoulder and then lived at 152, Liverpool Road, Irlam, Lancashire. He is commemorated on the Tyne Cot Memorial. Rifleman George Arthur Kitchen had volunteered early in the war and was in the 8th Kings Royal Rifle Corps. On July 29 1915 his unit was relieved near Hooge in the Ypres Salient and were heading for reserve positions when the Germans launched the first ever attack using flamethrowers. His battalion were hurried back and took part in two days of heavy fighting. George was killed on July 30. He had lived at 33, Coles Lane and was twenty years old. He is commemorated on the Menin Gate at Ypres.

Second Lieutenant Stanley Benjamin Westwood had a remarkable career in the 1/4th Loyal North Lancs. He was wounded on five occasions and spent a total of nine months in hospital. He was awarded the Military Cross and the Croix de Guerre. On the night of February 17 1918 the officer with him during a reconnaissance of a German crater was killed. Stanley was wounded in the wrist but still carried back the body of the officer. In March 1918 all the officers around him were killed and he led a handful of men to drive back the Prussian Guard. They held on for fourteen hours. This was probably during the German spring offensive. He was then a serjeant and soon received a battlefield commission. On April 15 1918 he was killed whilst rescuing a man trapped in barbed wire. He was 21 and had lived at 'The Birches', Park Road. He is buried in Vieille-Chapelle New Military Cemetery. All three men described are also commemorated on the Sutton Coldfield Memorial.

P. J. Lawrence did some research into the memorial in 1991.

10.
Erdington

St Barnabas, Erdington Churchyard. There are twenty nine CWGC graves as well as private headstones. A good example of the latter is Corporal Edward Minahan, aged 21, who died of wounds received on August 18 on September 22 1916 whilst serving in the 1/6th Warwicks. He had attended King Edward's at Aston. The headstone includes the words 'Here lies one of Britain's Heroes'.

Three members of one family feature on the headstone of Elizabeth Flintham who died on July 16 1915 aged 60. The four names on the headstone reflect a complicated family history as both Elizabeth and her husband, James, had been married before with James probably having six children by his first wife and Elizabeth probably six children by her first husband. In 1911 Elizabeth was living at 3, Church Road, Erdington. Also living there were her two sons, William, 23, and Charles Haynes, 19, and two from her husband's first marriage – Francis, 27, and Harold, 16. One of the names on the headstone is that of Lance Corporal Charles Haynes Flintham who died of wounds on October 8 1915 whilst serving in the 1st City Battalion. He is buried in Mount Huon Military Cemetery, Le Treport. A second name is that of Rifleman Harold Joseph Flintham who was a son of James first marriage and was killed in the Battle of Loos on September 25 1915 whilst serving the 2nd Rifle Brigade. According to his CWGC entry James Flintham was living Albany, New York. Harold is commemorated on the Ploegsteert Memorial in Belgium. The final name is that of Private Walter Flintham who was a product of the same marriage and was killed in the 2nd/Warwicks on the first day of the Somme. He left a wife, Lily, at 6 Back, 111, Lichfield Road, Aston. He is commemorated on the Thiepval Memorial.

There is a private memorial to Lieutenant Horace Wood, aged 23, named with four other family members including his mother. He was killed whilst serving with the 2nd/10th London Regiment and is buried in Dive Copse

British Cemetery, Sailly-Le-Sec. His parents lived at 'The Sycamores', Wood End Road, Erdington. His headstone includes the words 'A Volunteer who gave his life for his country'.

On the Gray family headstone there is the name of Wireless Operator 1st Class Horace Gray. He was only 15 when on the tug J.W Thompson travelling between Cardiff and Kola Bay, a fjord on the Barents Sea near Murmansk, on February 28 1917. It was torpedoed so that his 'grave is the sea'. He is commemorated on the Tower Hill Memorial, London, dedicated to merchant seamen of both world wars. One of the CWGC graves is that of Staff Serjeant Davis Turner of 6th Field Bakery of the Army Service Corps who died on May 26 1918. James Webster Tattersall was aged 37 when he died on February 13 1917. He was in the Army Pay Corps and was based at their Warwick office. His wife, Blanche, lived in West Bromwich after the war. Private Charles Perkins, 22, died of wounds in a Huddersfield Hospital on September 11 1916 after being wounded on July 24 on the Somme in the 1st Birmingham Pals. Before joining up in November 1914 he had been a telephone operator for Birmingham GPO. He was given a military funeral at the churchyard.

In recent years St Barnabas Church was badly damaged by a fire. There had been a memorial board in the nave which listed 138 men. Above their names were the words 'The Peace of Heaven is Theirs that life their Swords in such a just and charitable War'.

Chris John 'First World War Burials and Memorials in Erdington churchyard'. Hellfire Corner website.

Kingsbury Road and Holly Lane. Councillor Bernard Alderson and Mrs Alderson were responsible for the building of fourteen houses there for the occupation of disabled ex-servicemen administered by a trust. The councillor was probably living with his family at 25, Turville Road, Handsworth in 1911; he was an estate agent.

Erdington Abbey. When the war broke out there were twenty-six Germans living at Erdington Abbey which had been built in 1879-80 next to the Roman Catholic church of St Thomas and St Edmund. It had become a daughter house of Beuron Abbey in Wurttemberg and the Germans in Erdington had left possible persecution behind under Bismarck's Falk Laws. We can identify the twenty-six as they were required to register with the Birmingham police under emergency legislation. Six were described as priests, ten as lay brothers and seven younger men as students of theology.

One was the Father Superior and two had a status which could not be identified. The lay brothers had other occupations to help make the religious community self-sufficient – tailor, shoemaker, wheelwright, cook, kitchen worker, carpenter and bookbinder. Nine other men, probably non-Germans, are listed as Reverends there in the 1913 Kelly's Directory. Most of the Germans registered with the police on August 10 or 11. One registered as a 'guest intending to join the community' and another as a student of theology registered at the end of March 1915. Three weeks later Adolf Schumann registered and was described as the Father Superior, lay brother and gardener. He had moved from London.

There is a column in the aliens register which is devoted to the fate of each man registered. Twenty of the Germans had a tick in this column which suggests that they had been allowed to continue their vocation at the Abbey. Three were noted as 'exempt/repatriated' and a further two men had dates of leaving Britain via Folkestone by the end of 1914. One was Anton Lutz who had arrived in Birmingham from Beuron in 1901 and had served in the German infantry between 1894-6 in ambulance work; he had a tick next to his name and gave an undertaking on September 24 1917 not to take part in the war. The Very Reverend Henry Molitor was described as the prior in Kelly's Directory. He had only been there since April 1912. The most senior person when the war began was Abbott Ansgar Hoeckelmann who was soon 'interned' at Colwich Abbey, Staffordshire. Francis Izard, an Englishman acted on his behalf. In 1919 twenty-eight out of 39 German monks returned to Germany with the rest leaving in 1922.

'Erdington Abbey 1850-2001'. Michael Hodgetts. Benedictine History Symposium. 2001. Aliens register, 1914-1918. West Midlands Police Museum, Sparkbrook.

256, Kingsbury Road, Erdington.
This was the family home in 1911 of twelve year old Frank Thornton Birkinshaw who was at that time a pupil at the King Edward VI Grammar School at Aston where his family paid fees of one pound ten shillings each term. His father, Herbert, was Bradford born and was an 'agent for Bradford Goods' and was married to Isabella. Frank had been born at Ovingham, Northumberland on June 16 1898 and had two younger siblings, Mary, 7, and William, 6. There was one live in domestic servant. Frank left school at the end of 1913 and became an apprentice at an engineering company.

Soon after the outbreak of war Frank enlisted into the 1/8th Warwicks whose drill hall was near his old school in a former Aston Lower Grounds building shared with Aston Villa. He was still sixteen so lied about his age.

Sometime after October 16 1914 he wrote home to his father from Coggeshall in Essex where the battalion had been sent for further training and the defence of London. He was billeted with Mrs Grey and, in his first letter, revealed that it was luck whether you had received a pair of khaki trousers yet. He was also writing to his mother with details of a night alarm, his new boots and moans that plum and apple jam tasted like 'strawberry and turnip'. He thought that the doubled income might ruin his father. His next letter was to his mother and thanked her for a parcel and asked her to get a flashlamp for him from Halfords in Birmingham as no lights were allowed for fear of invasion. He was kept busy with trench digging, route marches, bayonet and rifle drill.

Frank, not yet seventeen, went to France with his battalion in March 1915; he was in 'C' company. Writing to his mother on April 3 he requested Oxo cubes, the weekly edition of the Mirror or Sketch and as many 'edible luxuries as you care to send out'. Eight days later he wrote to his sister Mary and told her to tell their father not to send cake from Barrows as it arrived stale but rather sardines in tomato sauce. He wrote to his mother on April 25 from a moated farm house north of Ploegsteert Wood and about a mile and a half from the front line. When he wrote again on May 3 he had just completed a four tour in the trenches 'in a very quiet part of the line'. "We had a bath a week ago. We had to march ten miles there and back to have it but it was worth it". He received a letter from his younger sister, Sheona, and wrote back on May 24. There was to be a trench relief that night followed by the 'joke' of four days rest as there was twice as much work to do.

In a letter to his mother on July 10 he stated that he had not been impressed by a ten mile march to form a guard of honour for Lord Kitchener which meant ten hours without food or drink. Writing from the Somme on August 17 to his father he asked him to "see if it were possible for me to get a transfer now to the Royal Flying Corps or the ASC or the RGA or the Motor Transport. This is important. Do your best". In his next letter he reassured his father than he was not fed up but desired a change "for something more interesting or exciting". During the autumn of 1915 Frank developed rheumatic fever from trench conditions and found himself at the Connaught Hospital, Aldershot.

By December 1915 he had returned to duty and was writing from Southminster, Essex, where the 2nd Line Territorials were based. In early January 1916 there was a move to Newcastle but before leaving he looked up people he knew at Coggeshall.

His desire for a transfer was met and on February 23 he joined the Royal Flying Corps as an Air Mechanic 2nd Class. He trained at Larkhill Camp on

Salisbury Plain and was then attached to 13 Depot. A letter from the latter expressed a desire to get out of England and 'do something again' as 'England is horribly tame'. He must have fulfilled this wish as he was in a Boulogne hospital with a knee problem at the end of January 1917 followed by transfer to a hospital in Birmingham. He returned to service by April and a letter dated September 12 1917 shows that he was in Italy in a rest camp next to the sea. He wrote to his brother in October from Taranto and giving notice of a move. He arrived in Aqaba at the northeastern tip of the Red Sea in early November to join 'X' Flight of seven aeroplanes as a driver mechanic. This was a secretive special unit which aimed to give T.E Lawrence and his Arab irregulars air support against the Turks. In an undated letter he explained that he had been at an advanced aerodrome "doing nothing except lying under my mosquito net and dividing my time between swatting flies and wishing I were in the Arctic regions".

On January 1 1918 he was promoted to Air Mechanic 1st Class. A letter to his mother on March 3 described a 'ripping' adventure 'up country' in February. He set off with Lieutenant A.D Makins and six or seven camel men; he rode a camel for the first time. The expedition was to search for a downed Turkish aeroplane that had been brought down by Arab fire east of Kalat Aneiza on the Turkish side of the Hejaz railway line. The Arabs had cut off the plane's wings but the British wanted to salvage the engine. The last part of the journey was supported by local Arabs; they blew up the railway line when they crossed it. The plane was found and the engine recovered although the Arabs had used it for target practice. Frank received the Meritorious

Air Mechanic Frank Birkinshaw is on the back row with his hand over his mouth. Sitting second left is Colonel T.E. Lawrence

Service Medal for his "great ability, cheerfulness and endurance in driving cars for long distances over bad country" in a dangerous operation. He was also awarded the Medaille d'honneur for the same reason. It is likely that during 1918 Frank drove Colonel Lawrence in a Crossley Tender as the war diary of 'X' Flight notes his appearances.

In June the unit moved thirty miles north from Aqaba to Guweira. In a letter written after his promotion to Corporal on September 1 he noted victories in the Hejaz and how interesting the 'small local wars' were as you could identify the outcome.

However, the whole flight of ten officers and 55 other ranks were doing nothing as "the nearest Turks are miles and miles away from us". The war against the Turks was nearly over. The Flight were sent to Suez and disbanded in early October and then reorganised for anti-submarine duty at Haifa. On November 5 Frank wrote to his mother from Cairo where he had brought a convoy of cars to exchange for three new ones. On November 10 he was hospitalised in Suez until December 31 1918 suffering from a mosquito bite on the leg which had turned septic and the Spanish flu.

Frank probably arrived back in England on early 1919 and joined his parents, now living at Hall Green. In September of that year he enrolled on a medical degree course at Birmingham University and lived during the course with his parents who had moved to Alvechurch. In 1922 Frank met Margaret Jepson in London and completed his medical studies there in 1925. In 1923 he became a Second Lieutenant in the 6th Royal Warwicks, a return to the Territorials but this time in peacetime. In May 1928 he married Margaret, then aged twenty, in London. Three months later Frank and his brother, Bill, almost died in a yachting accident in the Thames estuary. In 1929 a daughter, Jane, arrived. The parents now decided to emigrate to New Zealand and arrived on January 13 1930. They settled at Napier in North Island and Frank set up a medical practice. The family survived a severe earthquake in 1931. Frank had to start again as the town was in ruins but Margaret returned to England with Jane for the birth of a second child, Fay. In 1932 the family settled near Christchurch. Frank began to broadcast on the radio and Margaret wrote radio plays. He also contributed to a radical magazine including an article which advocated a national health plan for New Zealand. In 1936 Frank and Margaret separated and he returned to England for two years. In London he met a fellow doctor, Edna Mackenzie, who returned to New Zealand with him and became his wife in 1940. He now took up the post of superintendent of a hospital at Coromandel on North Island. In 1944 the couple moved to Auckland and a son, Alan, was born. In 1946 there was another child, Barbara. On October 2 1949 Frank collapsed and died. Two years later Edna and the children made a permanent move to England. She died in 1977.

'The Life and Times of Frank Thornton Birkinshaw', Barbara Rudoe. Rudoe Press. 2010. Barbara was Frank's daughter.

11.

Castle Vale/Castle Bromwich/ Shard End

Castle Vale Estate. This was the site of a Royal Flying Corps/RAF aerodrome which trained squadrons for active service and carried out test flights on newly manufactured aircraft. The War Office took over what had been Castle Bromwich Playing Fields in 1914 which the City Council had rented from the Birmingham, Tame and Rea District Drainage Board. It was used initially for training 19 Squadron and then for testing Handley-Page bombers and other new aeroplanes made in the district. Overall eleven squadrons were based at Castle Bromwich; most were formed there before moving to operational bases. One was Australian. The aircraft which the pilots were trained to use included Maurice Farmans, Avro 504s, BE2Cs, Sopwith Pups and Sopwith Camels. From the birth of the RAF in April 1918 many aircraft made in Birmingham, including Austin made SE5a's, went first to No 14 Aircraft Acceptance Park at Castle Bromwich which examined them and equipped them for operational use.

At the end of the war the Park had twenty-one storage sheds of 200 feet by 60 feet and nine large hangars. Jose Jukes later remembered Americans arriving at the aerodrome and an air crash which took place at Ryman's Farm, Ward End, later Ward End Recreation Ground, when a plane came low over Bromford and had its nose sunk into the ground near some cottages. An American stepped out unhurt.

Two pilots were killed on January 23 1918. Lieutenant Douglas Hamilton, aged 19, was flying a machine that day when a formation of four others came over. Hamilton made an Immelmann turn and one of the other machines collided with him at about 4000 feet. Both planes crashed. The other pilot was Lieutenant Ralph Hall, a Canadian, also aged 19. Hamilton is commem-

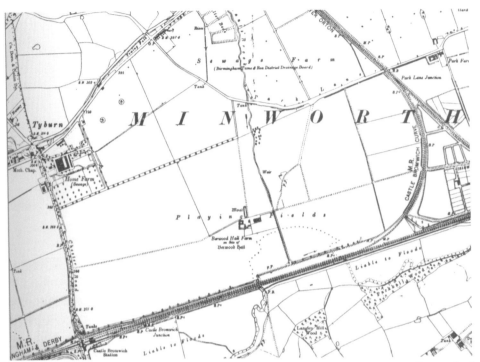

Castle Bromwich aerodrome was built on pre-war playing fields and Berwood Hall Farm had to make way. The Plants Brook was diverted

orated on the screen wall at Key Hill Cemetery and Hall was buried at Montreal, Canada.

The most notable pilot to pass through Castle Bromwich was Captain William Leefe Robinson VC. He was the first pilot to shoot down a German airship over Britain and was awarded the VC as a consequence. He was born in India in 1895, the son of a coffee estate owner. In 1909 he joined St Bees School, Cumberland and was a member of its OTC. In August 1914 he went to Sandhurst and was gazetted into the Worcestershire Regiment. He transferred to the RFC and went to France as an observer in March 1915. He was wounded over Lille and returned home to train as a pilot. He gained his wings in September 1915 and on the 20th reported to Captain R.M Rodwell at Castle Bromwich. While there for seventeen weeks he was billeted at 'Roseville', Sutton Road, Erdington where his hostess was impressed by the fact that he was a non-smoker and teetotaller.

By late October 1915 he was a flight commander responsible for five machines and 35 men. His job was to instruct observers and trainee pilots and deliver aircraft to home bases like Farnborough and Northolt. He was feted wherever he landed such as when he landed for lunch at Banbury one day. In a letter to his mother on October 21 he detailed what happened when he landed at Kenilworth with a passenger. "We had the time of our lives. Talk about autograph books and cameras. By gad I was positively sick of seeing and signing my own signature. When I swore I would not sign another book one girl caught hold of my machine and said she would not leave go until I signed. So after much amusing argument I told her to give me the book whereupon I placed my filthy hand, writing 'the mark of an aviator, W.L Robinson' over the top of the landmark – my hand was all dirty with the oil of the engine. The girl I liked best of all was a sweet little Flapper of about 17 called Kathleen Lennox for whom I drew our aeroplane. Another girl lent me her camera with which I took some photographs. She developed them and has just sent me some printed. We stayed at Kenilworth two days and a night".

Whilst at Castle Bromwich Robinson also mastered the art of night flying. In December 1915 he was sent south and joined a London defence squadron for 'Zepp Strafing'. In September 1916 he was based at Sutton's Farm airfield near Hornchurch. On the night of 2/3 he shot down SL 11 zeppelin over Cuffley, Hertfordshire. He was now a national hero. In April 1917 he was posted to France as a flight commander and was shot down during his first patrol near Mericourt. He was wounded and captured. His health deteriorated in captivity and, upon release, died on December 31 1918 at his sister's home at Stanmore from the Spanish flu. He was buried at All Saints in Harrow Weald.

Captain A.H Jackson had seen early service in the trenches but transferred to the RFC after recovering from a wound. He trained as a pilot at Castle Bromwich in June 1915. The aerodrome was a grass field with one hangar and tented accommodation. There was a big marquee for a mess. There were only 3-4 aircraft at that time. There were only about six trainees whilst he was there. Early morning flights were common when the air was still. At first he went up with an instructor in front of the trainee in an open cockpit. The trainee put his hands over the shoulders of the instructor with his hands on the controls. This was to get a 'feel' then the trainee graduated to dual control. There might be two flights a day – morning and evening but adding up to a total of no more than forty minutes.

William Fry trained at Castle Bromwich in the spring of 1916 as one of No 5 Reserve Squadron. Years later he felt the site was unsuitable because of the main railway line with telegraph poles and wires down one side and the sewage farm on another side. Roads on other sides also had telegraph poles and the only approach from the main road to the hangars, offices and workshop ran straight across the middle of the aerodrome. At least it was flat! He was billeted in Erdington and collected each morning by a lorry. Instructors were mainly pilots back from France for a rest, some in a nervous state. A few were outstanding pupils who had been retained to instruct. He began on a Maurice Farman 'Longhorn' and then the 'Shorthorn'. Engines and aircraft kept going until something went wrong. He thought the fitters and riggers were first class and were mostly volunteers from the motor and engineering trades. Instruction was ad hoc and relied on the method and judgement of each instructor. His first solo flight was on May 24 1916.

Flying training at Castle Bromwich appears to have been very hazardous. In addition to the thirteen men buried at nearby Castle Bromwich and Curdworth churchyards a further eighteen deaths have been identified by the Midland Aircraft Recovery Group. They have also identified 39 other men injured in accidents at and around Castle Bromwich between December 1915 and the end of the war. There are also eleven possibles. Some were lucky and only sustained slight wounds; others were seriously injured. The reasons for accidents and crashes were varied.

'spun into the ground'
'structural failure during aeronautics'
'stalled at thirty feet and crashed'
'landed fast in fog and ran through a hedge at Castle Bromwich.
'crashed while attempting to return to Castle Bromwich aerodrome with a failing engine'
'lost control in a violent squall'
'engine failure while landing'
'hit a tree when landing'
'tried to turn to avoid a machine on the ground at Castle Bromwich but crashed when a wingtip struck the ground'
'crashed in trees and wires when the engine failed on take-off'

In addition to those described in the entries under the two nearby churches the following men can be identified who were killed in accidents at Castle Bromwich......

Lieutenant Percy Wright, 29, from Ontario. 5 Reserve Squadron. Buried in Lodge Hill Cemetery (December 21 1916)
Second Lieutenant Frank Garner, 21, from Runcorn 5th Squadron. Buried at Runcorn. (December 20 1916)

Second Lieutenant Walter Pilling from Haggate, Lancashire, where he was
    buried (April 3 1917)
Second Lieutenant Cyril Thornton, 18, from Bournville. Buried in Lodge
    Hill Cemetery (October 5 1917)
Second Lieutenant Granville Lewis, 26, from London where he was buried
    in St Pancras Cemetery (October 5 1917)
Second Lieutenant R.F.S Christie who was buried in Lodge Hill Cemetery
    (October 15 1917)

More is known about three other casualties. Second Lieutenant Bertram
Joseph Venn died on July 11 1917 in the 1st Southern General Hospital as a
result of an accident in a Maurice Farman Shorthorn. The aircraft was being
force landed in a field next to the airfield after the engine stopped and struck
a hedge causing the pilot to be thrown out when the nose hit the ground. He
was 27 and born in Essex and before the War had been an assistant examiner
in the Patents Office of the Board of Trade in London. By December 1914
he was a lance corporal in a Wireless Signal Company and afterwards rose
through the ranks and joined the RFC. He was buried in Bristol. Air
Mechanic 2nd Class Sidney Larkin, 25, was an Australian in 71st Squadron
and died of accidental injuries on August 14 1917 in an Avro 504 which
crashed in gusty conditions; his pilot survived. He was born in Sydney and
attended a Catholic School. He had been an electrical mechanic before the
War, joined up in October 1916 and sailed from Sydney on January 17 1917.
He was buried in Lodge Hill Cemetery in Birmingham.

Serjeant Mechanic Harry Joseph Birtles, 22, of 28th Training Squadron
was killed in a Sopwith Pup which dived into the ground whilst attacking a
target in Sutton Park on April 22 1918. He had a complicated family
background in India and both his parents had died by the time he was killed.
He had joined the RFC on October 17 1917. He was buried at Odd Rode on
the Staffordshire/Cheshire border.

However, the worst accident was when a Handley Page 0/400 crashed at
Maxstoke on August 19 1918 killing all members of the six man crew. It was
on a test flight from 14 Aircraft Acceptance Park at Castle Bromwich when it
lost fabric from a wing and crashed. It was the worst accident in the first year
of the Royal Air Force. The aircraft was a biplane bomber and the largest built
in Britain. It had two 360 hp Rolls Royce engines and a wing span of 100 feet.
It had a maximum speed of 97 mph and could carry up to 2000 pounds of
bombs. The pilot that day was Lieutenant Robert Edward MacBeth, 28, who
had been born in Toronto and attended the University there where he gained

a science degree. He then became the assistant roadways engineer for the City of Toronto. When he was killed he had only been passed fit to resume operational flying nine days earlier after being injured in May 1916 after crashing into the North Sea. His long recovery took place in Canada before being posted to an aerial school in the Bahamas where he worked on surveying. Back in England he became an instructor in the theory of flying and was offered a post as the Chief Compass Officer in England. He wanted to return to active flying so turned the job down. In July 1918 he was a ferry pilot between London and Boulogne. That month he wrote an interesting five page letter which has survived. He described his brother, an artillery officer, who was in a rest camp in France suffering with the 'Spanish flu'. He talked about a friend, William Hubbard, also from Toronto who had been awarded the DFC for shooting down ten German planes. He was buried in St Michael's churchyard at Maxstoke. He hoped to meet another artillery officer friend when the latter was able to gain leave to London. He explained that he was testing two Handley Page bombers each day.

The second pilot on board was Lieutenant Frederick Bravery, aged 22, who was under instruction on the type. He was buried in Worthing. Three air mechanics were also killed on this flight. Charles Offord was 18 and was buried in Acton Cemetery, London. His role was to test the dynamo and lighting system. Albert Winrow, 22, was buried in his home city of Manchester. His role was that of 'a passenger to make up war load to pilot's instructions'. George Greenland was the passenger in charge of the petrol pumps. He came from London where he was buried. Aircraftman 2nd Class H.Simmonds, 31, was also there to make up the war load and was also buried in Maxstoke churchyard.

Website of Midland Aircraft Recovery Group formed in 1983.

'Aviation in Birmingham'. Geoffrey Negus and Tommy Stadden. 1984.

Birmingham Weekly Post September 9 1916.

'Air of Battle'. The autobiography of Wing Commander William Fry MC.

Captain A.H Jackson. Sound Archive, Imperial War Museum.

Castle Bromwich churchyard. This is opposite St Mary and St Margaret church. Here there are eight Commonwealth War Graves Commission graves from the First World War in a churchyard which overlooks the airfield where these men were based. Some of those buried have private headstones. They are all the result of training and flying accidents at the First World War airfield and seven of the eight were officers.

CASTLE VALE/CASTLE BROMWICH/SHARD END

In chronological order of their deaths the first one is Second Lieutenant Frank Dudley Evans, aged 18, on June 9 1916. He was a local man whose parents lived at 'Fairlea', Castle Bromwich. The next with a private headstone was Second Lieutenant William Moorwood Staniforth, 32, on March 23 1917. He was better known as 'Billie' and came from Hackenthorpe, Derbyshire. He was also married to Gladys and his headstone includes the words 'killed while on flying duty'. He was originally commissioned into the Queen's Own Yorkshire Dragoons probably on November 27 1915 and was serving in 28 Reserve Squadron when killed.

Corporal Clifford Newton Ryder, 24, was the only man not to be an officer. He died on April 10 1917 and was in 4 Squadron of the Australian Flying Corps. He was a fitter working in aircraft maintenance. He came from Sydney and two photographs have survived showing his funeral and pallbearers carrying his coffin. In the same crash Second Lieutenant John Williamson was killed.

Second Lieutenant Lucien Herbert Higgs came next; he died on June 8 1917. Also a private memorial and 'Airmen Died' suggests that he was a 'native of Brussels'. He was in 5 Training Squadron and crashed at Blisworth when he became lost. Second Lieutenant David Kitto Billings of 71 Squadron died on September 14 1917 after his Avro 504 crashed in a wood at Water Orton. He fell out of his cockpit when the straps broke during aeronautics. He came from Chicago in the USA where his father was a clergyman. Lieutenant Percy Charles Moynihan died on May 22 1918 as a member of 54 Training Squadron. His memorial is a private stone with the words 'killed while flying'. He was in a SE5a which collided with a tree on take-off. There is also a special memorial to Lieutenant Raymond Tenney Balch, 23, of 74 Training Squadron who died three days after Moynihan. He appears to have been a Canadian who left Phillips Academy at Andover, Massachusetts in 1914. He had become a temporary Second Lieutenant in November 1917. He was killed when coming out of a dive over Sutton Park. His parents came from Newbury Port, Massachusetts.

Finally there is the only one of the eight who had seen service at the front and the only post-war death. Captain Edwin Tufnell Hayne DSC DFC, aged 24, died on April 28 1919. He was born in Johannesburg on May 28 1895. He attended the King Edward VII School there and joined the Royal Naval Air Service in 1916. In 1917 he was posted to 3 Naval Squadron in France and flew Sopwith Camels. He became their 'top scorer' with fifteen victories. His first 'victory' was in August 1917 when he shot down an Albatross D.V south of Middelkerke in Belgium and his last was on June 16 1918. On

November 30 1917 the London Gazette recorded his Distinguished Service Cross for 'services with a wing of the RNAS at Dunkirk between March and September 1917'. "He had numerous engagements with enemy aircraft and on 16th August 1917 attacked an enemy aerodrome and placed a whole flight of machines out of action by machine gun fire. During a flight of over two hours, during which time he attacked transport and railways, he never exceeded a height of 1000 feet".

On September 21 1918 the London Gazette noted the award of his Distinguished Flying Cross. He was now in 203 Squadron of the Royal Air Force. The citation read "During the recent enemy offensive, this Officer carried out 48 special missions. Flying at extremely low altitudes he has inflicted heavy casualties on massed troops and transport. In addition, he has accounted for ten enemy machines, destroying three and driving down seven out of control; in these encounters he has never hesitated to engage the enemy, however superior in numbers. On one occasion he observed ten hostile aeroplanes harassing three Dolphins; he attacked three of the enemy, driving one down in flames". Hayne survived the war but met an accidental death when flying a Bristol F2 from Castle Bromwich which stalled and crashed whilst landing after his engine cut out. Major Maurice Perrin in the back seat died afterwards in hospital. In the cemetery Hayne has a large private memorial with these words at the bottom – "Let those that come after, see to it that his name be not forgotten".

See the article by Chris John on the Hellfire Corner website entitled 'Royal Flying Corps Burials and Memorials, Castle Bromwich aerodrome, Birmingham'.

Norman Chamberlain Playing Fields, Shard End. Were named after Captain Norman Chamberlain, a city councillor. He was killed at Cambrai on December 1 1917 in the 1/Grenadier Guards and buried in Fins New British Cemetery, Sorel-Le-Grand, France. Norman was a cousin of Neville Chamberlain. Born at Augustus Road, Edgbaston, in 1884, he was the son of Herbert Chamberlain, a nephew of Joseph Chamberlain. He attended Eton and studied History at Oxford University where he introduced his Uncle Joe at the Oxford Union. After leaving he became interested in social work and moved back to Birmingham in 1907 to live at Calthorpe Cottage, Edgbaston. Before his arrival he had resided at Toynbee Hall where he conducted a Working Lads' Club at Limehouse. He had also served on the Education Committee of the London County Council.

Back in Birmingham he initially became secretary of the West Birmingham branch of the City Aid Society. He also served on the committees of the

Housing Reform Association and the Working Boys Home. He was also associated with the work of the Middlemore Homes. He was active in several welfare organisations for deprived young people, including the Street Children's Union at Ryland Street. He set up a Boys' Club for paper sellers and unemployed youths who could be found in and around New Street Station. Austen Chamberlain thought that he was 'getting very socialistic, very wild'. He promoted help for adolescents after they left elementary schools through an after-care scheme which he started in 1911 and was eventually based on about a hundred School Care Committees in the city with over 2000 voluntary workers. He wanted to counter the demoralising effect of unemployment and poor nutrition and financed the emigration of several boys to Canada. He also helped at Birmingham Juvenile Courts by speaking up for defendants and organising probation work for those convicted. At the time of the 1911 census he was a boarder in a house at 1, Oakley Square, London where he lived on 'private means'.

He was elected to the City Council as a Liberal Unionist in 1909 for St Thomas' Ward and became Chairman of the Parks Committee between 1912 and 1914 having already set up a programme of organised games in parks during the summer of 1910. In 1912 the Parks Department funded the scheme. As chairman he increased the number of playing fields and recreation grounds available for organised leisure activities. "The driving principles of his welfare work were informed by social imperialism; he thought it was essential to improve the character and stamina of Birmingham's working class youth through moral guidance and structured physical activities so that they would be fit to defend the British Empire. He would presumably have seen his war service and death as a contribution to the same". In 1910 he had failed to win a Cornwall seat in the general election.

In 1914 he was the first member of the City Council to volunteer for active service and in January 1915 he was commissioned into the Grenadier Guards. However he found this elite regiment uncomfortable and in 1916 wrote about silly orders and ineptitude. On June 2 1917 Beatrice, sister of Austen, wrote to him – "I think that the men who are fighting our battles now are more heroic than the soldiers of any previous war ever waged because a large proportion of them hate it, hate everything about it and do it because they know it's right". Before his death he wrote from France a letter addressed to the boys of the Boys' Club which stated that "you won't get this unless I'm knocked out". He talked of "wishing you a happy life and one as worth living as mine" and having seen "all the pluck and cheerfulness and unselfishness and real uphill struggling to keep your end up and make headway which I've seen in all of you one time or another". He sympathised "with your bad luck and all the unfairness and difficulties that surround one when one is trying to make good – even if I'm not there to tell you and keep you at it". About the beginning of October 1917 he felt he was a 'failure and wash out' when his Colonel told him he would not get a company as he was not satisfied with his work despite a period of acting command. The playing fields are 40 acres in extent and were established, after landscaping, on an old gravel pit after the Second World War.

Suburban Birmingham website.

Birmingham Post February 15 1918. Library of Birmingham.

The Castle Bromwich war memorial. Is on 'The Green' and lists 33 names. One name listed is that of Commander the Honourable Richard Orlando Beaconsfield Bridgeman DSO of HMS Hyacinth who was killed on January 9 1917, aged 37, and is buried in Dar-Es-Salaam War Cemetery. There is also a plaque in his memory in Zanzibar Anglican Cathedral. He was the son of the 4th Earl of Bradford of Weston Park who died in 1915 and brother of the 5th Earl. The family estate also included Castle Bromwich Hall and land in the area. His DSO dated from 1915 when he was command of two whalers on August 19 which boarded under fire the SS Markgraf in Tanga Harbour.

In January 1917 his two man seaplane on a reconnaissance mission made a forced landing with engine trouble in a creek of the Rufiga Delta; he was the observer. With Germans nearby they burnt it and then spent three days walking and swimming towards the river mouth. Bridgeman died from exhaustion and exposure after their raft was swept out to sea. Flight Lieutenant Edwin Moon, the pilot from the RNAS, was taken prisoner. Bridgeman was born on February 28 1879 and pursued a naval career. At the very beginning of the war he was appointed to the Cape of Good Hope Station and soon became Flag Commander. During the war he served on seven different ships. He was also an observer during several flights in operations against the Konigsberg. He was well known as a big game hunter.

Commander Richard Bridgeman's memorial death plaque which was sent to the next of kin by the Government. They were commonly called the Dead Man's Penny.

The Castle Bromwich Victory Hall. Near the Green and adjacent to the Parish Church Rooms which is an earlier building dating from 1900. The Victory Hall is now a Community Church Centre. The foundation stone was laid by the Ida, Countess Dowager of Bradford, who then lived at Castle Bromwich Hall, on June 3 1922. She was the mother of R.O.B Bridgeman; her husband, the 4th Earl had died in January 1915 and his older brother had taken the title. The stone notes the 'victorious ending of the Great War 1914-1918' and that the Countess had the assistance of Private William Henry Morle. What the stone does not tell us is that Morle was in the 1st Battalion of the Royal Warwickshire Regiment and had gone to France with them on August 22 1914 but at some stage had become a prisoner of war.

William had been born at Raleigh's Cross on the Somerset border with Devon in c1887. In 1891 he was living with his grandparents at Lydeard St Lawrence, also in Somerset. By 1901, aged 14, he was living with his parents and four younger sisters at 76, Manor Road, Witton (near Witton Station). His father Joseph, aged 37, was working as a 'trollier' in an ammunition works, probably the nearby Lion Works of Kynochs. In 1907 William Morle married Alice. Three sons followed and the family were living in one of the terraced houses in New Street, Castle Bromwich in 1911. William worked as a 'general labourer'.

12.

Yardley/Acocks Green/ Greet/Stechford

Yardley Cemetery in Yardley Road. The CWGC commemorates 266 men who are or were buried in the Cemetery. If their graves have been lost they are still listed on a memorial screen wall. 124 deaths were post-war. Some of the total were men who did not see active service but others died of wounds or illness as a result of military operations abroad. Five had been awarded medals – 2 DCMs, 2 MMs and a Meritorious Service Medal. Unsurprisingly the highest number of men served in the Royal Warwickshire Regiment with 43. In addition 32 had served in various branches of the artillery, 20 in the Worcesters and 19 in the Royal Engineers. Four had served in the RFC/RAF and nine in the Navy. A wide variety of infantry regiments were represented. Only seven were officers but none above the rank of Lieutenant. The men detailed below are taken in the chronological order of their deaths.

Private Charles Fewtrell, aged 19, had been training in a reserve battalion of the Warwicks for six months and then died of acute bronchitis in a Bristol hospital on January 31 1916. He was given a military funeral with a gun carriage and the regimental band. He had lived at 6, Laburnum Villas, Poplar Road, Sparkhill and worked at the Globe Steam Laundry on the Stratford Road. The employees were given an afternoon off for the funeral and the firm sent its own wreaths. Private Harold Hackett, aged 26, died of wounds at Eastbourne and had already been a regular soldier for seven years in the 2nd Warwicks. He was also given a military funeral with a firing party of Royal Engineers from Great Brook Street Barracks. His father had a harness making business in Warstone Lane. Private William Warder, aged 20, had been badly wounded on the first day of the Somme whilst serving in the 1/6th

Warwicks. Unfortunately he died from his wounds on October 13 1916 in Netley Hospital fifteen weeks later. He lived in Greswolde Road, Sparkhill.

Corporal Lincoln Thompson, aged 29, was called up as a single man under the Derby Scheme in February 1916 but had not completed his training in a reserve Warwicks unit. He had attended Stratford Road Council School and before call up had run a hairdressers at 95, Kyrwicks Lane, Sparkbrook. He also lived in Sparkbrook at 10, Main Street. He died from heart failure after pneumonia at Priory Hospital, Cheltenham. He also received a military funeral. Lieutenant Frederick Wigan Jones had gone to France with the 1/8th Warwicks in March 1915. He died of wounds on December 21 1915. By the time of his death he had worked his way up through the ranks. He was also a freemason and lived at 'Sandown', 270, Station Road, Stechford. Private Victor Meade, aged 25, was the only Australian buried at Yardley and died on May 11 1917. He was in the 13th Battalion of the Australian Infantry and had been born at Geelong, Victoria. Private Albert Hawkeswood had originally joined under-age but was 19 when he died of wounds on June 9 1917 at the age of 19 in the 1st Royal Warwicks. He had lived at Towyn Road, Springfield, Sparkhill.

Private Edward Beavon, aged 37, was one of nine men of the 5th Reserve Battalion of the Royal Warwicks who drowned at Blyth Sands on August 24 1917. Over six hundred men had been on a route march on a hot day when they stopped at the beach to cool off. A heavy swell carried seven of them out to sea, including Beavon, and two rescuers also drowned. He came from Saltley. Private John Currah, aged 37, was attached to the depot of the Royal Welsh Fusiliers when he died on November 6 1917. His parents lived in Church Road, Yardley and he was 'a repatriated prisoner of war' who had been wounded in 1914. Serjeant David Watts, aged 29, was attached to the Depot of the Worcesters on December 1 1917 when he died. He was one of two Military Medal winners buried in the cemetery and came from Hay Mills.

Second Lieutenant Alfred Victor Flavell, aged 25, died in a flying accident on May 4 1918 whilst training in 8th Training Squadron. His plane developed wing trouble and when trying to land hit the top of a hangar which set the petrol tank on fire. Flavell was badly burned and only lived for twelve hours. His father was the head of Yardley Road Schools and lived in Golden Hillock Road. Alfred had left Birmingham University with a science degree and had initially served in a City Battalion for eighteen months in France before his commission. He had attended his father's school and Waverley Road Secondary School. He was given a military funeral. His brother, Herbert, had been killed on the Somme in 1916.

Boy Seaman F.C Lamb was buried with naval honours in July 1918. He was only 17 and had enlisted on October 1917. He trained on HMS Impregnable before transfer to the HMS Royal Oak. On the Royal Oak he contracted pneumonia whilst at sea. He fainted on three occasions before the ship's doctor was sent for. He was landed at a port and placed in hospital but died on July 1 1918. He had attended Holy Souls Roman Catholic School at Acocks Green where his widowed mother, Tabitha, lived at 49, Francis Road. The Reverend Father Gibbon noted his fine spirit in offering himself for his country before he need have done so.

Lieutenant Wilfred Walter Meddings also died in a flying accident on July 8 1918. He was with 201st Training Depot Station. He was 18 and lived with his parents at 101, Coventry Road, Small Heath. His father was works manager at the Delta and Extruded Metal Company of Dartmouth Street and the firm sent a floral tribute in the form of a propeller. Eight officers attended and there was a firing party.

Serjeant Charles Saunders, aged 32, was the other man who had been awarded the Military Medal. When he died four days before the Armistice he was part of the Special Brigade Depot of the Royal Engineers. His wife, Elizabeth, was buried in the same grave. Private Sidney Tabberner, aged 32, had originally joined the Royal Berkshire Regiment but died of pneumonia as a result of severe wounds on November 27 as a member of the 10th Warwicks. He was living at Camp Hill when he died and had previously lived in Acocks Green. Before joining in 1915 he had worked as an attendant at the Great Western Hotel. He was given a military funeral. One of the mourners was his brother, Frank, who had been a prisoner in Germany and arrived on the day of the funeral. A.Ogden was a shoeing smith in the 1st/1st Heavy Battery of the Royal Garrison Artillery when he died on February 20 1919.

Our final two examples were both awarded the Distinguished Conduct Medal. Company Serjeant Major F. Ariss died on April 19 1919 and had lived in Templefield Street, Small Heath. His award related to service in the 1/Royal Warwicks when they were stationed at St Yves near Ploegsteert Wood in Belgium during the four months after late November 1914. This period included the famous Christmas Truce in the same area. His citation described the "great zeal and devotion to duty from the commencements of the campaign, especially in the trenches at St Yves. CSM Ariss has set a splendid example to the men of his company". Serjeant H.J Salter, aged 44, is named on the screen wall at Yardley. He died on May 7 1920 and we know little about him apart from his DCM citation. This outlines that when he was a lance corporal in the Mounted Military Police he showed "great bravery and consistent good work from the 9th to 28th May 1915, near Ypres. He was employed, both day and night, in collecting stragglers, directing traffic and collecting war material. During the 24th May he assisted to places of safety several hundred men, who were suffering from gas poison. Most of the time, and especially on the 24th and 25th May, the town was being heavily shelled".

London Gazette for DCM citations.

Kevan Darby and other members of the Great War Forum.

Percy Road Greet. Here, near the junction with Warwick Road, the Motor Radiator Manufacturing Co made radiators for aeroplanes after January 1918 for the Ministry of Munitions.

Stoneleigh, Victoria Road, Stechford. Was lent by Mr G.H Tomlinson of Castle Bromwich. It opened in July 1916 and was named the Stechford and Yardley VAD Hospital with 62 beds.

Victor Mckey, one of the first two Brummies to be killed in the war

1252, Coventry Road, South Yardley. This was the family home of Able Seaman Victor James Mckey who was one of the first two Birmingham servicemen killed in the war in the same event. Their ship, HMS Amphion, a Royal Navy scout cruiser, struck a mine off the Thames estuary whilst heading for Harwich. Around 150 sailors were killed as the boat sank. Victor was 21 and is commemorated on the Plymouth Naval Memorial. The other man was Able Seaman William Nicholas, aged 29, who had lived at 6/53 Peel Street, Winson Green. His parents had moved to Bristol. He is commemorated on the same memorial.

The Crossways, Sherbourne Road, Acocks Green. This was the family home in 1911 of Eustace Leonard Hill, aged 16, who was to take part in a notable naval event in April 1919. He was born at Dursley, Gloucestershire. His father, George, was a physician and surgeon and there were two domestic servants. Ten years earlier the family were living in nearby Clifton Road. Eustace attended King Edward's between 1906 and 1913 when he left to become to a naval cadet on September 15. On August 2 1914 he became a midshipman and joined HMS Endymion which became part of the 10th Cruiser Squadron enforcing the northern blockade of Germany. On December 15 1914 he joined HMS Ajax, a King George V class battleship, which formed part of the 2nd Battle Squadron. In March 1916 he became an acting Sub-Lieutenant. He left the ship on April 4 1916 a few weeks before its only major action at Jutland. After a short spell on the newly launched destroyer, Patrician, Eustace joined HMS Hydra, also a destroyer, in August 1916.

He served on the Hydra until March 7 1917. This period of service was interrupted by two spells in a Plymouth hospital in November 1916, when he was now a full Sub-Lieutenant, and January 1917, suffering from syphilis. To add to his woes a senior officer commented adversely in January 1917 that "he does not show great intelligence and is slow to acquire knowledge by experience and observation. Is improving. At present not fitted for a position of responsibility".

After leaving the Hydra he spent two more short spells in hospital for the same reason. In April 1917 he attended a torpedo control course at HMS Vernon at Portsmouth. On April 23 he joined HMS Bellerophon, a Dreadnought class battleship, although two months later there was a further short spell in hospital for the original reason. He left the ship on October 24 1917. In November 1917 a Captain Watson recommended Eustace for promotion and on the 19th he became an Acting Lieutenant. He served on two more destroyers before the armistice, HMS Moon and HMS Laurel which he joined as full lieutenant.

On January 31 1919 Lieutenant Eustace Hill joined the battleship HMS Marlborough. In this capacity he was on the ship in the Black Sea in April 1919 when some members of the Russian royal family were evacuated. It arrived at Yalta from Constantinople on April 7. It carried a letter from Queen Alexandra, mother of George V, urging her sister, the Dowager Empress Marie Feodorovna, mother of the Tsar, to leave Russia as soon as possible. Her son, his wife and their four daughters had been executed in July 1918. The officer's cabins were made ready for the royal guests. Embarkation took place a few miles away at Koriez cove, closer to the Harax, the Empress's summer palace.

Other members of the Imperial family to board included Grand Duchess Xenia with her five sons (each with a bag of Russian soil), the sister of Tsar Nicholas, and the Grand Dukes Nicholas and Peter, the Tsar's cousins. The Marlborough left Koriez with fifty evacuees and docked at Yalta. Other members of the party included the Oxford educated Prince Felix Youssoupoff who had been involved in the murder of Rasputin and brought a tube on board containing two Rembrandts. The twenty members of the Imperial family came from three other summer palaces. A British sloop left first carrying about four hundred of the Imperial Guard. It steamed around the Marlborough with its passengers saluting and singing the royal anthem. The ship was able to leave on April 11 with refugees crowding into Yalta as the Bolshevik forces drew closer. The ship reached England via Malta and the Empress returned to her native Denmark after a short stay with her sister. In a diary she kept on her rescue ship she had written "I have to do everything myself".

Eustace Hill left HMS Marlborough on November 1 1920 and served elsewhere until being 'placed on the retired list at his own request' two years later. He served as a lieutenant commander in the Second World War, mainly on shore service.

'Service Record of King Edward's School, Birmingham during the War 1914-1919'. Cornish Brothers. 1920.

National Archives. Service records at ADM/196/120 and ADM/196/146.

31, Francis Road. Stechford.

31, Francis Road. Stechford. This was the home in 1911 of Arthur Sydney Langley and his wife Helen and their newly born son Edmund. The parents were both born at Chesterton, a suburb of Cambridge, Arthur in 1882. He joined the teaching staff of King Edward's School in 1905 and became a housemaster in 1910. In February 1913 he was a captain in the OTC there. In May 1916 he was commissioned into the Royal Naval Volunteer Reserve as a lieutenant and joined the Royal Naval Air Service depot at Stratford, East London, one of four officers and sixty men. It was then chiefly engaged in the small-scale production of anhydrous prussic acid and research on poisonous gases. The depot grew in strength and became the centre of chemical research and production for naval purposes.

It supplied large quantities of poison gas liquids to the army and various kinds of smoke-producing gear to the three services. In June 1917 Arthur was promoted to Lieutenant Commander and five months later became 'First Lieutenant' under Wing Commander Frank Brock of the famous fireworks family, the founder of the experimental station at Stratford. Brock devised and executed the massive smoke screen used during the Zeebrugge Raid to cover the approach of the raiders. He insisted on going shore himself and was killed on the Mole. Arthur Langley now took over command at Stratford from May 1918, when he was mentioned in despatches, until at least November of the same year. By the latter date he held the rank of lieutenant commander and the Stratford command now included a similar base a Dover, the RN Anti-gas section with depots at Tottenham and Stamford Hill, inspection and repair of anti-gas gear at Kirkwall, Rosyth, Harwich, Dover and Portsmouth and instructional Gas Schools for naval officers at Rosyth and Dover. At the same date he became a member of the Admiralty Anti-Gas Committee and in June 1919 acted as the Admiralty representative on the Chemical Warfare Organisation Committee.

On April 1 1919 his CMG was gazetted for his 'valuable services at Stratford'. He was not the only man with Birmingham connections who served at Stratford during the war. William Harold Juggins Vernon had received his scientific training at the Aston Manor Technical School, the Birmingham Municipal Technical School and Sheffield and Birmingham Universities. He served as a leading mechanic and petty officer in the RNAS at Stratford and later became an analyst in the Admiralty laboratories at Birmingham.

See 'Corris', Maney Hill Road, Sutton Coldfield, for Thomas Salter Price who also served at the Stratford Experimental Station.

'Service Record of King Edward's School, Birmingham during the War 1914-1919'. Cornish Brothers. 1920.

Clifton Road, Acocks Green. Before the First World War James Neville Marshall MC VC lived with his family in Acocks Green. Two of their homes were in Clifton Road – 'Melrose' and 'Beechcroft'. This road is now Oxford Road. They also lived at Springfield in 'The Avenue'. His father was a haberdasher in the city centre. He was one of six children and was born in Manchester; the family moved to Birmingham in the early 1890s. James attended King Edward's at Camp Hill and probably left for financial reasons in 1902 and became a clerk at the Midland Institute and later worked in the Medical Faculty of Birmingham University. On May 27 1910 his father committed suicide 'whilst of unsound mind'. The family home was then at 'Eastbourne House', Warwick Road. His widowed mother opened a private school with the help of two daughters.

This death of his father prompted James to leave the area and in early 1911 he was at Harlow, Essex, and described as a veterinary worker who worked with horses. Later press reports described him inaccurately as a veterinary surgeon. In September 1911 he married Edith Taylor at Epping; she was also interested in horses. This is where he shows signs of being rather a 'Walter Mitty' character because the marriage certificate falsely describes his father as a soldier and does not acknowledge that he had died. His own rank or profession was noted as a 'gentleman'! His age was given as 32 rather than 24 which fits with his later false claim to have served in the Boer War! He appears to have set himself up as a breeder of thoroughbred horses with contacts at Newmarket. A report he made in 1913 about a lame horse has survived. Before the outbreak of war he appears to have gone to Argentina to buy horses for the Army Remount Department; he may be the Mr J Marshall who left Southampton for Buenos Aires in December 1913.

By mid-September 1914 he was serving in the artillery of the Belgian army and was wounded several times and awarded two decorations; he had Belgian friends. After convalescence he was commissioned into the Irish Guards at the end of 1915, arrived in France in May 1916, served in the Ypres Salient and won an MC there. On July 14 1916 he was wounded with a bullet in the lung and spent seven months in England convalescing. He served in several battalions probably because he was a disciplinarian who could bring a battered battalion back into shape i.e. a 'stiffener'. In May 1917 he was appointed second in command of the 1/6 Lancashire Fusiliers. In May 1918 he returned to the 2/Irish Guards but within a month was posted to the 2/Manchesters as second in command.

He was attached to the 16/Lancashire Fusiliers from the Manchesters at Ors on November 4 1918 as an Acting Lieutenant Colonel when he was killed in the action which merited the posthumous award of the VC. He lies buried close to Wilfred Owen who called him the 'Mad Major' and 'the Major of the Ten Wounds'. In a letter home to his mother, Susan, he called Marshall "the most arrant, utterly soldierly soldier I have ever come across….bold, robust, dashing, unscrupulous, cruel, jovial, immoral, vast-chested, handsome-headed, of free, coarse speech". His tenth wound was reported in the Times on August 28 1918. His citation stated that it was for "most conspicuous bravery, determination and leadership in the attack on the Sambre-Oise Canal, near Catillon, on November 4 1918 when a partly constructed bridge came under concentrated fire and was broken before the advanced troops of his battalion could cross. Lt.Col. Marshall at once went forward and organised parties to repair the bridge. The first party were soon killed or wounded but, by personal example, he inspired his command and volunteers were instantly forthcoming. Under intense fire and with complete disregard of his own safety he stood on the bank encouraging his men and assisting in the work and, when the bridge was repaired, attempted to rush across at the head of his battalion and was killed while so doing. The passage of the canal was of vital importance and the gallantry displayed by all ranks was largely due to the inspiring example set by Lt.Col. Marshall". Edith, his wife, collected his VC at Buckingham Palace in April 1919. He later inspired a character in Pat Barker's war novel, 'The Ghost Road'. Arthur Graham concludes his biography by saying that "From the time of his arrival in Harlow to the day he died Neville Marshall was never all that he seemed to be and certainly not all that he often claimed to be".

Times February 14 1919.

'James Neville Marshall VC MC and Bar. A Biography'. Arthur S.Graham. Harlow Council. 1998. Heritage, Library of Birmingham.

'VCs of the First World War. The Final Days. 1918'. Gerald Gliddon. Sutton. 2000.

Tape recording by Captain G.A Potts, his adjutant. Imperial War Museum.

There is a photograph of him in the clubhouse of Camp Hill RFC.

Stechford war memorial. This is situated on a traffic island at 'Five Ways' where five roads converge – Yardley Fields Road, Albert Road, Lyttleton Road, Richmond Road and Stuarts Road. Fifty-two names are listed and also the words "They nobly responded to the call of duty and died that Britain might honour her pledged word to protect the weak and defenceless against aggression and that good faith truth and justice should prevail among the nations". The examples below can stand for them all.

Second Lieutenant Walter Benbow, aged 29, was killed on August 23 1918 whilst attached to the 7th/Berkshires from the 7th Kings Shropshire Light Infantry. He had been born at Brueton, Somerset but the family must have moved to Birmingham and he attended King Edward's, Camp Hill. After leaving school he became a clerk. He joined the 1st Kings Royal Rifle Corps in late August 1914 and went to France a year later. After a gunshot wound on March 7 1916 he returned to England, returning in August the same year. In March 1917 he was awarded the Military Medal for bravery in the field which contributed to the capture of the Grevillers trench line and Bailleul village. He had risen to the rank of Company Quartermaster Serjeant. He now went home to take a commission in the 7th Kings Shropshire LI although he was attached to the Berkshires when he returned to France. He lived at 'Chadshunt', Lyttleton Road, Stechford and lies buried in Bienvillers Military Cemetery.

Two Freer brothers are listed. In 1911 they were living with their family at 34, Albert Road and their father was a boot maker and repairer. There were six other brothers and one sister. Robert was a fifteen year old errand boy in a fruiterers and George Horace was still at school, aged 13. Private Robert Freer was killed on May 5 1916 in the 10th West Yorkshire Regiment and was buried in the Cite Bonjean Military Cemetery at Armentieres. Private George Freer was serving in the 1st Wiltshire Regiment when he was killed on May 27 1918. He is commemorated on the Soissons Memorial. Private Harry Collicott was 35 when he was killed in Belgium on August 19 1917. He was a member of the X Corps Cyclist Battalion. He left a wife, Lavinia, at 'Sweetbriar', Richmond Road, Stechford. Before the war he had been a tailor. He lies buried in Voormezeele Enclosure No 1 and 2. In 1911 George Bex was 17 years old and living at 111, Albert Road. He was working as an invoice clerk; his father was a carpenter. He died of wounds as a private in the Royal Army Medical Corps on July 25 1917 as part of 1st (South Midland) Mounted Brigade Field Ambulance. He had joined up at the end of October 1914. He was buried in Dozinghem Military Cemetery. It is likely that he was based at one of three casualty clearing stations nearby.

Second Lieutenant Cyril Elmore Pells was more fortunate than most men to have survived until he was killed in France on May 27 1918 because he had been a passenger on the Lusitania when it was torpedoed on May 7 1915. He had been born at Beccles, Suffolk in 1891. In 1911 he was working in the optical scientific instrument trade and living as a boarder at 4, Bury Street, Ruislip in the London area. He emigrated to Canada in March 1914 with his wife, Mary, and infant son, John. They settled in Vancouver and were returning to England on the Lusitania so that Cyril could join the British Army and Mary could train as a nurse. The ocean line was sunk by a torpedo from a U-boat when eleven miles off the south coast of Ireland. Sixty per cent of those on board were drowned. Cyril and Mary were in the second class dining saloon at the time that the ship was hit. They returned to their E deck cabin to retrieve their son and Cyril made a second trip below for lifebelts. They did not expect to survive and took seats together on one of the upper decks. They sank with the ship according to Cyril and lost their son. Mary reported that they had jumped from the ship. The parents made it to an overturned lifeboat and were later rescued. Upon arrival in England they went to live in Kensington and Cyril joined the London Regiment. He was later commissioned into the 2nd Devonshire Regiment as a second lieutenant. According to the CWGC Mary was living in California after the war but later returned to Canada. Cyril is also commemorated on the

Soissons Memorial. The final point to make about Cyril Pells is that there are no clues to explain why his name is on the Stechford Memorial or any connection with Birmingham.

Private William Summers, aged 23, lived at 66, Victoria Road, Stechford. He was a member of 'B' company of the 1st Birmingham Pals when killed on July 23 1916 in the attack on Wood Lane on the Somme; 187 others were killed in the same operation. His mother twice appealed for news of her son in the 'Missing Soldiers' Bureau of the Birmingham Weekly Post but to no avail. His name is on the Thiepval Memorial. His service number is interesting as it was '14' which shows that he was amongst the first men to join the Pals. Two days before Private Summers' death, Private Cyril Willday died of wounds at the age of 23. He was killed in the 2nd Birmingham Pals and is buried in Dantzig Alley British Cemetery at Mametz. He probably died as a result of shellfire on a day when his battalion moved up to the line for their attack on Wood Lane on the following day. Cyril had lived at 190, Station Road, Stechford. Private T.Tams was in the 3rd Birmingham Pals when killed on September 3 1916 in their attack on Falfemont Farm on the Somme. He was aged 19 and his parents lived at 28, Northcote Road, Stechford. He lies buried in Delville Wood Cemetery at Longueval.

186, Church Road, Yardley. This was the home of Private Charles Alfred Vigurs of the 11th Battalion of the Royal Warwickshire Regiment. He was one of two men killed in the front line around Loos, near Lens , in France, on February 22 1917 at the age of 28. He was born in Birmingham on July 11 1888 and later became a keen gymnast at the Birmingham Athletic Institute on John Bright Street. He shared eighth place in a team event at the 1908 London Olympic Games and also shared a team bronze medal at the Stockholm games in 1912. In 1911 he was living with his parents at the Yardley address and was working as a stock keeper in the hardware trade. His father worked as a press tool maker. He had other international honours and had a preference for the 'horse'. He is buried in Maroc British Cemetery at Grenay.

13.

Northfield/Longbridge/Rubery

City Asylum, Rubery Hill. The City Council handed over the City Asylum at Rubery Hill, built in 1882, as a war hospital as well as the nearby Hollymoor Annexe. Rubery Hill became the 1st Birmingham War Hospital (Rednal) with its first patients arriving on July 30 1915. This hospital and Hollymoor nearby were managed by the War Hospitals Committee which answered to the Asylums Committee of the City Council. All existing patients were to be transferred to asylums outside the city. Fewer alterations were needed at Hollymoor as it was a more recent building. The main structural alteration at Rubery was the provision of two operating theatres on part of the former 'female airing court'. Colonel Barling became senior surgeon and Dr Suffern the administrator of both hospitals. The latter had arrived in 1889 and during the war was given the rank of Colonel. Miss Turner was matron at Rubery.

The hospital closed in the early 1990s and only the chapel, porter's lodge and the Medical Superintendent's house remain. The Superintendent's house is now called Leighton House and belongs to Headway, a private medical firm. A planning application was made in 2012 to turn the chapel into thirteen apartments. It was gutted by fire in 2000. The former hospital site is now known as Rubery Great Park and is a substantial residential area.

Hollymoor, Tessall Lane. Opened in 1905, became the 2nd Birmingham War Hospital (Northfield) with its first patients on July 5 1915 with initial accommodation for 640 patients. Later 946 beds were made available by erecting tents in the grounds. Patients would be brought from Rubery Station in motor ambulances and cars. Miss Buckingham became matron at Hollymoor. After January 1 1918 Hollymoor became the Birmingham Special Military Surgical Hospital for orthopaedic cases. Some of the earliest medical staff in this specialism were Americans. In December 1915 George Cadbury had provided the 'Beeches' as an auxiliary to the hospital with 40 beds at its height.

The Blackwell Recovery Hospital, near Bromsgrove, was used for convalescence and could look after 112 men. A Ladies Committee provided many extras, including a hut where two films a week were shown. The Tramways Committee, Aston Villa and Birmingham City Football Club gave the patients free tickets. At the end of the war Hollymoor became a Ministry of Pensions hospital.

21280 men passed through the gates of Hollymoor Hospital. They were not all totally happy. Sergeant J.H. Daly wrote to the Birmingham Post in September 1916 on behalf of Anzacs at the hospital. The medical treatment and nursing care were of the 'best' but there was a problem about 'freedom' – "the out of bounds being within a few yards of the fences and, from what I can gather, we have to thank those of days gone by for this. It seems they were allowed more freedom but did not know a good thing when they had it. They came in at all hours and also the worse for drink; consequently those of us who follow have to suffer through men of that description". It is not clear whether he was referring to earlier patients or inmates. The hospital closed in July 1994.

'History of Hollymoor Hospital'. Fay Crofts. Brewin. 1998.

Many of the hospital buildings still exist including the entrance building, the chapel (now called St Bartholomew's) and prominent water tower. Some of the buildings are used as a surgery, pharmacy and a nursery.

Herbert Austin's Longbridge motor works. He took over in 1905 and they were greatly extended during the war. In 1914 it employed 2638 people and made 882 cars each year. In wartime it made aeroplanes, ambulances, engines, shells, armoured cars and tanks under Government contracts. After initial uncertainty as the car market slumped the first Government order was for 700 wooden limber wagons and 200 horse-drawn ambulances. Small orders soon became a flood including a large order for motorised vehicles from the Russian Government (lorries, armoured cars, ambulances). In 1918 the West Works employed 5000 people on 18 pounder shells – this had been built between December 1916 and June 1917. The record shell production in a working day of 9½ hours here was 13000. Each day 1200 tons of steel arrived in two special trains, one of which took away a complete load of swarf. Tanks were made at the North Works until 1918.

The East Works made aero engines and complete aircraft. By March 1917 the South Works was making 5000 shells a week.

Herbert Austin had sacked six men in succession as head of his aircraft manufacturing department before hiring 23 year old John Dudley North in late 1915. With 100 men, many former crate-makers, he had prepared the initial order for RE7s. From late 1915 RE7 biplanes and RE8 planes were built. North left the firm in 1917. A large order which eventually led to 1550 SEs was made in 1918 with production averaging 30 a week. Between 1914 and 1918 the factory made 200 lorries, 500 armoured cars, 650 guns and ambulances and motor cycles for the War Office or the Ministry of Munitions. Over 8 million shells and 2000 aircraft had been manufactured. The expansion in production capacity was financed by the Ministry of Munitions. The Ministry also helped the purchase of 123 acres of farmland in June 1917 between the works and Longbridge which developed into the Longbridge Estate of 252 dwellings, mostly prefabricated wooden bungalows with materials from the USA. Amenities were provided in 1918 with a block of old farm buildings converted into a village hall and club rooms. There was also a steam laundry and a temporary Church of England Mission room. This 'garden suburb' project was designed to meet problems of recruitment into the expanding workforce.

In 1917 a circular flying ground was built at the top of Cofton Hill on 73 acres of waste ground south of the works, which was levelled to remove bumps. This was next to Rednal and just on the other side of the Lickey road and north-east of Cofton Hackett Park. After the war it became a test track for cars. By 1918 the factory employed 21000, many of whom were women. Belgian refugee workers had also been employed. At the beginning of that year 10000 workers staged a four day strike over their bonus scheme and the failure to give aircraft workers the same pay rise awarded to other munitions workers. They also thought that the Works Committee chairman, Arthur Peacock, was being victimised. On October 19 1917 Zeppelin L42 dropped a bomb on the works which damaged the end of an outlying building and injured two people.

Herbert Austin's only son, Vernon, died as a result of injuries at La Bassee on January 26 1915; he was a lieutenant in 34 Brigade, Royal Field Artillery. Vernon was a keen motor car racer and was due to sail for Russia for a race when war broke out. He landed in France on August 17 1914. Although he was killed by a sniper his body was, unusually, brought back to England and buried with full military honours at St Martin's Church Canterbury. The headmaster of King's School, Canterbury, which he had attended, officiated.

The church has a plaque presented by Austin employees which reads "This tablet was erected in memory of a brave soldier by the employees of the Austin Motor Company of Birmingham, London and Manchester". His original grave marker is in the King's School Memorial Chapel and he is also commemorated at Moseley Rugby Club. In October 1918 Herbert's eldest daughter, Irene married a young Australian army officer, Captain Arthur Waite. Herbert himself was knighted at Buckingham Palace on 27 September 1917. Albert Ball VC, the air ace, had been an apprentice at Austin until 1914 where his father was a director. He may have persuaded the firm to take up the idea of a single-seat fighter but it did not reach the production stage.

The Manor House, Bristol Road, Northfield. This was the family home of George Cadbury (1839-1922) who was the son of the founder of the firm of Cadburys of Bournville. He was a manufacturer and social reformer. As a Quaker pacifist George had already opposed the Boer War and taken up Lloyd George's suggestion to buy the Daily News for £40000 in order to influence public opinion. The outbreak of the First World War led to a crisis of conscience for him. It was a test of conformity to the beliefs of the Society of Friends. He had seen the Boer War as unjust but whilst he acknowledged that the causes of the war were complex and there were faults on the British side German aggression was mainly responsible and needed to be 'crushed'. On the other hand he remained a strong believer in peace. The issue was made more urgent because his three sons were all young adults. Egbert, known as 'Bertie', born 1893, immediately left his roots behind and signed up as an able seaman with the Navy where he worked on minesweepers, initially on the yacht 'Zarifa' loaned to the Navy by his friends, the Garnetts. He had joined with seven other men of the First Trinity Boat Club of Cambridge University where he was studying law. His brother, Norman, was working as an engineer for the Electrical Mechanical Brake Company in West Bromwich. He was later head of the firm which manufactured shell components and, later, gears and track links for tanks.

Only the third and eldest son, Laurence, remained true and followed his father's wishes and became one of the forty three volunteers who went out to France with the Friends' Ambulance Unit after training in Buckinghamshire. They began service at Dunkirk in late October 1914 and then Ypres. Later, in the same unit, he became responsible for eighty vehicles in Flanders. He served throughout the war. He received the Croix de Guerre and the OBE. In 1919 Laurence became managing director of Cadburys. Their sisters also did war-related work. Molly trained as a nurse at Queen's

Hospital and later worked in a military hospital in France. She married William Greeves, a Northern Irishman serving with the Friends' Ambulance Unit. Dolly worked as a nurse at the Fircroft Working Men's College in Selly Oak which became a war hospital.

In 1915 Egbert joined the Royal Naval Air Service and became a major by the end of the war with the DSC and DFC. His work involved the interception of Zeppelins as they crossed the North Sea. He shot down L48 when flying a Sopwith Pup on June 16/17 1917. He also escaped a crash into the North Sea off Norfolk with minor injuries when he lost control after his goggles had slipped. In a letter to his father dated August 6 1918 he reported how his 'lucky star' had worked. He was at a concert with his wife when he heard that three Zeppelins had been sighted fifty miles north-east of Great Yarmouth. Only one plane was available so he rushed to the airfield in his Ford car, picked up clothing and 'took a running jump into the pilot's seat' of a DH4 and beat a competing fellow pilot. His gunner, Captain Bob Leckie, shot down one of the three Zeppelins. It was L70 and among those killed was Peter Strasser, the head of the German Airship Service. L70 was a long range zeppelin with six engines and the raid may have been a practice for an attack on New York. This was the last Zeppelin attack on Britain. He had downed his first Zeppelin in November 1915.

Some of the activities of the elderly George Cadbury during the war can be identified. He had faced hostile attacks in the 'warlike press' in the autumn of 1914. In a letter it criticised them because "for years they have been threatening Germany and writing sensational articles as to the preparations we should make for a German attack. They have thus played into the hands of the German Jingoes". His family letters were largely concerned with the expedients for helping the sick and wounded and avoiding the war's controversies and passions. This did not stop a visit from a detective in November 1916 who asked to see his cheque book. Cadbury told him that he was not ashamed to show him as he gave away three-fourths of his income. He regarded such activity as a threat to liberty. He had already switched his financial support from the Liberal Party to the Independent Labour Party which was anti-war. He had also helped to form the Union of Democratic Control in 1914 with E.D Morel, Charles Trevelyan, Ramsay MacDonald and others. It was critical of secret diplomacy and restrictions on civil liberties and opposed conscription. In October 1915 he was listed as one of the Vice-Presidents of the Armenian refugee fund of the Lord Mayor of London. Three months later the appeal talked about 'atrocities in Armenia'.

In January 1917 the Cadbury Brothers gave £500 to the Friends' War Victims Relief Fund. The same month he supported one of his favourite causes with £100 to the Strength of Britain Movement which wanted 'one more Big Push' to prohibit the liquor traffic. Before the war George Cadbury had constructed a barn like building in the grounds of The Manor which could seat 700 people. Every summer he provided food and entertainment for about 25000 children annually from the poorer parts of the city. George Cadbury died at the Manor House on October 24 1922. He was worth about £32 million in modern terms.

His second wife, Elizabeth (1858-1951), was an important figure in her own right. She came from the affluent Quaker family of Taylor from London and married George Cadbury in 1888. She was an active welfare worker and philanthropist with particular interests in education, youth work and the welfare of women. She was an active pacifist when the war broke out and became the first chair of the Peace and International Relations Committee of the National Council of Women. She also chaired the Peace and Arbitration Committee of the International Council of Women from May 1914. In the days just before the war she sent telegrams on their behalf to Asquith and Grey urging neutrality. In January 1916 she went to London for the annual meeting of the Society of Friends. The most important issue was the position of Quakers of military age faced with conscription. Elizabeth felt that the 'conscience' clause was a breakthrough and afterwards found it difficult to accept the refusal in the name of Quakerism of non-combatant service by Friends called up. Part of the 1916 meeting was disrupted by members of the Anti-German Union who accused a speaker, Charles Roden Buxton, a former Liberal MP and one of the founders of the UDC, of being a pro-German traitor. Mr Richard Glover shouted out "You know that the money of Mr George Cadbury is paying you, you dirty little boys and cowards".

The Belgian government honoured her in 1918 for her work with refugees in Birmingham. She was a member of the Executive which planned for the reception and care of Belgian refugees arriving in the city. She chaired the Allocation Committee which interviewed families and found them homes. She later took the chair of the Committee which looked after the Serbian refugee boys for which she later received the Serbian Red Cross of Honour. Years later she met twelve of the 'boys' in Belgrade. With other women she pressed for the inclusion of women's issues at the post-war Versailles conference. In late 1919 she was elected to the City Council.

'The Life of George Cadbury'. A.G Gardiner. Cassell.

'Elizabeth Cadbury 1858-1951'. Richenda Scott. Harrap. 1955.

Dame Elizabeth Cadbury died in 1951 at the Manor House. Two years later it was sold to Birmingham University who developed the site as a hall of residence. In 2007 the University sold it and the building became derelict despite a local campaign to save it. Some of the grounds are now Manor Farm Park.

St Laurence Church, Church Road, Northfield. The organ was given in 1937 by Lord and Lady Austin in memory of their son who was killed in the First World War. The organ was rebuilt in 1983. There is only one First World War burial in the adjacent churchyard, that of Major Frederick William Lister MC. He died on February 24 1919 at the age of 26. Frederick had originally served in the Queens Own Worcestershire Hussars (Worcestershire Yeomanry) as a private but was later commissioned into the 1st Battalion of the Tank Corps. His Military Cross was reported in the London Gazette on December 2 1918 and referred to a time when he was a Temporary Captain at Beaucourt-en-Santerre on August 8 1918. Its citation stated that the award was for "gallantry in leading his tanks into action and personally directing them to their objectives up to the moment of their engaging the enemy. Throughout two actions (August 8 and 23) he was on foot with his tanks and showed an absolute disregard for personal safety".

He was born in Northfield as the son of Wooldridge Lister, a wholesale jeweller in gold. In 1901 the family was living at 43, Woodland Road, Northfield; there were three sisters, one brother and a live in servant. In 1911 Frederick was living at The Cottage, Church Road, Northfield, with his widowed mother. He was working as a manufacturer's clerk. He is also commemorated on the Bexhill-on-Sea, Sussex, war memorial which is on the seafront as his parents had once lived at 20, Marine Mansion there.

Longbridge House, Northfield. Arthur Elia Impey was born here on April 29 1885, the son of Frederic and Eleanor Impey. In 1874 Frederic and Eleanor and their first child, Frederic, moved to Longbridge, Worcestershire from Edgbaston. Here he renovated an old moated farm-house in Longbridge Lane, originally called Longbridge House, which now became known as Longbridge Place, less than a mile from and east of both the railway and the road to Bristol. Unlike the area today the house was surrounded by countryside. After improvements the house had fourteen bedrooms. Arthur was the youngest of seven children. In 1891 their comfortable middle class lifestyle was emphasised by the tennis court and croquet lawn in the grounds where the gardens were four acres in extent.

His father was a partner and managing director of White and Pike, a Birmingham printing firm which had a works in Moor Street. In 1894 the firm built a new 'out of town' factory where Longbridge Lane joined the Bristol Road but within a year, however, it had burned down in a devastating fire. The site was purchased by Herbert Austin in 1906 for his motor vehicle business.

Captain Arthur Impey of the Royal Field Artillery

Both of Arthur's parents were Quakers so it was not surprising that Arthur was sent, between 1898 and 1901, to attend Bootham School, York. At some point after leaving Bootham School Arthur qualified as an accountant with Impey, Cudworth and Co of Birmingham. In 1910 Frederic Impey left Longbridge Place and the family moved, now reduced 'in fortune', to a smaller house, 'The Island', in nearby West Heath. Longbridge Place did not survive much longer for it was demolished in 1937 and a housing estate built on the site.

On September 28 Arthur was appointed to a Regular Army Special Reserve Commission in the Royal Field Artillery. On July 12 1915 he embarked from Southampton for the Western Front and on August 27 he was posted to 78th Brigade, RFA. It is likely that Arthur's first major test of action was at Hooge in the Ypres Salient from July 30-August 9 1915. We know from his diary that on July 1-3 1916 he saw action at Fricourt as the Somme battle opened. When his battery crossed the 'old Somme' battlefield in 1918 he passed familiar places. In October/November 1916 Arthur's battery was in the Thiepval, River Ancre, Grandcourt area during the final stages of the Battle of the Somme. His six week stay in his battery position was still 'the worst six weeks of my life'.

On April 28 1917 Impey was admitted to Hospital with PUO (pyrexia of unknown origin – a fever) but rejoined his unit on May 25. On July 1 1917 he was posted to 'A' Battery' of 79th Brigade, RFA from 78th Brigade. In September 1917 he had an accident in a dugout at his battery position in the Arras sector when, in the darkness, he slipped on the steps of his dugout and fell down to the bottom. It meant a fractured fibula and a return to England for a protracted recovery.

On August 15 1918, about to return to France, Arthur began his war diary which was to cover the last phase of the war which took his battery across the old Somme battlefield, south of Cambrai towards the Forest of Mormal, which involved crossing the Canal du Nord, the St Quentin Canal and the rivers Selle and Sambre. On September 29 he had gone forward with two batteries and he recorded what he found at Gauche Wood....

> "On entering the wood it became beastly, the nastiest sight I have ever seen. The trench was shelled all to pieces and the bottom and sides was composed entirely of the shattered and decomposing remains of men, all of them ours, lying as they had died. For 500 yards one could hardly take a step without treading on them. Good shooting by the Huns and, as the trench was in direct enfilade, it must have been hell to hold and was our front line of two days ago."

On October 9 he witnessed civilian scenes at Selvigny....

> ".....hundreds of old men and old women, young women and children, were flocking into the street, tricolours come from heaven knows where, were hanging from the windows of nearly every house. All were chattering, laughing, occasionally cheering, and passing round us, asking so many questions and so quickly that it was impossible to understand. Bunches of flowers were produced and given to everyone, the men grinning and making friends in the way peculiarly their own. I felt excited and happy and wondered where the devil the Hun had got to and what I had better do next. Then two men came up to me very excited and told me the curee 'veut beaucoup parlez a un officer Anglais'. So I was led away up a street towards the church, where stood a grimy unshaved, cheery old man in a cassock beaming through horn spectacles. He came up to me, pursed my hands, thanked me, blessed the British army, and said a lot of nasty things about the Bosch."

On November 11 1918 he informed the men from his battery on parade that the war was over. In his diary he wrote....

> "No news first thing so after breakfast I wandered into the village and met some of 17 Div Infantry marching back. I asked them where they were going to and someone said 'Home'. They looked rather happy and I wondered if it could be true – Then an extraordinarily relieved and happy looking Brigadier trotted along. I asked him if it meant Peace. He said 'Yes, I've just been talking to the Corps, its official'. So I went back to the battery and told Serjeant Major to fall the men in, in the orchard. They all seemed to know what it was and fell in a hollow square, grinning and expectant. Just as I was going to tell them an orderly appeared with a message which said 'Hostilities will cease at 11.00 hours' so I read that – Nothing much happened. They cheered, not wildly. We all felt it to be

so very unusual and in a short time they were back at work cleaning harness and guns and grooming the horses. After lunch I rode over to call on Mac who was in a comfortable Estaminet, a mile the other side of the village. A cheery crowd there, Straafer, Torrence and One and we played bridge – A quiet evening and early to bed."

In March 1919 he was released from the army. He probably joined Morland and Impey, his brother's firm, in the same year. By the early 1920s he had become managing director of Societe Anonyme des Etablissements Kalamazoo in Paris, a subsidiary company. Impey appears to have lived in France for all of the inter-war period until the German invasion of May 1940 made flight inevitable.

On September 26 1926, aged 41, Arthur married Lillian Cotton, an American painter, at St Jean de Luz in France. In January 1932 'Boiling Pot', the Kalamazoo works magazine, reported that the firms's works in France had moved to a modern factory at the end of 1930 in the south Paris suburbs. In May 1940 with the fall of France imminent Arthur left Paris for Bordeaux and England. On July 25 1940 he enrolled into 2nd Battalion of the Buckinghamshire Home Guard and in 1942 was promoted to the rank of Lieutenant-Colonel. When peace came in 1945 he resumed contact with the French firm as a director but continued to live in Britain. In 1946 he married again.

In February 1953 Arthur became chairman of Kalamazoo Ltd of Northfield when his brother retired. It was to be a short chairmanship because in October 29 1954 Arthur Impey died after a short illness, aged 69. He had lived for some time at 'The Old House', Guilsborough, Northamptonshire. His gravestone still stands alongside those of four other members of the family in Cofton Hackett churchyard.

Longbridge House is now the site of Greenlands Club.

The full text of Captain Arthur Impey's diary with analysis and his biography can be found on the 'Hellfire Corner' web site under the title 'Open Warfare'. The original diary is in the archives of the Library.

14.
Hagley Road/Bearwood/ Quinton

Plough and Harrow. A blue plaque records the short stay of J.R.R Tolkien, author of 'The Hobbit' and 'The Lord of the Rings'. who stayed there on Saturday June 3 1916 with his new bride, Edith Bratt. This was just before he left for the front. They had been married in a Catholic church in Warwick on March 22 1916. Before the war he attended Exeter College, Oxford University. In 1915 he joined the Lancashire Fusiliers and trained with their 3rd Reserve Battalion on Cannock Chase from mid-October 1915; he returned to one of the Chase camps between April and June 1918. On June 4 1916 he left for France with their 11th Battalion as a Second Lieutenant and the Signalling Officer. He was not involved on the first day of the Somme but was part of the attack on Ovillers on July 14 and a later attack on the Schwaben Redoubt. On October 27 1916 he fell ill with trench fever and on November 8 arrived in England on his way to the 1st Southern General Hospital in Birmingham a day later. He probably left the hospital in early December that year. His second medical board was held at the hospital on January 23 1917. He never returned to the front and did not fully recover with recoveries and relapses as he was moved from camp to camp on home service.

Two of his three close friends in the TCBS (Tea Club and Barrovian Society) from King Edward's in 1911 were killed by the end of the war. One was Robert Quilter Gilson, the son of the Headmaster of King Edward's School from 1900 to 1929; Robert was killed in action in July 1916. Another was Thomas Kenneth Barnsley, nicknamed 'Teacake', the son and grandson to two leading building contractors in Birmingham, both called John Barnsley. His father had been a longstanding member of the Volunteers and commanded the 1/5 Royal Warwicks at the outbreak of the war; a Territorial unit based at Thorp Street. Brigadier Sir John Barnsley did not see active service because of his age but became the Chief Recruiting Officer in Birmingham. His son was killed near Ypres in July 1917 whilst serving in the Coldstream Guards. He was a man of 'brilliant wit' and from Cambridge hoped to be a Wesleyan minister. Tolkien himself died on November 29 1971 and was buried in Oxford.

'Tolkien and the Great War. The Threshold of Middle Earth'. John Garth. Harper Collins. 2004.

St Philip's Grammar School. The editorial in the school magazine, 'Pietas' in the autumn of 1914 stated… "It is a particular pleasure to be able to record that one of our Old Boys went to the recruiting office on the first day of the war; and that another, with a defect in eyesight, would not take 'No' till he had been rejected six times; and that five of the last eight Captains of the School have joined the colours. Here are men and youths who, seeing before them a rare opportunity of doing a thing out of the common, demanding energy and enterprise with self-sacrifice, and involving risk of life and limb; and the opportunity of doing their country service such as comes but once in a hundred years, have seized it cheerfully, and careless of consequences, knowing only that circumstances being as they were, it was simply the best choice within their reach. These worthy 'saints' do not want our panegyrics; they avoid heroics on their own part; but we have a right to be proud of them".

Amongst those who served were Bill Slim and J.R.R Tolkien. Alfred Knight VC had attended the school between 1900 and 1903. In January 1918 he was given a civic reception and was presented to a large crowd in Victoria Square. He then visited his old school which was bedecked in the flags of the Allies and red, white and blue streamers. He was given a certificate and a clock. Early in the war encouraging letters arrived from the Archbishop of Birmingham and by the autumn of 1915 more than 160 Old Boys had joined the army. Mr Walsh, a Mathematics master joined up and was later killed in action. During the war a digging squad was formed which grew vegetables in a field at Vernon Road.

By the end of the war about 400 Old Boys had served in the forces with forty gaining commissions. Thirty-eight Old Boys and one master did not return. Private Vincent Reeve, aged 19, was killed on June 15 1916 whilst serving with the 2nd City Battalion on the Arras front. He came from Kings Heath.

Private George Beefy, aged 26, was serving with the 99th Field Ambulance of the RAMC when killed on November 2 of the same year. He left a wife, Lilian, at Kings Norton. Corporal Gerald Gascoyne, aged 20, was killed on July 16 1916 whilst serving in the 5th Ox and Bucks. He had lived in Moseley. His older brother, Francis, died on March 22 1918 whilst serving with the 11th Royal Warwicks in France. He was a subaltern. Private William McPike from Handsworth had joined the 1/6 Royal Warwicks under-age early in the war and was only 19 when killed on April 16 1917 near Epehy. Gunner Reginald Ives, 20, from Bearwood was killed on August 16 1918 with 'B' Battery of 311th Brigade, Royal Field Artillery.

'A History of St Philip's from beginning to beginning'. Margaret Worsley. 1997.

Quinton Municipal Cemetery, Halesowen Road. Lance Corporal George Onions VC lies buried here. The medal was won in the service of the 1/Devons at Achiet-Le-Petit in 1918. He died at his home on the Hagley Road in 1944. George Onions only lived in Birmingham in later life although his father had lived in Edgbaston at an unknown date and was an iron and steel merchant in the city. He was born in Bilston on March 2 1883, the son of Zacary and Amy Onions. In 1891 he was living at Stalybridge. He attended West Monmouthshire Grammar School, Pontypool, and became an apprentice steelmaker. This was after giving up plans to become a mining engineer after a short spell at Pirpentwys Colliery at the time of a serious mine accident. On the 1901 census he is recorded as an assistant to an analytical chemist at Abersychan in Monmouthshire. In 1904 he emigrated to Australia and three years married Florence in Brisbane. A son, George, was born in 1909; he died in 1932.

Having returned at an unknown date he later enlisted at Sale, Cheshire, where he lived at Cranford Avenue, and served in the 3rd Hussars Reserve regiment and the 3rd King's Own Hussars which were cavalry regiments. He saw service in the Easter Rising in Dublin in 1916. At some point he was attached to the 1/Devons in Belgium and France and by August 1918 was a lance-corporal. He was awarded the Victoria Cross for an act of heroism at Achiet-Le-Petit on the Somme on August 22 1918. The citation in the London Gazette on December 14 stated… "having been sent out with one man to get in touch with the battalion on the right flank, he observed the enemy advancing in large numbers to counter-attack the positions gained on the previous day. Realising his opportunity, he boldly placed himself with his comrade on the flank of the advancing enemy and opened rapid fire when the target was most favourable. When the enemy was about 100 yards from him the line wavered and some hands were seen to be thrown up. Lance Corporal Onions then rushed forward and, with the assistance of his comrade, took about 200 of the enemy prisoners and marched them back to his company commander. By his magnificent courage and presence of mind he averted what might have been a very dangerous situation".

He was later commissioned into the Rifle Brigade. On February 22 1919 a large crowd turned out at Sale Town Hall to greet their hero. He was presented with a gold watch, a cheque for £185 and a framed address from the local council. His wife was given a gold brooch displaying the crest of her husband's regiment. After the war he served as a Major in the Auxiliary Division of the Royal Irish Constabulary which existed from 1920-2. During the following period he was a publicity agent for the Colliery Guardian Company, who published a journal, in London. In 1929 he attended the VCs dinner hosted by the Prince of Wales at the House of Lords. In 1936 he moved to Birmingham and in 1939 became a captain in the Royal Defence Corps attached to the Warwicks but resigned in 1941 because of ill health. He had helped to set up this unit before it was absorbed into the regular army; in September 1938 it had about 200 trained veterans of the First World War. He died on April 2 1944 in Dudley Road Hospital after complications from a motor accident a few weeks earlier. He was then living at 4, Hagley Court, Hagley Road and was a member of the South Staffordshire Home Guard at Bilston.

Birmingham Biography 1944. Library of Birmingham.

Bourne College. Once stood in Spies Road, Quinton. It was a minor private school with a Primitive Methodist basis. Originally in Summer Lane it moved to the countryside and the new building opened in 1882. It attracted some local pupils otherwise they came from all over Britain and the world. The College closed in 1928 and the buildings were acquired by the Birmingham Guardians who renamed it Quinton Hall and used it as a home for aged men. In July 1921 a marble plaque was unveiled after a public subscription. It commemorated thirty College boys who died in the Great War. One of those named was Second Lieutenant Ewart Richards who died of wounds in No 10 CCS near Kemmel on May 11 1918 whilst serving in the 10th Warwicks. He was 27 and came from West Bromwich where his parents were living at the time of his death. He had been educated at Bourne and before the war was working at the Wednesbury branch of Lloyds Bank. He had originally joined the 3rd City Battalion in October 1914 and had gone to the front with them. In 1917 he returned home for officer training and returned to another battalion in January 1918.

170 other former pupils served in the forces. The memorial was later moved to the Methodist Chapel in College Road nearby. All that remains of Quinton Hall are two landmark pine trees which stand on the Chantry estate on the site. They were planted for the coronation of George V in 1911. The Hall was demolished in 1978. The memorial disappeared when the chapel was demolished to make way for the M5 motorway. At the beginning of this century the Quinton Local History Society campaigned for a new memorial which was unveiled by Carl Chinn in the Quinbourne Centre on June 30 2001.

Article in the Birmingham Historian 2001. Quinton Local History Society website.

The building was demolished in the early 1980s and the site was redeveloped for residential use.

11, Bissell Street, Quinton. Lance Serjeant Horace Hadley family home. The Quinton church magazine in September 1916 identified him as 'the first Quinton young man to lay down his life for King and Country'. He was aged 20 and the son of Frank and Lydia Hadley. The family had been at the same address since 1901. In 1901 his father was a bricklayer's labourer but ten years later was a baker and provision dealer. Horace in 1911 worked in the manufacture of ship lamps. He was also born in Quinton. He had an older brother, Frank, and two sisters, Maud and Dorothy. He was killed on July 19 1916 in the 2/6 Warwicks attack at Fromelles. He is commemorated on the Loos Memorial. By early 1915 over 150 men from Quinton parish had volunteered and at Christmas 1916 350 servicemen from the parish received gifts and cards.

Many of the neighbouring terraced houses have survived but No 11 has been redeveloped for modern housing.

Christ Church, Quinton. During the war the rector was the Reverend W.A Rowlands. Many years later it was noted that, in addition to his clerical duties, he was one of team of four clergymen "who worked on a lathe turning shells at a munitions factory and acting as special constable, postman and even grave-digger in what was then largely a rural parish". As a true patriot he believed that 'the successful prosecution of the war had to come before everything else'. He devoted three days or nights each week to making shells. His curate, Reverend J.Sweetman, did the same. Rowlands' predecessor before 1912 was the Reverend C.R Martyn who spent almost four years in France as an army chaplain and was twice mentioned in despatches. He died of pneumonia in March 1919. Inside the church there is a memorial plaque with 73 names.

There is also a marble plaque to Private Charles Parish of the 15th Royal Warwicks who was killed near High Wood on the Somme on July 23 1916, aged 38. He enlisted in the first month of the war and is commemorated on the Thiepval Memorial. He had been a solicitor. His parents lived at The Hollies, Halesowen. There are a small number of war graves in the churchyard. One belongs to Sapper William Grove of the Inland Waterways and Docks branch of the Royal Engineers who died on August 25 1918 aged 41. His wife, Mary, lived at 14, College Road, Quinton. He probably did not see overseas service.

'Quinton' by Bernard Taylor. Tempus. 2004.

141, Poplar Avenue, Bearwood.

Was the family home of Second Lieutenant Herbert James M.C VC, Birmingham's first such award in the Great War and also the first for his Regiment. Although he was not living there according to the 1911 Census his parents, Walter, 60, and Emily, 57, were there with their daughters, Eveline, 25 a teacher, and Beatrice, 22, a clerk. Walter James was Coventry born and worked as an 'engraver jeweller' with his own business in Warstone Lane. He was married in 1883. Ten years earlier, the family, including 13 year old Herbert, were living at 76, Three Shires Oak Road, Smethwick. His sister Doris, 5, was also listed. Herbert was noted as Birmingham born. They were at the same address in 1891. Herbert was born on November 30 1888 and attended Smethwick Central School and for a short time worked as a teacher at Bearwood Road and Brasshouse Lane Schools. On April 13 1909 he joined the 21st Lancers as a trooper and was sent to Egypt. He continued his studies and won several prizes for languages.

He was in India when the war broke out with the rank of Lance Corporal. He obtained a commission and was posted to the 4/Worcesters. On March 22 1915 he embarked with his regiment for Gallipoli where he landed on W Beach on April 25. He was soon wounded in the head and spent six weeks in a Malta Hospital. He was to win the Victoria Cross for an attack on Gully Ravine on the Gallipoli peninsula on June 28 and July 3 1915. The citation stated… "For most conspicuous bravery during the operations in the Southern Zone of the Gallipoli Peninsula. On the 28th June 1915, when a portion of a Regiment had been checked owing to all the officers being put out of action, Second Lieutenant James, who belonged to a neighbouring unit, entirely on his own initiative gathered together a body of men and led

Neville Chamberlain, the Lord Mayor, honours Second Lieutenant Herbert James VC. in December 1915

them forward under heavy shell and rifle fire. He then returned, organised a second party and again advanced, His gallant example put fresh life in the attack. On the 3rd July, in the same locality, Second Lieutenant James headed a party of bomb throwers from the Worcesters up a Turkish communication trench and, after nearly all his bomb throwers had been killed or wounded, he remained alone at the head of the trench and kept back the enemy single-handed till a barrier had been built behind him and the trench secured. He was throughout exposed to a murderous fire". For the first event he was acting as a liaison officer to the 5/Royal Scots and for the second event he was one of four of thirty men unwounded.

He was invested with the decoration by King George V at Buckingham Palace on January 15 1916. It was published in the London Gazette on September 1 1915 at which time his address was given as Poplar Avenue. Two days later Mr Harris at Bearwood Road School wrote in the school log book – "Proud to record that Lieutenant Herbert James, an old soldier and teacher in this school, has been awarded the Victoria Cross for most conspicuous bravery". A half day holiday was given to celebrate. His portrait was displayed in other local schools. James had been wounded in the foot in Gallipoli on the night of September 25/26 and went, firstly to Cairo, and finally arrived at Southampton on sick leave on November 15 1915. After treatment at a London hospital he returned to Birmingham on Saturday November 27; coincidentally he arrived at New Street on the same train as Private Arthur Vickers, 2/Warwicks, who had an excited reception for his VC at Loos. Reporters went to Poplar Avenue but James turned down interviews.

On Saturday December 11 the Lord Mayor, Neville Chamberlain, presented a framed resolution from the City Council in a ceremony in Victoria Square. His mother attended the event. On Monday December 20 he was guest of honour at the Christmas Dinner of the Smethwick Teachers' Association at the Blue Gates Hotel, Smethwick. Some of the ladies asked him to sign their menus. On December 22 he returned to Bearwood Road School where he was given a presentation. Mr G.H Harris, the headteacher, recorded in his log book – "A red letter day in the history of the school. Lieutenant Herbert James VC, who for nearly twelve years was a scholar and teacher at this school, was presented by the teachers of the three departments with a sword of honour as a token of esteem and in honour of his being awarded the Victoria Cross... The Mayoress (Mrs Ryder) made the presentation and the gathering included the scholars of this school, the teachers of all departments and some of the leading citizens of Smethwick... ...The gathering and presentation were unique in the annals of Smethwick and the ceremony lasted from 3 to 4 p.m". Harris pointed out that "It is true that Lieutenant James first saw the light in Birmingham...and that, therefore, Birmingham claims him as their VC. But so far as that goes Birmingham have only got his birth certificate". Once again he said little himself but did hope that if there was another war the boys would "follow the example of those who had gone without having to be fetched".

Herbert James returned to the front in March 1916 as a company commander in the 1/Worcesters but was wounded on the Somme in July 1916 in an attack on Contalmaison. He was sent to two different hospitals in England. During the recovery period on September 5 he married Gladys Lillicrap at Stoke Deverel church in Devonport. A son, Anthony, later followed.

On May 1 1917 he was awarded the Croix de Guerre at a time when he had returned to active service. On August 18 1917 he was promoted to a GSO3 staff post as a captain. In April 1918 he was promoted again to Brigade Major. In 1918 he was mentioned in despatches on May 20 and awarded the Military Cross on October 16 for an action near Amiens when serving in the 1/Worcs. He was also mentioned in despatches on December 20. When the war ended he remained in the army. On June 26 1920 he attended the VC party at Buckingham Palace and on November 11 the same year he was part of the Honour Guard for the burial of the Unknown Soldier in Westminster Abbey. Just before Christmas 1920 he joined the East Lancashire Regiment as a Captain and Brevet Major before entering the Staff College and serving as a Staff Captain at the War Office.

With failing health, most probably as a result of his wartime head wound, he was placed on the retired list in March 1930. He separated from his first wife and remarried to a woman named Jessie on November 26 1929. In the late 1920s he transferred to the York and Lancaster Regiment as a major. The circumstances of his death were tragic. He was found ill and starving in a flat at Brunswick Gardens, Kensington, by his landlord and died in hospital on August 15 1958. There were twenty-three oil paintings on the walls which he had been involved in buying and selling. He had lived there for 15 months and had suffered a seizure six days before he was found. He was living the life of a recluse and his landlord was astonished to find clues to his VC after his death. His funeral at Kensal Green Cemetery was attended by General Sir Richard Gale, Deputy Supreme Allied Commander in Europe and Colonel of the Worcestershire Regiment, and other dignitaries. When he died his son, Anthony, was a major serving with the Worcestershire Regiment in the West Indies. In June 2008 his VC was sold for £211000 to a private collector.

Smethwick Heritage Centre Web site – Heroes of Smethwick.

'VCs of the First World War – Gallipoli'. Stephen Snelling. Alan Sutton. 1995.

144, Poplar Avenue, Bearwood.

This road is off Sandon Road, Bearwood. A blue plaque commemorates the house as the pre-war home of 'Bill' Slim (1891-1970), a Lieutenant in the 9th Warwicks, who was wounded at Gallipoli and served in Mesopotamia. In 1911 he was a 19 year old assistant teacher living at home with his father John, a commercial traveller in hardware, and his mother Charlotte. His Aunt Mary Tucker and one servant were also there. He is better known as the commander of the 14th Army in Burma in 1943-5.

Slim was born near Bristol on August 6 1891. In 1903 his family moved to Birmingham where his father set up as a hardware merchant and factor. He attended St Philip's Catholic Grammar School and, then, in 1908 transferred to King Edward's where he joined the OTC. He became a pupil teacher in an elementary school and then a junior clerk. In 1912 he enrolled in the University OTC as a lance corporal despite not being an undergraduate. He was offered a job with a Shell subsidiary to start on September 1 1914 but the war intervened. He was on holiday in Germany in July 1914 but left as the international situation deteriorated. On August 22 1914 he was gazetted as a second lieutenant in the 9th Warwicks. In June 1915 his battalion left England for Gallipoli. On August 9 he was wounded during the Anzac attack. He later recorded the details.

"At that moment something hit me hard between the shoulders like a huge, flat shovel….The blow pitched me heavily on my face but, after a dazed moment, I managed to sit up. I felt no pain and was surprised to see blood spurting from the point of my left shoulder and already spreading in a dark, damp patch over my jacket….I sat there wondering for a second and then Gregson, one of my two surviving officers, was kneeling beside me. The firing was heavier now, clapping just over our heads, and as Gregson leant towards me to speak, he suddenly slumped forward across my feet."

Slim was able to put his remaining subaltern in command and then his servant shuffled him sliding down the hill to an Aid post where he was bandaged with muslin wrapping from his topee. Lieutenant Slim was taken to a barge on the Anzac beach and then to a ship which sailed for Lemnos and then onwards on the hospital ship, 'Aquitania', bound for Southampton. There he was taken to the nearby Netley Hospital. The bullet had gone through his left shoulder and into his lung; he could easily have died at Netley at this point if the wrong surgical option had been taken.

In September 1916 he returned to his battalion now in Mesopotamia where he was to win the MC in February 1917. He was wounded in the right arm in March 1917 and sent to India where he saw out the rest of the war. He remained in the army after 1918 and by 1939 had risen to the rank of Brigadier who had commanded Gurkhas.

George Dixon School, City Road. Some member of the boys' school staff entered military service so Miss Davis became the first female teacher in 1915. Four more women had been appointed by the end of the war. During the war some boys went to special camps to help with fruit-picking. Second Lieutenant George H Smith, 8/Worcs, wrote from the front after Easter 1916 with thanks for a copy of 'The Crown', the school magazine. The editorial in the Easter 1916 issue was surprising for the time – "We have to record with inexpressible sadness more of our old boys who have made the final sacrifice. This brings home, even to the youngest of us, the horror of war. Our daily papers supply us with the brighter side of the picture, as a rule, and in their records of heroic deeds and daring exploits we are carried away from the tragedy. A glamour distorts our vision of things as they are".

Driver A.Chervas of the ASC had already written in February 1915 to the girls with thanks for a football. The girls' school magazine, 'The Magpie', made appeals for clothes and food parcels for Belgian refugees and the girls themselves did a great deal of knitting. In late 1915 Form 2B made 27 knitted articles. When news of the armistice came Mr Brown, the headmaster, took the whole school into St Germain's Church for a service of thanksgiving. When the boys returned the Union Jack was raised in the playground.

Post-war £500 was raised for a memorial to Old Dixonians who had fought and those who had fallen. About 400 staff and old boys served and 46 had died. Four of those who died had lived in Willow Avenue – Second Lieutenant Joseph Groutage, 22, had lived at 196; he was attached to the 61st Division HQ from the 2/5th Warwicks. He was killed on March 29 1918. Corporal Thomas Sturrock, 20, had lived at 187. He was killed in Salonika serving in 17th Brigade RFA Ammunition Column. The Cutler brothers lived at 112; they were both privates. Harold, 21, was killed on the first day of the Somme in the 1/6th Warwicks. His brother, Reginald, was 19 when killed in Belgium on April 13 1918 in the 3rd Coldstream Guards.

Two other sets of brothers also died. The Hunston brothers were both killed on the Somme in 1916 – Lieutenant John on July 15 in the 6/Bedfords and Second Lieutenant Robert on September 28 in the 7th/Bedfords. John was 20 and Robert a year older and they had lived at 32, Hallewell Road. The While brothers from 38, Station Road, Harborne, were both subalterns. Charles was killed on June 26 1916 in the 8th Warwicks and Frank on July 15 in the same year in the 1st Middlesex Regiment. Lieutenant John Holmes was killed two days before the war ended, aged 19, whilst serving in 15 Squadron RAF in France. He had lived at 41, Holly Lane, Smethwick. Private Hubert Pressly, 23, was serving in the 58th Australian Battalion when he was killed on January 23 1917. His parents lived at 40, Summerfield Crescent. Lance Corporal Bertram Wales, 30, had been a manual instructor at the school and was killed on July 23 1916 on the Somme whilst serving in the 14th Warwicks.

'100 Years at City Road. A History of the George Dixon Secondary School'. Laurence Reading and David Housley. 2006.

15.

Kings Norton/Brandwood End/ Selly Oak/Bournville

Cadbury's of Bournville. Became much more than cocoa and chocolate manufacturers when producing food for the war effort. 218 Cadbury workers were killed in the services of the 2148 that joined up. Thirty eight men became members of the Friends' Ambulance Unit. Unlike other great Birmingham firms the number employed at Bournville shrank during the war from 6800 to 4900. In 1914 the company manufactured 706 lines which by the end of 1915 had been reduced to 195. A major problem for the firm was the loss of its main source of sugar in Central Europe. At the end of the war about 1500 demobilised men returned to the firm. During the war the company had looked after the anxious dependents of its workforce who had enlisted. A married man would receive two-thirds of his pre-war wage and a single man one-third. £2171 was spent on gifts to war widows of Cadbury men and £354 was spent on food parcels for Bournville prisoners of war. Parcels of two or three books were sent out to serving men. Men were given the chance to state their book preferences. The top three were Rider Haggard, Conan Doyle and Jack London. Twice a year one pound of Mexican chocolate was sent in the parcel sent to every permanent employee.

Bournville girls also made comforts for serving men, often from their own department. For example, in December 1914 the Stock Office equipped all the men on two torpedo boats with woollen scarves. Also in 1915 seventy three girls at different times volunteered to do washing and laundry work for soldier patients at 'Fircroft' and 'The Beeches'. Three ceremonial reunions were held in the first year of peace. At the first one of 600 men George Cadbury declared that in future a peaceful spirit should make war impossible. Pre-war many employees had gained recognition by the St John Ambulance. Early on fourteen girl employees with ambulance training left to work as probationary nurses at the City Hospitals. Some eventually became sisters. During the war the Bournville Nursing Division was formed and led by Miss F.N Dunscombe. Some women did weekend duty at military hospitals – three at Highbury, four at Fircroft and two at Harborne Hall. Six did occasional work at the Snow Hill Rest Station.

Seventeen men who had attended ambulance classes at the works volunteered for service at the front despite being over military age. Other such men joined the St John Ambulance Brigade in the city and were mainly involved in conveying the wounded from the ambulance trains to hospitals. Some men and VAD nurses provided refreshments to the wounded passing through Snow Hill Station. For a short stop there was tea, cake and fruit. There were also various societies at the works which played a part on the home front. The Musical and Dramatic societies put on a large number of concerts and entertainments for local hospitals. The Camera Club gave help to the YMCA Snapshots from Home League by providing family photographs for sending to absent fathers, sons and brothers at the front. Forewomen supported a Belgian family – the De Haes. In 1916 Mr W.A Cadbury was part of a Friends' War Victims Relief Fund mission to Russia which led to support for refugees from evacuated areas of Poland and Lithuania.

'Bournville Works and the War 1914-1919'. Special number of the works magazine. Library of Birmingham.

Kings Norton Metal Company.

Was visited by the King on the first day of his visit to Birmingham – July 22 1915. 100000 Lee Enfield rifles were produced during the war by its workforce of about 2000. The firm also had a cartridge factory at Blackpole, Worcestershire. It had originally been a rolling mill plant founded in 1858. During the war the most dangerous processes were carried out in temporary buildings on nearby marshes. This firm before the war had been the first makers of six pounder shell cases for the Nordenfeldt gun. In 1920 the firm became Nobel Industries and from 1926 part of ICI. It closed on the site in 1932 and the plant moved to Witton.

The site is now the Kings Norton Business Centre with about eighty companies in 2007. A later road, Melchett Road, has been built through the site.

The Beeches, Bournville Lane, Selly Oak.

This house was used as a Red Cross Auxiliary Hospital. It was lent by George Cadbury rent free and opened on December 1 1915. 46 beds were later provided. It was staffed by

Northfield Red Cross and supported by Cadbury workers via weekly collections. It was known as Worcestershire VAD 22. In March 1918 the Red Cross took over full financial responsibility. Between 1918 and 1919 it was used for facial injuries. During its time as a hospital 982 patients were treated. Before the war the house and grounds had been used as an invalid home in the winter for Salvation Army officers and others and in the spring became a camp where children from the slums could enjoy a two week holiday. Thirty children stayed at a time.

The building survives and is now used as a management centre.

A hostel opened in Selly Oak. In May 1916 for Serbian refugees in a house loaned by Mrs Alfred Wiggin of Bordesley Hall, Alvechurch. She was the wife of a barrister and railway company director. Twenty-five boys were looked after following a hazardous journey. They were aged between 9 and 17 and were the sons of peasants. They had fled from the advancing Austrian army. One aged 11 had fallen in with a Serbian mountain battery that gave him a uniform and called him 'The General'. The boys were sent to the Bournville Village Schools and Kings Norton Secondary School. The exact address of the hostel is not known.

Elliot's Metal Works, Elliott Road, Selly Oak. This works manufactured, smelted and rolled metal namely copper, brass and 'yellow metal'. It was named in an article on 'Canteens for Munition Makers' in Edgbastonia in August 1915 where it was stated that "the canteen which many Edgbaston ladies have already associated themselves with is at Elliott's Metal Works, Selly Oak, and has been organised by Miss Ida Cameron Adams". The early initiative for factory canteens had begun with a Lady Lawrence early in the 1914. "It stands to reason that if our munition makers are to remain fit and well, they must be properly looked after as regards their food and nowhere can they obtain better and more wholesome refreshments than from a canteen specially established upon the premises where they are at work". Canteens were organised by local sub-committees of ladies with voluntary women helpers. The article also cited a canteen at the Birmingham Metal and Munitions Company, Landor Street, run by the Women's Volunteer Reserve; another at Messrs Thomas Smith and Co, Saltley, run by the British Women's Temperance Association; and at the BSA a canteen was run by the Birmingham and Midland Women's Suffrage Society. Such developments had more to do with worker efficiency than big-hearted paternalism. Lloyd George later remarked that it was "a strange irony that the making of weapons of destruction should afford the occasion to humanise industry".

'Edgbastonia' August 1915. Library of Birmingham.

Fircroft Working Men's College, Bristol Road, Selly Oak.

Originally the home of George Cadbury junior the college was founded in 1909 and was managed by the Works Hospital Committee at Cadburys. In September 1918 its work was changed from the care of wounded soldiers to discharged disabled soldiers and sailors. Matron Rose received the Royal Red Cross medal from the King.

It is now Fircroft College of Adult Education.

Broad Meadow House, Broad Meadow Lane, Kings Norton.

Was used to accommodate Belgian refugees.

St Nicholas Church, Kings Norton. The lych gate Great War memorial was erected in 1922 with 37 names. There are six CWGC graves of the Great War in the adjacent churchyard none of whom have a medal index card which suggests that they did not see overseas service. Private Archibald William Beaufoy died on May 3 1916 in the 5th Wiltshires in Mesopotamia. He may have been killed by the Turks or died from the conditions around Kut. He was buried in Amara War Cemetery. He was born in Wigston Parva Leicestershire, in 1891 and in 1911 was a groundsman on a golf links living with his widowed father, a gardener, a brother and two younger sisters at 90, Wychall Lane, Kings Norton. Private George Cogbill was killed on April 10 1918 whilst serving in the 3rd Worcs. He left a wife, Agnes, at 18, Camp Lane, Kings Norton; his parents lived at 19, Dell Road, Cotteridge. In 1911 his family, including two very young daughters, aged 2 and two months, were at the same address. He was working as a labourer in a screw works. He is also commemorated on the Ploegsteert Memorial.

Lieutenant Richard Reeve Emmens was killed on the Somme, aged 22, on September 4 1916 whilst serving as a member of a Trench Mortar Battery. He was buried in Caterpillar Valley Cemetery at Longueval. Post-war his widowed mother lived at 'Springthorpe', Redditch Road, Kings Norton. In 1911 he was living at the same house with his mother and stepfather, John Kerr, who was an accountant. There were also a stepbrother and two stepsisters and two servants. He was an articled clerk possibly in the same profession. Private Harold Latimer Posnette died of wounds in the 3rd

Birmingham Pals on the Somme and was buried in Heilly Station Cemetery at Mericourt L'Abbe. There were three Casualty Clearing Stations nearby. Private Edwin Reginald Keey, aged 30, was killed in the 1st Somerset Light Infantry on May 15 1918 and is buried at Mont-Bernanchon British Cemetery at Gonneheim. In 1911 he was still living with his family at The Redlands, 161, Northfield Road, Kings Norton and working as a printer's assistant. His father was the stationery superintendent in the Council House.

Driver James Bolstridge is named on the lych gate and on the Tramways Department Memorial at Kings Heath. He is buried in the churchyard behind the church with a CWGC headstone with a date of death of May 4 1917; he was 32. He left a wife, Emily, and two children at 42, Ripple Road, Stirchley; they were married in the church in July 1908. He may not have served at the front and was a member of 661st Horse Transport Company of the Army Service Corps based at Park Royal, London. He had enlisted on May 8 1915. In 1911 he was at the Ripple Road address and was working as a 'tramway motor man'.

16, Baldwin Road, Kings Norton. One of the names on the St Nicholas lych gate memorial is that of Corporal Joseph Oliver Lowe of the 2/Royal Fusiliers who was killed on October 25 1916 and is commemorated on the Thiepval Memorial. He was aged 20 and lived in Baldwin Road. A letter was found on his body with a request that it should be forwarded in the event of his death. It read – "My dearest Pa, Ma, Emily and Leslie – again I am called upon as a true soldier of dear England to advance and attack the enemy. I pray that Almighty God may protect me and save me from all harm......Dear folk at home, my heart burns with the pride of a soldier. I am trusting in our Heavenly Father to help me to play the man in this next engagement. I hope that some day we may all meet in Heaven. Best love to all from your loving son, Joe".

Letter cited on page 185 of 'King's Norton: A History' by George Demidowicz and Stephen Price. Phillimore. 2009.

This house still exists as part of a terrace.

Moundsley Hall, Walkers Heath Road, Kings Norton. Was the home of the wartime 'squire' of Kings Norton, Charles Pelham Lane. Built in the 1890s it was demolished in 1936 and a new building erected in its place. Lane's son, Lieutenant Commander Arthur Geoffrey Lane, died of illness on November 8 1918 when commanding HMS Assistance, a naval repair ship. He may have died at home or nearby because he was buried in St

Nicholas churchyard four days later. He was 35 years old. The family are commemorated by a stained glass window in the church.

The later building is now part of a large care home complex. The lodge at the entrance probably dates from the time of the squire.

Woodbrooke Quaker Study Centre, 1046, Bristol Road.

This institution is linked to Alfred Barrett Brown who came to lecture there in 1912. The substantial 'Georgian style' house was built by Josiah Mason and sold to George Cadbury in 1881. The latter later moved to the Manor House and in 1903 gave Woodbrooke as a Quaker study centre which it still is today.

Alfred Barrett Brown was born at Headingley, Leeds, in 1888, the son of Alfred Kemp Brown and Emma his wife. He had two older sisters and in 1891 his father was working as a private tutor. The family was prosperous with a governess and a live in servant. At that time they were living at 19, East Shrubbery at Westbury on Trym near Bristol. Ten years later the family were living at 11, Exeter Buildings, Bristol. His father was now described as a private

Two of the leaders of the No Conscription Fellowship from Birmingham. On the left Will Chamberlain and on the right Alfred Barrett Brown

tutor living on his own means. By 1911 there had been another move to 'Broxholme', Bigwood Road, Hendon. His father was now a widower 'partially retired'. Alfred Barrett was described as an Oxford undergraduate. Earlier he had attended the Quaker Bootham School, York. In 1912 he married Doris, the daughter of J.J Cockshott of Southport. They were to have two sons and two daughters. In 1912 he also became a lecturer in philosophy at the Woodbrooke Settlement in Selly Oak and probably lived in. He held the post until 1921.

The No Conscription Fellowship (NCF) was formed in December 1914 and two Birmingham men were important national leaders, William

Chamberlain and Alfred Barrett Brown. Conscription began in February 1916 when the first Military Service Act became law. The two leaders from Birmingham were amongst those imprisoned for 61 days for failing to pay a fine. In October 1916 Chamberlain and Barrett Brown appeared before the Birmingham Tribunal. The latter stated that he believed all war to be both un-Christian and immoral. He was then questioned about his Quaker activities. The chairman said that he regarded Brown as a danger to the state but thought he was the type of person who had caused the Government to put a conscience clause into the Act. He was granted absolute exemption.

In November 1916 Barrett Brown presided over a NCF conference in Birmingham where Bertrand Russell and Fenner Brockway spoke. Barrett Brown was beginning to diverge from other leaders of the NCF and in March 1917, from the safety of Woodbrooke, was lamenting the NCF policy of seeking amelioration of the condition of absolutists in prison as a 'lamentable lapse from its principles of No Compromise'.

In July 1917 Barrett Brown resigned from the NCF Council but remained chairman of the Midlands Division and the Birmingham branch. In responding to events in Russia he believed in an 'unarmed revolution'. At Christmas 1917 the Friends Service Committee issued a statement, which he signed, explained why the Society of Friends had issued no appeal to the Government for the release of conscientious objectors. It argued that to gain release before the public had accepted the pacifist position would 'injure the greater cause'.

In January 1918 Barrett Brown's absolute exemption was revoked after a case brought by a military representative on the Birmingham Tribunal who wanted the exemption to be changed to work of national importance. He did not appear in person and sent a letter stating that he felt uneasy at having to apply under the Military Service Act for his certificate of exemption as this would indicate his acceptance of the Act. The military representative stated that Barrett Brown was at 'Woodbrooke Settlement preaching sedition'. The chairman then said that 'Well we had better withdraw the exemption if he does not care to appear'.

In April 1918 Barrett Brown was arrested and taken to Budbrooke Barracks, Warwick, where he was court martialled. For some reason it was quashed and another held. The second court martial was held in May 1918 and he was sentenced to 112 days hard labour and taken to Wormwood Scrubs. He also spent time in Canterbury Prison and was released in June 1919. In Canterbury he edited the fortnightly 'Canterbury Clinker' with verses contributed by Barrett Brown.

In 1921 Alfred Barrett Brown left Woodbrooke and became Vice-Principal of Ruskin College, Oxford. Five years later he became Principal, a post he held until 1944. Between 1940 and 1947 he acted as a Regional Welfare Officer for the Ministry of Labour. He published four books between 1929 and 1938 on the themes of religion and democracy. His last known address was The Malt House, South Stoke, Goring on Thames. He died on October 2 1947.

'Socialism in Birmingham and the Black Country 1850-1939'. George J. Barnsby. Integrated Publishing. 1998.

Who was Who 1941-50.

42, Hay Green Lane, Bournville. It has not been possible to find a wartime address for Miss Julia Varley, a leading woman trade unionist of the time. This was her address in November 1952 when she died at the age of 81. She was born at Bradford, the daughter of a worsted mill worker. She left school at twelve and became a weaver. At the age of 15 she was branch secretary of the Weavers and Textile Workers' Union. She became the first woman member of the executive committee of the Bradford Trades Council in 1899. In 1904 she became a Bradford Poor Law Guardian. To investigate the life of tramping women she tramped from Leeds to Liverpool to find out first hand. She did the same for licensed women's lodgings houses in London. She was twice imprisoned in 1907 as a suffragette. She now became involved with Mary Macarthur and the National Federation of Women Workers and, in particular, the cause of the women chain workers of Cradley Heath.

In 1909 Edward Cadbury invited her organise women workers at Bournville and a branch of the NFWW was established. In January 1910 she became the first woman to be elected to the executive of the Birmingham Trades Council and was to serve for ten years. In 1911 she failed to win election to the new Greater Birmingham Council after standing as a socialist in Kings Norton. By 1912 she had joined the Workers' Union which sought to organise both sexes.

Two days after the declaration of war Julia Varley was part of a Birmingham Trades Council deputation to meet the Lord Mayor to discuss the steps which might be needed to deal with the dislocation of trade and employment created by the war. She became one of five from the Trades Council who joined the Emergency Committee. Julia was also part of Trades Council initiatives to help Belgian refugees as well as trying to ensure that their employment conformed to trade union practice. This work was praised by Vandervelde, the Belgian socialist, who visited in November 1914.

During the war she served on the Munitions Tribunal and the Citizens' Committee.

She was the only woman organiser in Workers' Union until August 1915 and was an active organiser throughout the war despite having a major throat operation in early 1917. She disagreed with many men on the Birmingham Trades Council over the introduction of conscription which she accepted and joined a breakaway Birmingham Trade Union Industrial Council. In 1917 she was selected to serve on the Labour Advisory Board set up by the Ministry of Labour and which monitored the working of labour exchanges. In early 1918 she went to France as one of five women sent to investigate rumours of immoral behaviour by WAACs in France; they were groundless. The commission found "a healthy, cheerful, self-respecting body of hard-working women, conscious of their position as links in the great chain of the Nation's purpose and zealous in its service". Afterwards Julia spoke at a factory gate meeting at the Austin about the slanders on the women of the WAAC.

In 1920 Julia Varley took up the cause of female domestic servants. In 1917 there were still 1.25 million women in service, a drop of only 400000 since the war began. The fall was mainly in middle class households. In 1920 she formed in Birmingham a Domestic Servants' Union and set up their own social club in the city at 1, Loveday Street. The Daily Chronicle called the club a 'servants' paradise'. A charter of appropriate conditions of work was issued which covered hours, time off, a minimum wage, their own bedroom, the mistress should pay for uniform and servants should be addressed by their proper names. Julia was a member of a 1923 Ministry of Labour enquiry into the 'servant shortage'. She told them that one part of the problem was caused by parents wishing a better life for their daughters.

Post-war she continued to serve as the chief woman organiser of her union which became the Transport and General Workers. She was elected to the General Council of the TUC and also served on Government committees. In 1931 her public work was recognised by an OBE. In September 1935 Julia was part of a large international delegation to the League of Nations in Geneva on the subject of women's claims for equality all over the world. She was the principal speaker of the delegation in her role on the Women's Committee of the TUC and the International Committee of Trade Union Women.

She retired from trade union work in 1936 and began to live at Hay Green Lane. As she grew older she lost her sight. She died at the home of her sisters in her native Bradford on November 24 1952 and was buried in Undercliffe cemetery there. George Haynes, a Birmingham trade unionist, had always believed that she was a 'pocket dreadnought'.

'Socialism in Birmingham and the Black Country 1850-1939'. George Barnsby. Integrated Publishing, 1998.

'The Birmingham Trades Council 1866-1966'. John Corbett. Lawrence and Wishart. 1966.

Oxford Dictionary of National Biography.

'South Hill', Oak Tree Lane, Bournville.

This house was the wartime home of Wilfred Ernest Littleboy, an absolutist conscientious objector in the First World War based on his Quaker beliefs. He came before the Birmingham Tribunal in 1916 with Neville Chamberlain in the chair. Chamberlain asked him "You're an accountant; couldn't you go to a munitions factory into the office as an accountant? You'd be paid as an accountant". It was at this hearing that he was asked why he wouldn't regard the needs of the country. He replied "The need of the country is a better understanding of Christ". Chamberlain replied "It is the material need of the country not the spiritual that is in question at this Tribunal". Wilfred Littleboy then stated that he thought that his work as an accountant, plus the religious and social work he did, was witness to the spirit of peace to which Chamberlain replied that "while Littleboy was raising spirituality the Germans were thundering at the gate". His case was deferred for a month in order to give him time to consider whether he would take alternative work.

At the next hearing he was referred to the Non-Combatant Corps against his wishes and beliefs. He appealed against this decision and appeared before the Birmingham Appeals Tribunal in June 1917. He stated that in loyalty to God he could not become part of organised war. He was asked "If you worked under the Pelham Committee (i.e. recommendation to do work of national importance) would not this bring about the peace and good you desire?". The reply was no. He was then asked "If all your countrymen took the same position would this keep the Germans out of this country?". He replied that "This would liberate such a spiritual force as would advance the coming Kingdom of God". His appeal was dismissed.

He did not go to the Non Combatant Corps and was therefore arrested and taken under military escort to Budbrooke Barracks, near Warwick. He refused to put on the soldier's uniform he was ordered to wear and therefore faced a court martial where he was sentenced to 112 days in prison and sent to Wormwood Scrubs. He made a statement to the court martial at Budbrooke on January 16 1917 which ended with "I therefore refused to obey a military order in the firm belief that I was thereby obeying the voice of God within me". He believed that his conscience was being ignored when he was not granted absolute exemption from military service. He also said that "Neither the decision of a civil tribunal nor the authority of the army could discharge me from a loyalty which I owe to God". The prison had a harsh regime with a silence rule rigorously enforced.

After release he continued to maintain his stance and faced two further court martials for disobeying orders and received a further 2½ years in prison. He was sent to the small civil prison at Dorchester in August 1917 where there were 30-40 other conscientious objectors. He related his experiences to his parents and felt himself lucky to remain on good health and spirits unlike some of the others who found it difficult to cope. After final discharge in April 1919 he was also fortunate to be able to restart his business as he was self-employed. He recognised that his family had faced 'a much stiffer time' as his father, Francis, who was a bank manager in a small country town, was known as the man with four sons who would not join the war.

He was born into a Quaker family of several generations in 1885 at Newport Pagnell, Buckinghamshire. In 1901 he was a boarder at Bootham Friends School at York; he was there for three years. His younger brother Ronald was at the school at the same time as was Arthur Impey of Longbridge House (see his entry). In 1902 he came to Birmingham and was articled into a firm of chartered accountants. He became active in the activities of the 'Young Friends'. In 1909, having completed his articles, he spent nine months in Australia with a Birmingham colleague working with 'Young Friends' there.

He was asked what he would do if Britain introduced conscription. He answered with "I suppose I should be going to prison". In 1910 he set up his own accountancy practice and became more active in the Birmingham Quaker community. In 1911 he was boarding with his uncle, William Littleboy, at 'South Hill', Oak Tree Lane, Bournville. William was a retired gas and electric fittings manufacturer who, like his nephew's father, had been born in Hertfordshire. His Aunt Margaret was Edgbaston born. It was a house with three servants. In 1912 he became a Quaker elder. At the time of Kelly's Directory of 1913 he had an office at Ocean Chambers, 44, Waterloo Street in the city centre. In 1914 he became clerk to the Chair of the Monthly Meeting of Birmingham Friends.

The war came as a shock to him. He felt a personal conviction that there was a place for witness to the war as unchristian rather than joining the Friends' Ambulance Unit or working for war victims relief. He joined the No

Conscription Fellowship and became friends with men who had a different, and political, angle against the war. Wilfred was relieved when the exemption clauses of the Military Service Act of 1916 included political convictions as he did not want the Quakers to be isolated. He was thirty-one when he first came into conflict with the authorities. He later became the clerk of the London Yearly Quaker Meeting. During the Second World War he served as a firewatcher. He died in 1979.

Imperial War Museum sound interview, June 25 1974.

George J. Barnsby. 'Socialism in Birmingham and the Black Country 1850-1939'. Integrated Publishing. 1998.

Lodge Hill Cemetery, Weoley Park Road, Selly Oak. This municipal cemetery was opened in 1895 and has the largest number of First World War casualties of the five municipal cemeteries either in Section B10 or commemorated on screen walls if the graves of those who died were not individually marked. There are 501 with 122 of the total post-war, many doubtless victims of the flu epidemic. The total is high because Lodge Hill was the designated burial place for those who did not survive treatment at the 1st Southern General Hospital.

The five municipal cemeteries hold 1447 First World casualties with 32.6% falling after the Armistice on November 11 1918. Lodge Hill received men who had died from Australia, 53, Canada, 31, New Zealand, 8, and South Africa, 1. There were 61 Royal Warwicks, 21 Worcesters, 42 artillery, 28 Army Service Corps, 21 Royal Engineers. 18 were from the air force and ten the Navy and there were five women. There were twelve holders of the Military Medal, one of whom also held the Military Cross and two holders of the Distinguished Conduct Medal. The Military medallists were Private William Hodgens, 50th Australian Battalion from South Australia; Serjeant P.L Barton of the 2/6th Warwicks from Acocks Green; Sapper Thomas Prescott, Royal Engineers, from Ladywood; Lieutenant Sylvester Hannan, 3rd Canadians; Private Joseph Edmonds, 1st Birmingham Pals; Serjeant T. Hall, Worcestershire Regiment who lived in a court dwelling in Holliday Street; Lieutenant Henry Taylor of the Australian Flying Corps (also held the MC); Private L.Beaulieu, 38th Canadian Infantry; Private Richard Swift, 1/8th Warwicks from Acocks Green; Lance Serjeant Christopher Smith, 8th Royal Berkshires; Gunner Percival Walsh, RFA, from Balsall Heath; and Private John Walsh, Royal Munster Fusiliers from county Limerick. The examples which follow in chronological order of death can represent all those men and women in the cemetery.

Private Benjamin Nolan died in the 1st Southern General Hospital, aged 27, on March 13 1915 after being invalided home from France and the 1st Warwicks during the previous December suffering from rheumatism and the effects of exposure. He was born in Leamington and left a widow and two children in a court dwelling in Barford Street, Birmingham. Serjeant H.J Thacker from Bishopsgate Street died at home on October 5 1915 from natural causes whilst serving with the 2/5th Warwicks before they were sent to France. He was buried with full military honours and his coffin arrived at Lodge Hill on a gun carriage. The Reverend Stephen Sullings was a chaplain attached to the 54th Division RAMC when he contracted enteric fever at Gallipoli. He must have died in a Birmingham hospital on November 21 1915. He came from Essex but had served as minister of the Colne Road Wesleyan Chapel, Burnley; he is named on its war memorial. He had joined in October 1914 and left a wife, Edith.

Private H.Willock was one of seven RAMC staff of the 1st Southern General Hospital to die in wartime. He died aged 21 on December 5 1915. He was the adopted son of the Stoke family of King Edward's Road, Ladywood. On February 19 1916 Serjeant Samuel Stewart, aged 28, was taken ill at Albany Barracks, Parkhurst, on the Isle of Wight. He was serving in the 3rd Warwicks, a reserve battalion. A week later he died of pneumonia in the 'Dudley section'. He was buried with full military honours. Serjeant James Underwood died at home on September 24 1916 suffering from the effects of trench hardships. He had previously served nine years in the army and appears to have re-enlisted. He was aged 58 and appears to have been a member of the band of the 6th Warwicks. He had lived in King Edward's Road. Private Hugh Blair had come from his native Tryphena on the island of Great Barrier, 55 miles from Auckland, New Zealand, to have a lasting resting place in Birmingham. He was wounded at the front whilst serving in the 2nd Battalion of the Auckland Regiment and died on October 9 1916.

Corporal William Rickerby was 25 when he died on November 21 1916 from wounds received on August 18 that year whilst serving in the 1/5th Warwicks. He was wounded during his unit's attack on the Leipzig Redoubt near Thiepval on the Somme. He had volunteered early in the war. His parents lived in Thorpe Street, Birmingham and he left a wife and one child in Sherlock Street. When the CWGC contacted relatives after the war his wife had already remarried and lived in Balsall Heath. Lieutenant Percy Wright was killed as a result of an accident in a Longhorn plane flown from his 5th Reserve Squadron base at Castle Bromwich. On December 20 1916 he side-slipped at 400 feet and crashed and caught fire at Walmley. He died of his injuries on the following day. His flying colleague, Second Lieutenant Frank Garner, did not survive and was buried at Runcorn.

Staff Nurse Hilda Garlick was one of five women buried at Lodge Hill. She was one of three Territorial Force Nursing Service women buried there. Dublin born she was mobilised into the 1st Southern General on August 12 1914 but resigned as a staff nurse on November 11 that year as a result of nephitis (a serious kidney condition). She spent fourteen days in hospital. She must have stayed in the city to be buried there after her death on August 12 1917. She had lived at 16, Reservoir Road, Edgbaston. Her brother, William, received her memorial scroll in 1925 after it was returned from a Canford Cliffs, Bournemouth address, four years earlier. She is named on Belfast Cathedral roll of honour plaque on the west wall.

Lance Serjeant John Riley and Private Harry Southern were both killed in the Blyth sands drownings of 5th Warwicks Reserve Battalion on August 24 1917. Riley, 25, from Ladywood, was a rescuer and had just returned from France and was due to be married on the next day and his rail warrant was in his room. He was given a military funeral. Southern was 18 and his parents lived at 226, Slade Road, Erdington. Lieutenant Sylvester Hannan, 22, had been a clerk and enlisted in September 1914 at Valcartier, north of Quebec, Canada although born at Rochester, New York. This was Canada's largest military camp as it was near the port of Quebec. He had previously served in the militia for three years, probably around Toronto. He served in the 3rd Canadian Infantry, the Central Ontario Regiment. He died on December 12 1917 although his Military Cross was not gazetted until July 1918. He was a Roman Catholic.

There is an irony in the death of Captain Vernon Earle Busby, RAF, who was killed on June 8 1918 on a test flight whilst serving in the Accidents Department of the Air Ministry. His base was Marklesham Heath, Suffolk, but he had been sent to assist with flight testing at an aerodrome at Cricklewood in North London next to a Handley Page factory. He was one of six crew in a Handley Page V/1500 which stalled and spun out of control at Golders Green on June 8 1918. This aircraft was a four-engined heavy night bomber which was designed to attack Berlin but the war ended before the forty manufactured could mount a raid. Busby was 23 and was buried in Birmingham because his parents lived in at 'Fairfield', Serpentine Road, Selly Hill. He had attended King Edward's where he had joined the OTC and became an expert motor cyclist, including in TT races. He volunteered on the third day of the war and became engineer of his unit. After being wounded at Mons he was commissioned into the Royal Engineers. In 1915 he transferred to the RFC and went to France where he remained until December 1916. He was in hospital in England for several months with a leg injury. From early 1917 he worked for the Air Ministry.

Able Seaman William Howman died on July 17 1918, aged 36. He was serving on HMS Kent, an armoured cruiser launched in 1901. It is not totally clear where the ship was located. He died ashore and was buried in Birmingham where his parents lived. In June 1918 the Kent was on English Channel convoy escort duty until returning to the China Station in July 1918 so it was likely that he became ill during the former operation. CWGC notes that he served in the successful Battle of the Falkland Islands on December 8 1914 when a British force engaged with Admiral von Spee's cruiser squadron. Two German ships ran from the British fleet, including the Nürnberg, a light cruiser, at full speed. HMS Kent followed also pushing her boilers and engines to the limit. Needing maintenance the Nürnberg engaged but the Kent was superior in shell weight and armour. After two boiler explosions the German ship sank. HMS Kent then helped to corner the Dresden in the Battle of the Chilean island of Mas a Tierra on March 14 1915 before moving to the China Station. In 1916 HMS Kent was on the Cape of Good Hope Station.

On October 24 1918 Lance Serjeant Ernest Grimston, 22, died of wounds. He was born in Sydney, Australia, and before the war was an engine cleaner. He enlisted in his home town of Goulburn, New South Wales, in February 1916 and about twenty weeks later left Sydney in the 19th Battalion of the Australian Infantry. He was awarded the DCM for action during an attack at Mont St Quentin on August 31 1918. "His serjeant, having located a machine gun, the two decided to attack the post. They worked amongst buildings to within 15 yards and rushed the gun. Although the serjeant was immediately killed Corporal Grimston reached the post, wounded the two occupants, and captured the gun."

Sapper John Cattlin Leneham was a member of 1st Australian Tunnelling Company and died of wounds on November 6 1918 at the age of 24; his wounds were probably sustained in October 1918 when 32 men were hospitalised. With mining over the unit was then following the Allied advance and working on roads and bridges around Busigny south of Le Cateau. He was born in Sydney but his parents lived at Mount Lawley, Western Australia. Before the war he was a painter and then enlisted in July 1915. He left Sydney on February 20 1916. He probably also worked around Hooge, Hill 60 and Hill 63 near Ypres.

Armourer Quarter Master Serjeant William Melton Patrick of the Royal Army Ordnance Corps is our first post-war example. He died on February 6 1919 aged 47. He was an old soldier with twenty-two years service, including in China and India. He held long service and good conduct medals. He held the same position in November 1914 when he was living at 5, Viewfield Street, Stirling and married Edith Hyde from the same town. Immediately after the war she was at Malvern Park Farm, Solihull. Isaac Warner died on July 28 1920 aged 28. His parents lived in Milner Road, Selly Park. He had served in the Machine Gun Corps and was one of the two DCM holders buried in the Cemetery. The citation published in the London Gazette on October 21 1918 concerned a German counter-attack. "A party of about ten of the enemy reached within twenty yards of his gun and one threw a bomb, which burst under it, piercing the barrel casting and slightly wounded him. He instantly tore off his puttees, tied them round the hole through which the water was escaping, so keeping the gun in action until the remaining enemy were killed or wounded. His initiative and contempt of danger were consistent with his whole bearing during the operations".

Monyhull, Brandwood End. Was a war hospital under the aegis of the 1st Southern General and was opened on November 22 1916. The old Monyhull Hall, built in the 18th century, was the centrepiece of the building and still remains. The 'Monyhull Colony' followed a joint decision of the Poor Law Guardians of Birmingham, Kings Norton and Aston to provide an institution 'for sane epileptics and feeble minded persons'. It was nearing completion in 1914 with provision for children and their intended accommodation was converted for use as a 400 bed military hospital. Between 1916 and 1919 about 5000 patients were treated. Convoys of wounded soldiers, some from the Empire, arrived almost daily. One section of the hospital was set aside for severe shell shock cases. The hospital also admitted 'service patients' who were 'epileptic discharged' soldiers who had been sent there by local War Pensions Committees.

The first such patient was admitted in March 1917. Matron commented that "he had lost his voice on admission as the result of a fit but from the first he grumbled, was discontented and did not intend to stay; he was kept in bed for three days for observation; he was put into a small dormitory, had a fire there, an armchair for when he was up and was made as comfortable as possible. His meals were served specially in every way yet he was not contented and absconded on the 23rd. He had only been five months in the army, had seen no fighting but, of course, constantly said that 'this was all he got after having served his King and Country'". Such patients had strict rules, did outdoor farm work or gardening and could not leave without a pass. Service patients began to call Home 9 the 'Homestead'. Some were very troublesome. On September 25 1918 three of the 26 men in the Homestead were returned to their homes. One was 'very dirty in his habits and too mental to remain here'; one came in drunk and poured a jug of coffee over the attendant; and the third was very insolent and encouraged other men to join him in gambling. In July 1920 the service patients were discharged or sent to Hollymoor. By 1918 the colony of men, women and children who were the real 'colonists' rose to 650. The hospital closed in 1998.

'Monyhull 1908-1998. A History of Caring' by Deborah Hutchings. Brewin. 1998.

The hospital site has been redeveloped for substantial residential use. The old Hall, a large neo-classical building, still exists adjacent to St Francis Drive and is used as apartments. The red brick hospital chapel of St Francis still exists.

Brandwood End Cemetery.

Brandwood End Cemetery. Contains 108 scattered burials or names on a screen wall if graves are not individually marked of men who were Great War casualties. Eighteen served in the Royal Warwickshire Regiment, eleven were artillerymen, ten served in the Air Force and nine in the Army Service Corps. There were three Australians and one Canadian and only one medal winner. Half of the men died after the Armistice.

Lieutenant Arthur Edward Wilson was one of the Royal Warwicks and his story is very tragic. He died on December 3 1918 at the age of 29. Before the war he worked as a colonial traveller in the export department of The New Hudson Cycle Company, cycle manufacturers, with his father as managing director, and lived in Howard Road, Kings Heath. He joined the 1st Birmingham Pals at the outbreak of war and soon became an officer in the same battalion. At some point during the first two years of the war he had been badly wounded but recovered and then suffered severe shell shock during the Battle of the Somme and spent several months in a convalescent home in England. Alan Furse was in the same battalion and left an account of the circumstances of September 12 1916….

"September 12 was a terribly hot day and poor old Wilson got a terrible dose of shell shock. He was in charge of C Coy on my right. A whizzbang burst just outside the trench near him and he went completely mad, trying to scratch a hole in the ground and barking like a dog. We tried to calm him down but finally had to send him back over the top in daylight in charge of two men."

He did not return to action and the firm requested his release to work on urgent aircraft contracts for the Government. He appears to have kept his army rank. The firm had four premises in central Birmingham – 29-35 Summer Hill Street; Parade Mills, Sandpits; 1, Summer Row; and 40, Paradise Street. They were a substantial firm and were taken over by Girling Brakes in the 1930s and later by Lucas. Before his death he had well advanced plans to marry and had bought a house. However, he contracted influenza and died of pneumonia. He was given a military funeral at Brandwood End.

Private William Shakespeare, aged 25, died on November 6 1917 in Dewsbury War Hospital from wounds received three and a half weeks earlier when the 3rd Birmingham Pals were in the Ypres Salient. He had attended Mary Street Board School, Birmingham, and worked as a gas meter maker. He enlisted in June 1915 and had probably been reluctant to do so earlier as he had three young children after marrying Elizabeth in 1903. His case was also tragic as his fourth child was born a week after his death.

Private Jesse Blunn, aged 17, was another casualty of the Blyth drownings on August 24 1917 (see Beavon, Yardley Cemetery). He was also in the 5th Reserve Battalion of the Warwicks and was buried with military honours. He lived at 83, Highbury Road, Birmingham. Private Walter Taylor, aged 37, died on November 20 1919 and is listed on the screen wall. He was a member of the Royal Veterinary Corps. Second Lieutenant Frederick Clifford Alabaster is also buried in the Cemetery and is described under his home of 2, Amesbury Road, Moseley. Private Albert Hambleton was the Military Medal winner and is listed on the screen wall. He died aged 28 whilst serving in the Coldstream Guards on February 21 1917. His parents lived at 48, Greenway Street, Small Heath.

Furse account from page 212 'Birmingham Pals. 14th, 15th & 16th Battalions of the Royal Warwickshire Regiment. A History of the Three City Battalions Raised in Birmingham in World War One'. Terry Carter. Pen & Sword, 1997.

16.

Harborne

Harborne Hall VAD Auxiliary Hospital. Was opened in January 1916 after being originally located at Hill Crest, Richmond Hill Road, Edgbaston; the latter had been given by Mr William Roberts of Handsworth. The Hall was loaned by Walter Chamberlain, brother of Joseph Chamberlain. His son, Walter Basil, was a Captain in the 1/1st Worcestershire Yeomanry and was awarded the MC. He was commissioned in late October 1914 but became a POW in Turkey for 2½ years. His daughter, Pearl, became a VAD nurse. Walter was a businessman who was chairman and director of many Birmingham companies including GKN and Avery; for the latter he was largely responsible for the purchase of the Soho Foundry. He was a Liberal Unionist and was fascinated by new inventions e.g cars and X-rays. He was a keen ornithologist and there were penguins in the pool. He left the Hall and moved to Surrey in 1902 but kept it on and allowed Avery employees to use it for recreation. It was also an early host to Belgian refugees and a new committee had one week to prepare for its first group on September 19 1914. Gifts of furniture, clothing and household goods poured in. The Hall was managed by a group of refugee nuns from Antwerp led by Mother Josepha. Work was found for some of the men who contributed one-third of their earnings. In August 1915 the nuns returned to Belgium and new homes were found for 45 remaining refugees. Afterwards a letter of thanks noted the 'hospitable dwelling of Harborne Hall which has sheltered us in our exile. We thank you a thousand times'.

In the hospital there was room for 100 men and later another 68 in the grounds where an operating theatre was also built. In May 1917 Stapylton House in St Peter's Road, Harborne, was taken over as an annexe and provided 35 beds; it was loaned by Mr J.A Kenrick. Overall over 5600 patients passed through. Employees of Messrs W and T Avery of Smethwick contributed regularly to hospital funds and helped in its management, particularly Mr Cannell. The Newfoundland Government made an annual contribution to hospital funds. The hospital was run by Mrs Heaton, the Commandant. She was awarded the MBE in 1918 for her work. After the war Harborne Hall became a boys' preparatory school.

'The History of Harborne Hall'. Frances Wilmot. Library of Birmingham.

Lordswood, Harborne was opened as a VAD Hospital on May 15 1915 and was given by Miss Smith of Weston-super-Mare. In 1916 there were 70 beds.

5, St Mary's Road, Harborne. Was the home in 1913 of Gustav Adolph Boeddicker whose son, Major Hans Frederick, served in the Midland Field Ambulance before and during the war. In the same year his son was

Gustav Boeddicker, British naturalised and German born

listed as a surgeon at 97, Bradford Street; he also acted as the honorary local medical officer to Dr Barnado's. On June 22 1911 the then Lieutenant Boeddicker had commanded the Field Ambulance's men who attended the Coronation Ceremonial in London. Gustav's daughter-in-law served as superintendent of the VAD Hospital at Highbury. Gustav registered with Birmingham Police on August 10 under the Emergency Powers affecting enemy aliens. He was born at Iserlohn, Westphalia, on January 29 1850 and came to Britain with his wife, Martha, in 1877, in order to work as a chemist to Wiggin and

Co. They had been married two years before and brought the infant Hans with them.

Gustav had served in the German Fusiliers between 1869 and 1870, which included the Franco-Prussian War where he was badly wounded in the 35th Regiment and afterwards became a French prisoner. Many years later he gave a lecture about his war experiences to a local society. In 1881 he was living in Sandon Road, Edgbaston and was by profession an analytical chemist. In 1891 he was living at 'Arnsberg', Greenfield Road, Harborne and ten years later was at 'Iserlohn', St Mary's Road, Harborne. He was then described as a managing director of a cobalt works. Hans was living at home and this was the year that he qualified as a doctor in London. At some stage

Gustav became a director of Henry Wiggin and Co at George Street, Parade, Birmingham. Their works was at Vittoria Street, Smethwick and refined, cast and rolled with a variety of metals – nickel, cobalt, silver, red lead and tin oxide.

Following the sinking of the Lusitania in May 1915 Gustav organised a memorial for presentation to Lord Mayor Bowater on May 20. The memorial was signed by 33 'naturalised British subjects of German and Austrian descent' and was a strong protest against the inhuman methods of the German Government in killing non-combatants and using poisonous gas. Boeddicker contributed £10 himself to the Lusitania Relief Fund. The signatories included Paul Metz who had been resident in England for over forty years and had a son in the British Army, and C.H Laubenburg, who lived in St Bernard's Road, Olton, a resident for 43 years. The Lord Mayor stated that he had had many opportunities to understand their loyalty including sons fighting, marriages to English ladies and there should be no resentment against them and he hoped their property would not be damaged.

In 1911 Hans was living at 97, Bradford Street with a surgery at 424, Green Lane, Bordesley. Hans himself had become naturalised and married Julia who was born at Rainhill, Lancashire. When the 1st South Midland Field Ambulance left Moor Street Station in August 1914 'C' section was commanded by Major Hans Boeddicker. They became attached to the 'Warwick' Brigade of Territorials and followed them to France in March 1915. He set up an Advanced Dressing Station at Fonquevillers on the Somme and later saw service in Italy. Probably on his return he became registrar at the No 1 Birmingham War Hospital. In 1920 Hans was still in Bradford Street and in September 1925 went on a cruise with his wife to the Canary Islands. Julia died in 1933 and the same year he remarried Winifred Curr. However, he died himself within a year. Gustav and Martha had died in 1923 and 1925 respectively. Gustav's obituary in the Birmingham Post gave details of his early career. He had trained in chemistry and metallurgy at the Berlin Technical College and then at the Royal School of Mines in Berlin. He then became demonstrator and principal assistant to Dr Finkener, a leading authority on inorganic chemistry. Before he came to Birmingham he was a chemist at the Iserlohn Nickel Works and assistant manager of the Imperial Mint at Berlin.

Birmingham Post May 7 1923.

The Birmingham Territorial Units of the RAMC 1914-1919. Lieutenant Colonel J.E.H Sawyer. Allday. 1921. Library of Birmingham.

Metchley Abbey. This was not as the name suggests a religious house but an early 19th century romantic fabrication in Gothic style. At some point later in the century it was sub-divided. In 1916 it was the home of Lieutenant Colonel Edgar Innes, the Commanding Officer of the 1/8 Warwicks, the Territorials based at Aston. He was killed on the first day of the Somme in the only attack by the Regiment at zero hour. In the attack on the Heidenkopf, a German strongpoint, the Colonel went over the top and was killed within a few yards by a bullet through the head. He was at the side of Private Fred Lewis, his battalion runner, who survived the war. The battalion was hit with 230 deaths that day. Three-quarters have no known grave and like Colonel Innes are commemorated on the Thiepval Memorial. On June 13 1917 a ceremony took place in the Birmingham Council Chamber to commemorate the "heroism and sacrifice of two officers of the Warwickshire Regiment". The Lord Mayor, A.D Brookes presided and the opening remarks were by Major Townsend, the second in command, who had written to tell Mrs Innes of her husband's death. On behalf of his brother officers he asked the Lord Mayor to present to the Colonel's wife a framed and illuminated address and an enlarged photograph. The other officer was Major Caddick.

The address read – "We the undersigned, brother officers, survivors of this memorable day (July 1 1916), desire to place on record our keen appreciation of the valuable services rendered to the battalion by our late beloved Colonel and our admiration for his patriotism, endurance and devotion to duty under the most trying conditions. We pay a grateful appreciation to his resourcefulness, unselfish bravery and unwearied diligence. His heroism in the face of death was in keeping with the high standard of duty so conspicuous in his life. The officers and men are profoundly touched by the valuable help from Mrs Innes, whose interest in the sick and wounded, is unfailing and whose practical help to the families of the fighting men of the regiment can never be forgotten".

He had also been previously mentioned in despatches. In the New Year's Honours list in 1916 he had been awarded a CMG. Innes was born in Moseley on December 16 1872 and his father, John, was Scottish born. He attended a private school at Lytham and then studied in Paris. Afterwards he entered his father's business, joined the Birmingham Athletic Institute and the Edgbaston Rowing Club. In 1900 he was commissioned into the 1st Warwickshire Volunteer Battalion at Thorp Street becoming a captain in 1907. When the 8th Territorial Battalion was formed in 1908 he became Major and second in command. On April 15 1909 he married Nancy Wright who was born in Morpeth, Northumberland. A daughter, Edith, was born the following year when his address was given in the census as 93, Metchley Lane. Before the war Innes had owned a wines and spirits import company, Innes, Smith and Co, in the High Street and had acted as secretary of the local branch of the National Service League. He had succeeded Colonel Ludlow in command of the battalion in April 1913 when Ludlow had been promoted. His father had lived at Harborne Hill House. His wife was also active in the war and organised visits to the wives and families of 8th Battalion men, was a member of the Aston and Witton Committee of the POW Fund and was an officer of the VAD Hospital at Harborne Hall which opened in November 1914.

Metchley Abbey is now sheltered accommodation for the elderly and is a listed building.

Edgbastonia August 1916. Library of Birmingham.

17.
Miscellaneous

Hall Green and Shirley. On April 12 1918 a Zeppelin flew over these outlying districts (see Hilda Moss entry, 171-5, Moseley Road, for her memory of this).

Billesley Common. In July 1929 the City Council granted a lease of land on the Billesley Common estate for the erection of houses as a memorial to Earl Haig and to accommodate disabled ex-servicemen or their widows. Surrounded by an area bounded by Coldbath Road, Brook Lane and Yardley Wood Road the roads have the names – Jutland, Vimy and Menin. There is also a Menin Crescent and Menin Passage. Jutland was the major sea battle of 1916. Vimy was the ridge of high ground stormed by the Canadians on April 9 1917 and Menin the road out of Ypres towards the front line. The buildings are difficult to date but are definitely inter-war and many were built to the late 19th century pattern of tunnelbacks.

Alfred Knight Way, Attwood Green. After the redevelopment of Lee Bank a new name was given to the area north of the Bristol Road. One new road at the Bath Row end of Bell Barn Road was named after the Ladywood born VC, Serjeant Alfred Knight, and dedicated on November 9 2006 at a ceremony attended by his grand-daughter, Anne Walsh, and other members of his family. It was awarded for an action in the Ypres Salient on September 20 1917 whilst serving with the Post Office Rifles. He was born in Friston Street, Ladywood on August 24 1888, the son of Joseph, a glass cutter, and Annie Knight. He attended St Philip's Grammar School, Edgbaston. He had joined the clerical staff at the Post Office in 1909 and was a regular worshipper at the Oratory Roman Catholic Church. When the Post Office Engineering Department moved to Nottingham in 1912 he transferred there and was working in Carrington Street when the war broke out. He married

Mabel Saunderson in May 1915. On October 26 1914 he enlisted in the 2/8 Post Office Rifles of the London Regiment. The unit did not go overseas until January 1917 and in May of that year he distinguished himself by bringing in wounded men under fire at Bullecourt. As a result he was promoted to serjeant.

He was later awarded the Victoria Cross during an operation against German positions at the Battle for Wurst Farm Ridge, Alberta Section, Ypres on September 20 1917. The citation read…."Serjeant Knight did extraordinary good work and showed exceptional bravery and initiative when his platoon was attacking an enemy strongpoint and came under very heavy fire from an enemy machine gun. He rushed through our own barrage, bayoneted the enemy gunner and captured the position single-handed. Later twelve of the enemy with a machine gun were encountered in a shell-hole. He again rushed forward by himself, bayoneted two and shot a third, and caused the remainder to scatter. Subsequently during the attack on a fortified farm (Hubner Farm) when entangled up to his waist in mud and seeing a number of the enemy firing on our troops he immediately opened fire on them without waiting to extricate himself from the mud, killing six of the enemy. Again noticing the company on his right flank being held up in their attack on another farm Serjeant Knight collected some men and took up a position on the flank of this farm from where he brought a heavy fire to bear on the farm as a result of which the farm was captured. All the platoon officers of the company had become casualties before the first objective was reached and this gallant NCO took command of all the men of his own platoon and of the platoons without officers. His energy in consolidating and reorganising was untiring. His several single-handed actions showed exceptional bravery and saved a great number of casualties in the company. They were performed under heavy machine gun and rifle fire and without regard to personal risk, and were the direct cause of the objectives being captured".

Years later he recalled his survival as a miracle. "All my kit was shot away almost as soon as we were in it. Bullets rattled on my steel helmet – there were several significant dents and one hole in it I found later – and part of a book was shot away in my pocket. A photograph case and a cigarette case probably saved my life from one bullet, which must have passed just under my arm-pit". Knight received his VC at Buckingham Palace from the King on January 3 1918. He now became a minor celebrity and became a magnet for journalists when he returned to Nottingham in December 1917 and was given civic receptions in both Nottingham and Birmingham. The press liked his sense of humour and one Birmingham newspaper dubbed him 'the Jolly

VC'. He served until the Armistice and in March 1919 was commissioned into the Sherwood Foresters. After demobilisation he returned to the Post Office but was soon transferred to the Ministry of Labour.

From 1931-7 he managed the Employment Exchange at York and, afterwards, served in the Trade Board Section at Leeds. When he retired in 1951 he was Senior Wages Inspector in the Midlands section of the Ministry of Labour. On June 7 1951 he was appointed an MBE. He served as President of York and Birmingham Circles of the Catenian Association, the Catholic professional and businessmen's organisation. He later retired to Birmingham and died on December 4 1960 at the age of 72 at his home in Elvetham Road, Edgbaston. He is buried in Oscott Catholic Cemetery, New Oscott. In 1979 Terence Cuneo produced a painting of him winning his VC which was hung at Inglis Barracks, Mill Hill, London, home of the Royal Engineers Postal Depot. His VC is held by the British Postal Museum and Archive.

British Postal Museum website

King Edward VI Grammar School, Five Ways, Bartley Green.

The school was originally built at Five Ways in 1883 but moved to the city outskirts at Bartley Green in 1958. At Speech Day in December 1914 the Headmaster, E.H.F MacCarthy noted that 1200 Old Edwardians from the foundation's schools were serving with the colours, including 200 from his school. He added "Poor little Belgium. Little, but how really great. Great in sacrifice, great in suffering, great in imperishable honour". In the school a large war map was kept up to date with miniature flags and an active Cadet Corps was established in 1915. Staff shortages became apparent as some teachers joined up. At least two of the latter were wounded. Gaps were filled by the appointment of women and disabled men as temporary teachers. One school magazine described the war as a 'grim struggle' which was reflected in Arthur Barker's first speech day as a new headmaster in December 1916. It had to be held in the afternoon because of lighting restrictions so attendance was affected and, instead of the usual prizes, war certificates were awarded and the value of the prize was given in stamps to buy War Loan vouchers.

The school made collections for war charities, senior boys spent holidays on farms helping with food production, and a war allotment was cultivated in Portland Road. By the end of the war 637 Old Boys had seen active service and 123 of these had been killed. Forty-eight men received an award, including 25 MCs. Amongst those killed was Second Lieutenant Francis Freeman, aged 23, who died on the first day of the Somme serving in the

Lancashire Fusiliers. He was born in Edgbaston and his parents had moved to Malvern. On the same day Lieutenant Harold Foizey, aged 31, was killed. His parents were living in Tipton and he was in the West Yorkshire Regiment. Private Charles Barrow was also killed on the Somme on September 3 1916 as part of 'A' company, 14th Warwicks. His parents lived at 9, Francis Road, Edgbaston. Captain William Hunter, aged 31, had been a solicitor before the war and his father had been minister of Wycliffe Baptist Church on the Bristol Road. He was killed on July 31 1917, the first day of the Battle of Third Ypres. He was in the Lincolnshire Regiment and is commemorated on the Menin Gate at Ypres.

Second Lieutenant George Morley Smith, aged 22, had left school for Birmingham University and then joined the Leicestershire Regiment. He was killed in Belgium on October 6 1917. His parents were living in Dale End. Lance Corporal Laurence Dabbs was the same age when killed a few weeks later in Gaza serving in the Worcestershire Yeomanry. His parents were living at 'Sunny Bank', Raglan Road, Smethwick. Second Lieutenant Arthur Rosenthal had lived at 37, Beaufort Road, Edgbaston, and went missing in action serving in the 65th Squadron of the Royal Flying Corps on November 23 1917. He was aged 20. He was probably Jewish as his parents were Israel and Johanna Rosenthal. He is commemorated on the Arras Flying Services Memorial.

'King Edward VI Five Ways School 1883-1983'. David Wheeldon.

'Five Ways' – the school magazine – Spring Term 1917 and Spring Term 1918 – Library of Birmingham.

1 Back, 102, Sherborne Street, Ladywood. This was the family home in 1911 of Arthur Grove Earp whose wartime death in 1916 puts him in an unfortunate category of British soldiers. In 1911 he was a nineteen year old bedstead polisher who had been born in Moseley Street. His mother, Jane, was a widow and there were three daughters, Florence, Matilda and Ethel, and a younger brother, Thomas. Ten years earlier his father, Thomas, a gardener, was alive and the family were living at 'Lodge', Rookery Road, Handsworth. Arthur Earp went to war with the 1/5th Royal Warwicks and in 1916 was on the Somme. On July 21 1916 Henry Ogle, 1/7th Warwicks, was a witness to events surrounding a 'shot at dawn'…."the brigade was drawn up in a hollow square in a quarry. In the middle of the square was a small group of officers, NCOs and drummers and one figure who was already little more than a ghost. A minute ago he had been a private soldier in a regiment of the line, wearing that regiment's badges and buttons embossed with the Royal Arms. Now he stood deprived of badges and buttons and all honourable military identity and was under sentence of death. He was to be shot at dawn the next day. Some sort of indictment had been read out to us on parade to the effect that he had been guilty of cowardice in the face of the enemy. I was one of many who sympathised but acquiesced, unable to think of a working alternative. Now he was drummed out of the service and marched away to wait for the dawn. The morning's ceremony had made a deep impression on me".

The Medal Index Card of Private Arthur Earp reveals his fate

The man was Private Arthur Earp of 'D' company whose offence was 'quitting his post'. He was a Kitchener volunteer who had enlisted on September 14 1914. In the routine orders of the 1/6 Battalion it states that Earp....

> "was tried by Field General Court Martial on the following charge – 'When on Active Service, leaving his post without orders from his superior officer'. The sentence of the court was 'To suffer death by being shot'. The sentence was duly carried out at 4.30 a.m. on 22nd July 1916."

He was buried at Bouzincourt Communal Cemetery Extension.

Earp's case causes disquiet as the court martial on July 8 recommended that mercy should be shown. The President of the court was Major F.S

Hanson of the 1/7th alongside Lieutenant Gassett of the 1/6th and Captain A.S Alabaster of Earp's own battalion. Earp had left his post in Carench trench near Hebuterne on June 26. There were two witnesses for the prosecution. Serjeant Williams had taken his platoon into the trench at 4 a.m. and left Corporal Golby in charge of the left post garrison to which Earp belonged.

Both NCOs told the court that they had personally warned the men that they were not to leave the post until they were relieved. He was at his post at 12.30 p.m. but about 1 p.m. Golby noticed that he was missing. Williams came back half an hour later and searched for him unsuccessfully. Earp reported to the Corporal in Botha dugout behind the front line at 2.30 a.m. on June 27. In cross-examination Williams said that the platoon had been doing twenty-four hour periods of duty in the front and reserve lines for four days and 'they had a particularly trying time of it as the great bombardment was in progress and there was a lot of retaliation'. Golby added that 'the accused was in a highly nervous state when he went into the post. The trenches were shelled heavily from about 4 a.m. for about two hours…on June 27 he told me that he couldn't stand the shelling so went to Botha dugout'.

In his defence Earp said that when the trenches were being heavily shelled he got into the dugout. 'I was feeling giddy and did not know what I was doing. After the shelling ceased, I walked out and went a little way down the communication trench, the shelling started again and I could not get back… The next time our platoon went up into the front line I was sent out of the trenches by Captain Gell as I was unable to stand the shelling'. Serjeant Williams also gave evidence for the defence and stated that Earp was "always of a nervous disposition and was very nervous on that morning in particular. He had been sent down to the base for three or four months". This was the key point with the implication that Earp was shell-shocked but it was not followed up by the man himself or anyone else. There were also no entries on his conduct sheet and his character was 'good'.

The court martial had put in a recommendation that mercy be shown in Earp's case. His brigade commander, Dent, however, recommended that the death sentence be carried out as three other men from the battalion had been convicted of the same offence three weeks earlier and had their sentences commuted to two years imprisonment. In other words he wanted an example made to others. The 48th divisional commander, Fanshawe, disagreed. He wrote that "the battalions of the Brigade have done well and I do not think that an example is necessary". The Corps commander, Hunter-Weston, agreed. General Hubert Gough, commanding Reserve Army (soon to be 5th Army), thought that an example was 'very necessary'. 'This is a very serious military offence and if passed over the state of courage of the British soldier is likely to be lowered'. It was now up to the Commander-in-Chief, Douglas Haig, who received the papers as the disaster of July 1 was becoming clear. He wrote – 'How can we ever win if a plea like this is allowed?'. One final irony is that Serjeant Williams himself was killed in action on July 18 before the sentence was carried out.

'The Fateful Battle Line. The Great War Journals and Sketches of Captain Henry Ogle MC'. Edited by Michael Glover. Leo Cooper. 1993.

National Archives court martial file, WO/71/485.